Edna Lewis

Edna Lewis

At the Table with an American Original

Edited by Sara B. Franklin

THE UNIVERSITY OF NORTH CAROLINA PRESS

Chapel Hill

Designed by Jamison Cockerham
Set in Arno, Chaparral, Challista Script, and SignPainter
by Tseng Information Systems, Inc.

Manufactured in the United States of America

The University of North Carolina Press has been a member
of the Green Press Initiative since 2003.

Cover photograph courtesy of John T. Hill
Frontispiece: Pen and gouache portrait of Edna Lewis by
Amy C. Evans, 2017. www.amycevans.com.

LIBRARY OF CONGRESS CATALOGING-IN-PUBLICATION DATA
Names: Franklin, Sara B., editor.
Title: Edna Lewis : at the table with an American original / edited by Sara B. Franklin.
Description: Chapel Hill : The University of North Carolina Press, [2018] |
Includes bibliographical references and index.
Identifiers: LCCN 2017036473| ISBN 9781469638553 (cloth : alk. paper) |
ISBN 9781469638560 (ebook)
Subjects: LCSH: Lewis, Edna. | African American cooks. | Cookbooks — History and
criticism. | Cooking, American — Southern style.
Classification: LCC TX649.L48 E36 2018 | DDC 641.5975—dc23
LC record available at https://lccn.loc.gov/2017036473

John T. Edge's essay, "Paying Down Debts of Pleasure," originally appeared in the *Oxford American* (Fall 2013); Francis Lam's essay, "Edna Lewis and Black Roots of American Cooking," originally appeared in the *New York Times Magazine*, October 28, 2015; and Susan Rebecca White's essay, "On Edna Lewis's *The Edna Lewis Cookbook*," originally appeared in *Tin House* 15, no. 3 (March 2014).

*To all the women who have
ever put pen to paper,*

*or shared their knowledge and skills
through oral traditions,*

*to help us remember and perpetuate
the living art of cooking*

Contents

Foreword

KIM SEVERSON

—⁌⁌—

Death is the only sure measure of a person's worth. If you've lost some-body, you understand this. There you are at your grandmother's funeral, and someone you've never met before walks over and tells you about the day she stood up to a bully on an elementary school playground. Months after your husband passes, a note arrives in the mail expressing gratitude for the time he covered a friend's rent without ever asking that the loan be repaid.

Only in hindsight do the bits and pieces of a life get uncovered, the parts coalescing into a new and more powerful whole. The good, strong, and brave aren't always visible until they don't walk among us anymore. Then, like the winning numbers on a scratch-off ticket, the worth of a life is revealed. The prize was there all along, just under the surface.

The lens through which a person's life is viewed shifts with time. Con-sider Alexander Hamilton. He became a renegade hero to a generation of young people who drank up the Broadway musical in which the dusty story of America's founding fathers was reimagined with black and Hispanic actors and set to a hip-hop soundtrack.

This is where we find ourselves when we consider with new eyes the life of Edna Lewis, which began on a Virginia farm in a small settlement called Freetown in 1916 and ended when she took her last breath in 2006 in a little apartment in Decatur, Georgia, a few days shy of her ninetieth birthday.

The facts of Miss Lewis's life haven't changed since her death. She moved through the world as an African American woman only two genera-tions out of slavery. She was deeply committed to social change. She was an artist and a fashion designer, a writer and a cook whose reach stretched from California to Africa. Her life took her from the soft dirt fields of her beloved rural home, where gathering, growing, and cooking was a form of family entertainment, to professional kitchens in Washington, D.C., New York, and, finally, Atlanta.

But what her life meant, and her influence on subsequent generations, has a new urgency at a time when the nation is looking again into the causes and effects of racism, and the history of the brutality laced through so much of the South she loved.

Miss Lewis cooked at a time when the simple, pure country food she was raised on and sought to teach became twisted into the cartoonish, corn-pone version that Cracker Barrel and Paula Deen would come to exploit or became the greasy, reductive manifestations of barbecue and greens found in urban soul food restaurants.

Miss Lewis knew southern food was neither of those things. She articulated, in a quiet, lyrical, and powerful way, that southern cooking could be as simple as a perfect peach pie but also as precise and elegant in its execution as any dish in the haute French culinary canon. Country cooking, when approached with unflinching purity and a dedication to technique, was delicious and important.

For students of southern culture, there is little argument that Miss Lewis was at the heart of a culinary renaissance that has led to a deeper appreciation of the regional nuances of cooking in the South. She helped nudge those in the North and on the West Coast to embrace the notion that eating must be connected to the seasons and the earth, and that country food should have a revered place on the American table.

The importance of Edna Lewis is shifting still. As the country finds itself again drilling down into its class and racial divisions, Miss Lewis and her story have taken on yet another layer of importance. Although food has always been cultural currency, it has never enjoyed the kind of crossover into the arts, politics, and health as it has in the past decade. How we eat has come to underscore issues of race, class, and environmental degradation. The pleasures of the table softly open hearts and give us a common language and a reason to have hard conversations about where our food comes from and who cooks it. Any knowledgeable eater these days knows that a bowl of shrimp and grits or a pot of gently simmering lady peas flavored with just a kiss of streak 'o lean, for example, has roots in the worst chapter of America's history.

As cooks and scholars debate anew who owns southern food, Miss Lewis and her story offer a clear-eyed look back and a path forward. The life of an African American woman whose roots were firmly planted in garden soil and who cooked in countless kitchens with purpose and play-

Kim Severson

ful elegance becomes even more important. Her simple prose, her careful recipes, and her unyielding devotion to that which is both delicious and true mean more than they ever have.

Edna Lewis was a great cook in life. In death, she has become an even a greater teacher.

Introduction

SARA B. FRANKLIN

—⁊⁊⁊—

For me, it all began with a page of a magazine. It was January 2008. I was frozen deep in a Boston winter, paging through the issue of *Gourmet* that had just arrived in my mailbox and dreaming of new things pushing up through sun-warmed earth and the bite of something—anything—green on my tongue, to shock me out of the dull gray of short, dark northeastern days. Instead of a taste, though, it was a question that awoke me—"How did Southern food come into being?"—and a simple refrain—"Southern is . . . ." The piece was titled "What Is Southern?" and the author was Edna Lewis, an apparently esteemed cook and food writer I'd never heard of from a region—the American South—of which I knew nothing.

Her prose was feisty and provocative, wrought with exacting fineness. In "What Is Southern?" Edna Lewis spoke of a place, not merely through ingredients, but through culture as a whole—Truman Capote and wild watercress, Tennessee Williams and baked snowbirds; Lewis noted the forced history of illiteracy among black Americans in the same breath as some of the greatest names in American art and literature. There was no intent of irony here, but rather a distinct effort to broaden the purview of who and what was counted and accounted for in the measure of culture—Bessie Smith, environmental stewardship, Louis Armstrong, culinary know-how—and deep, deep knowledge of place buttressed it all.

I was hooked.

I promptly ordered a copy of Lewis's famed cookbook *The Taste of Country Cooking*, and read it cover to cover, discovering a text that was equal parts instruction manual, history book, memoir, field guide, and philosophical treatise. I hadn't known food could be the thread that connected all of that, nor had I realized that such complexity and depth of culture could all be found right here in the United States.

My America was worlds away from Lewis's. A Yankee through and through, my people are blueblood Boston Brahmins, hardworking New Jersey farmers and grocers, and decidedly urban Eastern European Jewish immigrants who landed in Brooklyn. I grew up in suburban New York—my parents' idea of a compromise between my father's love of bustling cities and my mother's longing for the fields and woods of New England.

I grew up with a deep, though unspoken, sense that the place we lived was not the sort of place you *belonged* to. Most of the adults in town, my dad among them, boarded the morning train to be whisked off to New York City for work, and my mom packed my brother and me up to visit family with huge gardens, chickens, and horses in Maine and Massachusetts every chance she got. We were, it seemed to me, always en route to somewhere else. I couldn't tell you much about what made that little hometown of mine distinct (though perhaps, returning with an adult's eyes, I'd have more insight). The food we ate reflected that vague placelessness, like the crackling static between channels on the TV. It was "American" in the worst sense—frozen vegetables, hot dogs, and buttered pasta.

My mom was never much of a cook, and she hated the nightly demand of getting dinner on the table. But she loved to eat, especially from the little patch of garden she tended in our backyard. And it was growing up, during summers, that I first understood that simple, fresh food, left mostly alone, is very good. There was no dogma to accompany this message, only a working woman who hated a hot stove.

Plates of vegetables from the garden, humid late afternoons spent picking what mom needed for dinner, and the short but fruitful growing season of the Northeast all stuck with me, albeit tucked somewhere way, way down. In my teenage years, I began experimenting with cooking—learning from the early stars of the Food Network—and used my very first check to send away for a subscription to the now defunct *Gourmet* magazine, the publication that would eventually introduce me to Miss Lewis. In college, I spent my free time in hole-in-the-wall restaurants and tiny, decrepit student kitchens, secretly entertaining a life in food, though I hadn't the slightest idea what that would mean. When I started farming around the same time, the connections between place, flavor, and good eating—those dormant threads from my childhood—became clearer, and my longing to develop and understand them stronger. Lewis became, for me, a pivotal figure in my thinking about food, and about American culture at large.

To Lewis, who was southern in both her cooking and her writing—which, today, is considered some of the most important, as well as the most resonant and evocative in America's cultural history—approachability and clarity were tantamount. For Edna Lewis, born in 1916 in rural Virginia, beauty was found in rushing streams that kept butter cool, in the smell of earth newly turned by a plow. The history of her African-descended ancestors was made plain by the presence of guinea hens in the farmyard and the artful use of fatback. Her devotion to the culinary and literary arts continued almost to the very end of her life—her final cookbook, *The Gift of Southern Cooking*, written with Scott Peacock, was published just three years before her death in 2006.

In Lewis's experience, culture could be found in chats over coffee, served so hot one had to save breath to cool the steaming cup. Politics were revealed in the willful disregard of Thanksgiving and Independence Day as holidays. Craft was demonstrated by the light touch of a hand turning biscuit dough, and artistry in the golden crackle of chicken skin. And a clear desire to be heard and counted shone through in lyrical, yet unflinchingly direct, prose.

Lewis—heralded today as both the grande dame and grande doyenne of southern cooking—played a vital role in drawing serious attention to the cooking of the American South and was among the first southern African American women to pen a cookbook transparent about the author's true identity—race, gender, and even name. The late Miss Lewis, as she was frequently called, cooked and wrote of food as a means to explore and commemorate her childhood experiences and memories of everyday life and, later, to celebrate the diversity and richness of southern foodways. Today, she is considered a key source on the black experience in the post-Reconstruction South, as well as a trailblazer of the contemporary revival and popularity of regional agriculture and cooking generally, and of southern food in particular.

Edna Lewis was born in Freetown, Virginia, a small community founded by emancipated slaves, including Lewis's grandfather. Food work was at the core of life in Freetown. The community proudly strove to be self-sufficient, growing most everything its inhabitants consumed, saving purchases only for such processed goods as sugar, flour, and coffee. In Lewis's portrayals of her birthplace, food was a source not only of survival but also of great joy and meaning. The rhythms of the fields and woods marked the passage of the seasons, bound the residents to their land, and acted as the nucleus of social gatherings, both everyday and festive. Lewis's young life revolved around the labors and joys of those rhythms, and she learned how to cook by participating in food production from an early age. From the fields to the forests, the smokehouse to the springhouse, the cutting block to the kitchen table, Lewis grew up with food at the forefront of her daily life. She came to value place, flavor, and the embodied memories of human hands, the very characteristics that would eventually define her cooking and writing style.

At sixteen, she left home for Washington, D.C., and then made her way to New York City, where she worked briefly as a laundress in Brooklyn, then as a seamstress. She observed the haute fashions of the day, eventually sewing garments for celebrities, including Marilyn Monroe, while simultaneously developing her own style of African-inspired garb, which she would don for the rest of her life. She is said to have been deeply involved, during this period, with the communist cause, together with her husband, Steve Kingston. While speculations about, and allusions to, Lewis's political affiliations ripple through biographical sketches, she herself rarely spoke on the record about such involvement.

Through it all, she continued, always, to cook. Her meals were well known and celebrated among many lucky enough to partake. In 1949, two friends of Lewis's from New York's downtown scene — John Nicholson, an eccentric, entrepreneurial antiques dealer, and fashion photographer Karl Bissinger — invited Lewis to helm the kitchen at Café Nicholson, a new East Side restaurant they were opening as partners. It was Lewis's first paid cooking job. Café Nicholson, which focused on simple French-inspired fare, became a veritable salon for New York's bohemian elite. The café garnered a devoted following that included a handful of notable southerners — Truman Capote and Tennessee Williams among them — for whom Lewis often specially prepared nostalgic southern dishes like buttermilk biscuits and fried chicken.

Food, which had been so quotidian a part of Lewis's upbringing, became her creative work. After three years, Lewis left Café Nicholson in 1952, trying her hand alternately at pheasant farming in New Jersey and working as a lecturer at the American Museum of Natural History, all while growing her reputation as a chef and private caterer. She left lasting marks on the food at the prominent the Fearrington House Restaurant in Pittsboro, North Carolina, and Middleton Place in Charleston, South Carolina.

The small but burgeoning food scene of the late sixties and seventies — whose ringleaders included Craig Claiborne of the *New York Times* and the beloved downtown bon vivant James Beard — began to raise the profile of food culture in general, and cookbooks particularly. And as demand for Lewis's exceptional culinary talents grew, she decided to try her hand at writing a cookbook. *The Edna Lewis Cookbook*, which Lewis cowrote with socialite Evangeline Peterson, was a collection of recipes focused on simple French American food of the sort featured at Café Nicholson, peppered throughout with a few southern favorites. Peterson and Lewis struggled to perfect the manuscript, and when, in the early seventies, Lewis found herself laid up with a broken leg, she and Peterson went to seek the counsel of Judith Jones, the Knopf editor who had "discovered" and published Julia Child in 1961.

As Jones tells it, the existing cookbook was too near to publication for a major overhaul. At the editor's urging, though, Lewis began to reminisce about her childhood in Freetown. It took only a few moments of Lewis recounting her vivid memories for Jones to realize she had struck gold. Lewis's voice was distinct—melodic, at moments edging on rhapsodic—and she had a unique story to tell that, Jones believed, would resonate with the reading and cooking public of the time.

Together, Lewis and Jones began work on a new book. Lewis struggled with writing at first, so as a workaround, Jones had Lewis tell her stories aloud, as she had in their first meeting, while Jones furiously took notes. She sent Lewis home with the scribbles and instructed Lewis to write her stories down exactly as she had told them. Before long, the two had the narrative that binds *The Taste of Country Cooking*. Lewis filled the book with pleasure-infused vignettes of her upbringing, like the first plowing of the earth in spring, foraging for wild greens, pulling cooled milk and butter up from a rushing stream that flowed under the springhouse, annual Emancipation Day picnics, and communal hog killings. In her introduction to *In Pursuit of Flavor*, Lewis wrote, "I feel fortunate to have been raised at a time when the vegetables from the garden, the fruit from the orchard and the meat from the smokehouse were all good and pure, unadulterated by chemicals and long-life packaging. . . . I have that memory of good flavor to go by.

The Taste of Country Cooking, published in 1976, is now considered a canonical text in the long history of southern cookery books and a classic in American culinary letters, one, as *New York Times* writers Eric Asimov and Kim Severson noted in their 2006 eulogy, that "sits on the shelves of America's best chefs." It also, vitally, helped shift perceptions of southern cooking, both within the region and outside its bounds. Lewis's book heralded an explosion in the publication of southern cookbooks that reflected the "nouvelle southern" style of cooking, a southern iteration of the nouvelle cuisine movement under way in France, with its focus on the freshest ingredients and purity of taste. In the wake of Lewis's success, notable southern cooks, such as Bill Neal of Crook's Corner in Chapel Hill, penned their own books, updating and refining southern classics and paying particular attention to local specialties and history of place.

It's important to remember that when Lewis published her book, the South was commonly perceived as a region that symbolized the tremendous inequities of modern America — an almost naive abundance abutting abject destitution. As Marcie Cohen Ferris demonstrates in *The Edible South*, popular conceptions of the region and its food emerged from a truly complex amalgam of historical events and cultural constructions of memory. The long shadow of slavery and the trauma of the Civil War tainted popular notions of the South and its cuisine with shame. In more recent memory, media covering the South had focused on the upheaval of the civil rights movement, images from Lyndon Johnson's War on Poverty, and the groundbreaking 1968 CBS documentary "Hunger in America."

Within the South, white nostalgia for (largely imagined) plantation sideboards groaning with plenty still ran rampant. Such mythology had long rendered black southern cooks all but invisible. Despite a growing scholarship that documented how enslaved Africans and, later, African Americans deeply shaped what we now think of as southern food, in popular consciousness, southern cuisine belonged to the white elite. Soul food, borne of the Great Migration, was, in part, the African American response to such insulting gaps in memory. Soul food paid tribute to its roots and the African and African American influences on southern cooking, but it was also a distinctly urban phenomenon, the cuisine of a people moving away from subsistence living and toward city lives. In the increasingly industrial cities of the Midwest and Northeast, food played an important role in asserting and maintaining cultural identity but still was largely relegated to the sidelines in daily life.

The Taste of Country Cooking presented both an alternative history and a new, authoritative perspective on southern food. As a black woman who had, by then, made a name for herself as a professional cook, Lewis remembered back before the urbanization of black southern cooking, before land loss and industrialization forever changed the demographic makeup and economy of the South. *Her* South — the rural, postbellum South of autonomous African Americans — had largely been forgotten. Lewis's reflections did not seek to define a region but to elegize a tiny dot on the map, a

Sara B. Franklin

community that was deeply connected to the land upon, and off of, which it subsisted. *The Taste of Country Cooking* powerfully reframed southern food for American readers and cooks; as Severson and Asimov put it, the book "helped put an end to the knee-slapping, cornpone image of southern food among many American cooks."

The Taste of Country Cooking made an immediate splash, unusual in its transracial appeal and rare combination of a gourmand sensibility with progressive politics. The back-to-the-landers found that the book echoed their ethic of communal spirit, self-sufficiency, and good health produced by subsistence farming. It appealed, too, to the burgeoning environmental movement, spurred by the publication of Rachel Carson's *Silent Spring* in 1962, and furthered by the oil embargo in 1973. It also played into the race and gender politics of the moment, providing an example of black femininity that simultaneously demonstrated cosmopolitanism and a deep awareness of ancestry and roots.

But Lewis's fans weren't merely drawn to her book for political reasons; they came for the food. Many of the leading figures of the food world were early enthusiasts of the book's recipes and prose. Alice Waters, the Berkeley-based champion of the nascent farm-to-table movement, and the great innovator in California cuisine, found in Lewis a kindred spirit, as did M. F. K. Fisher and James Beard (both of whom were, at the time, working with Judith Jones themselves). The *New York Times* food editor and restaurant critic Craig Claiborne—who himself hailed from the Deep South (Mississippi, to be exact)—said of the book that it "may well be the most entertaining regional cookbook in America."

Not only did Lewis's professional prominence climb as she quickly became a "chef's chef," but her personal life, too, changed. Lewis's editor, Judith Jones, became a close friend and confidant, as did Jones's husband, Evan Jones, also a writer, one who often covered food. Evan and Edna were known to spend evenings together in the Joneses' apartment, sipping bourbon and listening to Bessie Smith records. Involvement with the Joneses introduced Lewis to other women whose lives had changed dramatically due to their involvement in food writing and publication, including Julia Child and Marion Cunningham. Marion went on to become the country's foremost proselytizer of home cooking. Bolstered by Jones's encouragement and the successes of her food-writing peers, Lewis went on to pen another cookbook, *In Pursuit of Flavor*, in 1988. And after years of cooking mostly in the South, she made a return to the New York restaurant scene, bringing prominence, and a distinctly southern fare to the Brooklyn restaurant Gage & Tollner.

In the early 1990s, Lewis left restaurants for good and settled in Georgia. In her later years, she became best known as the mentor and companion of the emerging southern chef Scott Peacock, who was then running the kitchen of the Georgia governor's mansion. The two shared a food philosophy still rare in restaurant kitchens at the time: a focus on fresh, local ingredients, and a bent toward preserving and reviving what they saw as the endangered ways of traditional southern home cooking. The two, widely viewed as the odd couple of southern cooking—Peacock was several decades Lewis's junior, in addition to being a white, gay man—lived together in Decatur for the last years of Lewis's life. Together they wrote *The Gift of Southern Cooking: Recipes and Revelations from Two Great American Cooks* (2003), which, too, has taken its place as a classic in southern food cultures.

But Lewis's life and legacy goes even deeper, and this volume seeks to explore and provide a critical appreciation of some of complexities commonly left out in celebrations of her memory. *Edna Lewis: At the Table with an American Original* strives to unpack the mythology that surrounds Lewis as well as to deepen our understanding of her tremendous contribution to American foodways. Lewis's life and story are rife with seeming contradictions. She was thrust into a limelight that she was reluctant to claim; observing her toward the end of her life, novelist Chang-Rae Lee wrote, "The more time I spend with Lewis, the more I begin to suspect that her well-deserved status and prominence in the field are our own wishful construct, and not necessarily hers." Likely engaged with the communist cause, she was reticent about her involvement. Deeply attached to the southern countryside, she was drawn to the cultural elite of New York City. Beloved and highly sought after, she nevertheless, by the end of her life, often struggled to make ends meet. Posthumously the unwitting bearer of the black southern culinary experience, Lewis was far more complex than the nostalgic rural idyll imagined by so many.

Reflecting on an interview he'd conducted with the then elderly Lewis, in 2001 Chang-Rae Lee wrote, "In a quiet fashion, as a chef, cookbook author, and champion of southern cooking, [Lewis] is as legendary in the food world as Julia Child." And yet, whereas Child has long been a darling of the media and, more recently, has become a subject of interest for scholars of food, cinema, and women's history, knowledge of Lewis's life and work remains surprisingly slim beyond the realm of the tight-knit world of dedicated food lovers and food writers. This is particularly surprising given the impact she's had on perceptions and knowledge of American food in general, and southern foodways in particular. Child became a household name, yet Lewis lingers in the wings of popular food history—a cult favorite and an underdog hero. Writer Tim Mazurek put it nicely: "If you already know Edna Lewis, you probably assume everyone does, but an informal poll of my friends found that only one or two people knew who she was and exactly zero owned one of her cookbooks."

Recently, however, as southern food has taken the nation by storm—heirloom grits, artisanal bourbon, succotash, and countless varieties of pickles and preserves now grace the menus of America's finest restaurants—Lewis's memory has enjoyed something of a revival. A thirtieth edition of *The Taste of Country Cooking* was released in 2006—the year of Lewis's death—with a new and highly appreciative foreword by Alice Waters. In 2014, the U.S. Postal Service honored Lewis, alongside the likes of Julia Child and James Beard, as one of five "Celebrity Chefs" in American history. The Postal Service wrote that she "revolutionized our understanding of food," was an "early but ardent champion of trends that many foodies now take for granted," and "encouraged us to undertake our own culinary adventures." Of the chefs honored, Lewis was the only one who focused her work exclusively on "American" food.

Lewis and her memory are enjoying a surge of popularity and posthumous celebration, effectively introducing her to a new generation to whom she is largely unknown. This is important especially because she has long meant so much to many different kinds of people. Her life and work have transcended categories of race, place, and class, gender, age, and political allegiance, providing one of the best examples of what I call the quiet power of cookbooks.

This book aims to capture, for the first time and with the thoughtful attention she deserves, the life and work of Lewis through the voices of some of those whose lives she touched during her lifetime and those she continues to influence in the here and now.

In Part I, our essayists recall their impressions, both early and lasting, of Edna Lewis, whether they were lucky enough to have known her or, like me, encountered her only on the page. Former *Gourmet* editor Jane Lear reflects on Lewis's now iconic essay, "What Is Southern?" which she purchased (sight unseen) and published in *Gourmet* in

2008. In her essay, Lewis used luminaries of the day as her touchstones—including Thomas Wolfe, Bessie Smith, Richard Wright, William Faulkner, and Tennessee Williams—along with the signs and seasons of the natural world. Lear uses the essay as *her* touchstone to explore how nature, seasonal rhythms, and folk traditions inspired Lewis to spread the gospel of genuine southern cooking and inspired, in turn, a generation of home cooks. *Washington Post* food editor Joe Yonan, who grew up in West Texas, reflects on his discovery of Lewis through *The Gift of Southern Cooking* to explore his imagined nostalgia for a cuisine he never experienced growing up, his longing to claim southern food as his own, and how coming to understand the complexities of southern food has led him to explore and connect with his own patchwork identity. One of today's leading writers working to uncover and demand recognition of African American contributions to American food culture, Toni Tipton-Martin, explores the impact of her relationship with Lewis and her life and work on the author's own sense of mission and urgency to pursue and publicize the long, underappreciated history and impact of black women cooks on American foodways. Renowned cookbook and food writer Deborah Madison recalls a lunch that Lewis and Scott Peacock prepared for her during a book tour stop in Atlanta and reflects on what it was to be in Lewis's presence, as well as on the lingering effects of that encounter. John T. Edge, writer and leader of the Southern Foodways Alliance (SFA), shares his provocative 2013 essay "Debts of Gratitude"—in which he explores questions of iconicity and tokenization—updating it with details of Lewis's influence on and relationship to both himself and the SFA. Famed restaurateur and farm-to-table pioneer Alice Waters details her first impressions of *The Taste of Country Cooking* and explores the impact Lewis made on her own cooking style at Chez Panisse in Berkeley. She concludes her essay with a recipe in "the spirit of Edna's bracing combination of diligence and elegance" that graced the table at the centennial celebration of Lewis's birth at Chez Panisse in 2016. Eminent food writer Francis Lam shares his profile—at turns contemplative, reverential, and painful—of Lewis, published in 2015 in the *New York Times Magazine*; he writes of coming to know Lewis, many years into a career as a food professional, and the impact she has wrought across regions, generations, and races. Atlanta native Susan Rebecca White, whose 2006 novel *A Place at the Table* is loosely based on Lewis, writes of living in New York City, young and going through a divorce, and delving into *The Edna Lewis Cookbook* to research her novel. In so doing, she recalls the comforts of home and learns that feeding oneself well can lead to healing. And writer and cookbook author Caroline Randall Williams tells of growing up in a family of women from Lewis's universe, who embodied, Williams finds, the grace and culinary tastes by which Miss Lewis also lived. Williams tells the story of shared heritage as it informs the present and future of southern food, black food, and a reclamation of both southern and black health, elegance, and eloquence through food and through history.

In Part II, writers explore and interrogate Lewis's role and broader context in culinary, racial, agricultural, labor, geographical, women's, and literary history and culture. Chef and food studies scholar Scott Alves Barton presents an essay in three acts, in which he details Lewis's import in the community of black professional chefs, positions her within the African diaspora, and examines and celebrates her cooking style and recipes alongside those of other African American cooks and cookbook writers, himself included. Historian Megan Elias argues that Lewis was herself a historian and that her cookbooks contributed "to the work of reclamation by identifying a black food history" during a period when African American history was first being explored in earnest, as both part of the American historical narrative and a story all its own. Culinary historian of the African diaspora Michael W. Twitty writes of Lewis as a subject and lens not only into southern foodways but into a much more regionally and culturally specific history. In so doing, he argues that while Lewis, indeed, helped destigmatize and popularize southern food in general, her work reminds us of the wide diversity among southern histories, identities, and cuisines. Performance scholar Lily Kelting takes on the perplexing paradox of Lewis's ubiquity as an inspiration for some of today's most prominent southern chefs even as her presence in the archives remains scarce. How, she asks, do we draw out the details of her life, given such a void in the record, and how do we study the life and impact of someone whose work was food, which is, by its very definition, ephemeral? How might we use Lewis to develop a more sensory approach to history in general and to culinary history more specifically? Patricia E. Clark, a literary scholar with a deep interest in African American cookbooks, takes up similar questions of absence and distance, this time the relative dearth of race in Lewis's work. In grappling with questions about Lewis's place and role in African American literature, she positions Lewis within a long history of African American authors and cooks who have made important marks in the history of published work and yet have left much of significance unsaid. Only recently have those in quest of American history and identity been given the latitude to rummage through cupboards and comb farm fields, stand at the stove and sit at kitchen tables in our search. Although food may be the most universal and the most frequently exercised of all cultural forms, it has long been seen as so quotidian, "so banal," as American studies scholar Marcie Cohen Ferris puts it, "as to be virtually invisible." The scholarly essays in this section thus contribute important work to the fledgling but growing interdisciplinary field of food studies.

In Part III, we see how Lewis's legacy lives on, most tangibly, today: on tables around the country. We become privy here to how, over more than four decades, Lewis has influenced prominent cooks, who also teach cooking. Through this channel, we assume, Lewis's legacy reaches into the kitchens of home cooks day after day. Cookbook author, cooking instructor, and southern food writer Nathalie Dupree offers insight into what it was to know, work with, and be inspired by Lewis up close at the height of her career and explores issues of race and bias in the world of food media. Delving into some of Lewis's most famed relationships, as well as her notable positions as head chef at restaurants along the Eastern Seaboard, Dupree offers a rare window into Lewis as a friend, colleague, public figure, fellow southerner, feminist, and struggling artist, all with a keen awareness of race and how it affected Lewis's image and treatment both publicly and privately. Chef Mashama Bailey, raised in the Bronx but with deep roots in the South, speaks of Lewis's impact as she switched careers from social worker to professional cook and how she discovered, in Lewis, a woman whose resemblance to the women in her family was not so much in the way they looked as in the way they cooked and in the centrality of food and the table among southern families. Bailey concludes with recipes for a meal she prepares as a way to lace the threads of her geography and ancestry, in which she finds belonging and comfort. Maine-based cooking teacher and farmer Annemarie Ahearn writes of the parallels she has discovered between agricultural life and the cooking of both the mountain South and the coastal North. She speaks of the inspiration she has drawn from Lewis, ranging from the art of preserving to the simple reminder to attend to one's surroundings. It has influenced her adjustment to farm life and cooking and also her approach to teaching others to source and prepare the best food possible. Ahearn concludes with a full seasonal menu, in the style of Lewis's *Taste of Country Cooking*, that serves as the foundation for an Edna Lewis–themed summertime class she has integrated into the curriculum at her cooking school, Salt Water Farm. Chef and television personality Vivian Howard writes of her return to rural North Carolina after beginning her cooking career in New York's fine-dining restaurants and of Lewis's role in her slow, humbling realization that, in order to connect and resonate with her hometown audience, she would need to find a culinary approach that reflected the skills and techniques she had picked up in the urban North while honoring the agriculture, traditional dishes, and deep-set culture of the rural South. Demonstrating the balance she's achieved, Howard includes a Lewis-inspired recipe of the sort that has struck a chord both regionally and nationally, leading to broad appreciation of Howard's approach to the revival of southern cooking in her own right. And, closing the volume, cookbook author and master preserver Kevin West speaks of what it is to be a southerner in exile himself, as Lewis was, and the deep longing and even deeper curiosity that those circumstances instill. In a haunting essay, he links the current resurgence of interest in traditional southern foodways and his own family's food traditions with the omnipresent march of technology and mobility that so affects, and in some ways threatens, the ancestors, ghosts, and cultures that characterize the mountain South.

"Recently," observed southern studies scholars William Ferris and Charles Reagan Wilson, "culture has been viewed as an abstraction." We look for high culture *in* abstraction, sniffing for symbolism and hidden metaphors as markers of magnitude and import; the fewer who understand, perhaps the louder the applause.

Food, of course, is the opposite of abstract. The thing on the plate is the thing itself; transformed by the alchemy of heat, the combining of ingredients, and the skill of human hands, yet remaining nothing other than that which it is. And if it fails to appeal — to be, literally, palatable — it fails to fulfill its purpose: to be consumed, to give nourishment, and ultimately to disappear. Food, and home cooking in particular, could not be any more tangible, any less abstract. Day after day, the onions must be chopped and the eggs scrambled, the meal served and the dishes washed. Food's inherent *neededness* makes it seem less a site of culture than one of drudgery; not only is it common, it is necessary, too. In the ignominy of repetition and the dullness of ubiquity, we often forget to look at the gleam. Edna Lewis looked at the gleam.

Through her voice on the page, Lewis started me on a winding path in food and an ongoing fascination with southern food and culture. Lewis lent me her insatiable curiosity about plant varieties, both wild and domestic, and reminds me constantly that the divisions between production and consumption are false. From Lewis, I learned that intimacy is as crucial, but undervalued, a pillar of our collective food system as it is of our private food cultures at home. She awakened me to the breathtaking power of tenderness, too—a truth I first experienced when a man gently folded feather-light biscuit dough for my breakfast. I married him.

This book, then, is a project of personal tribute of gratitude as much as it is of critical exploration and collaborative celebration. All of the writers herein have their own tales of how they first discovered Lewis. In some essays, that story takes center stage; in others, it recedes into the background, replaced by insights and questions that Lewis and her work have provoked. What emerges from this many-tongued volume is a nuanced picture of Lewis as deeply human, a woman whose spirit and impact is very much alive today, countering the notion that she is but an icon, a figure of the past, an untouchable archetype frozen in time. Although the voices, ages, races, ethnicities, regional provenances, and professions of our essayists range widely, each writer's sense of Lewis as muse, as visionary, and as immortal teacher shines through. And in this contested and divisive moment in American history, one in which the very idea of place—both physical place and the cultures of place, that is to say, *belonging*—is constantly called into question, Lewis's voice and lessons take on new resonance and offer important insight. We hope that this book will cement Lewis's place in history—culinary, African American, and women's—while emphasizing her impact, and that it will provide a suitable legacy for a remarkable woman whose vibrant work speaks to the power of food at the heart of American life and culture.

Sara B. Franklin

PART ONE

Encountering Miss Lewis

What Is Southern?

The Annotated Edna Lewis

JANE LEAR

More than a quarter century ago, Edna Lewis spooled out a lyrical essay she titled "What Is Southern?" on lined yellow legal paper and sent it along to friend and fellow food writer Eugene Walter. "How did southern food come into being? The early cooking of southern food was primarily done by blacks, men and women. In the home, in hotels, in boardinghouses, on boats, on trains, and at the White House.... What began as hard work became creative work," she wrote, economically ignoring the vertical margin on the left. "There is something about the South that stimulates creativity in people, be they black or white writers, artists, cooks, builders, or primitives that pass away without knowing they were talented.... Living in a rural setting is inspiring: Birds, the quiet, flowers, trees, gardens, fields, music, love, sunshine, rain, and the smells of the earth all play a part in the world of creativity. It has nothing to do with reading or writing. Many of those cooks could not read or write."

The cover letter, likely torn from the same pad and dated June 9, 1992, read in part: "For me the South is not just food. It is beauty, love, hate Art, Poetry and hard work. I love what is good.... It is what makes us who we are." At the bottom of the page, to the right of Miss Lewis's signature, is a water ring made by a chunky tumbler, and it has all the authority of a notary's seal. I can almost hear the chink of ice in bourbon as Walter set down the glass on what was at hand.

The essay—really, more of a manifesto—in which Miss Lewis defines her world was inspired by a cooking seminar in Seaside, Florida, that she put together with Scott Peacock, former chef for the Georgia governor and her protégé. Along with Walter and John Egerton, one of the South's most eminent writers on history and food, they became so caught up in the spirit of the thing that they all talked about writing a book together. Miss Lewis followed through with alacrity, then mailed her contribution off to Walter.

Fast-forward to 2007, when Miss Lewis, who had died the year before, was the subject of a remarkable phone conversation I had with Thomas Head, a pal from the Southern Foodways Alliance. He and Don W. Goodman, executor of the estate of Eugene Walter, had discovered "What Is Southern?" in a box of Walter's papers, and they wondered if *Gourmet*, where I was senior articles editor, would be interested in acquiring it. In 1984, the magazine had published a piece by Evan Jones about Miss Lewis (her signature chocolate soufflé was on the cover), so it seemed like a fitting home for their find, Tom said.

It certainly did. I snapped it up, sight unseen, in a New York minute.

Miss Lewis was the quietest, most enigmatic star in the culinary firmament, and I can't help but be amused at how many people today claim they knew her really, really well. I most assuredly did not, even though we met long ago, at the offices of Alfred A. Knopf, her publisher and my employer, a couple of years after *The Taste of Country Cooking* appeared in 1976.

I was new to the city and new to cooking for myself—a necessity on an entry-level publishing salary. So I dipped into the cookbooks I'd inherited from my mother, including a first edition of *Charleston Receipts*, published in 1950 by the Junior League of Charleston. Unlike so many of the community cookbooks that are published today—polyglot collections with no regional identity whatsoever—the book reflected a marked sense of place. Leaving aside the references to canned soup, oleomargarine, and so on, the recipes featured the abundant provisions of a subtropical region: seafood, game, rice, vegetables, fruit. The range was extraordinary. There were almost fifty recipes in the beverage chapter, for example, including one for the cordial called cherry bounce that begins: "Go to Old Market and get a quart of wild cherries." Other treasures included pepper jelly and pickled okra (now considered icons of the South but, in fact, created after World War II), oyster fritters, rice omelet, smothered marsh hens, and Huguenot torte. I read it in chunks, like a novel or guidebook, and I did the same with Miss Lewis's *Taste of Country Cooking*.

It was her second book, a cookbook-memoir, and an instant classic. The prose was fresh, immediate, and evocative; what saved it from sentimentality was the steely commitment to a farm-to-table connection that was decades ahead of its time. And the menus, organized by seasons, were convivial and celebratory, ranging from An Early Spring Dinner of braised mutton, a salad of tender beet tops, lamb's quarters, and purslane, and blancmange garnished with raspberries to A Winter Dinner of beef à la mode, wild watercress salad with vinegar and oil, and deep-dish apple pie with nutmeg sauce. Both reminiscences and recipes were testament to the broad sweep of American cooking when Miss Lewis, who was born in 1916, was a girl.

Miss Lewis and I had a nodding acquaintance throughout the years—we'd often see one another on the prowl at the New York City Greenmarket—but I didn't get a chance to enjoy her cooking until the late 1980s, when she presided over the kitchen at Gage & Tollner (established in 1879), in Brooklyn. I'd lived in Brooklyn Heights since my Knopf days and, when feeling flush, ventured across the vast expanse of Boerum Place to the grittier environs of Fulton Street, where the restaurant's Doric-columned portico, vintage gas-electric lighting fixtures, and dignified waiters welcomed all comers.

I get hungry just thinking about the menu: she-crab soup, crab cakes, broiled oysters on toast, broiled clam bellies and creamed asparagus, pan-fried quail with country ham, perfectly fried chicken, ultralight biscuits brought straight from the oven, and pies that longtime friends and I still reminisce about. For me, an expat southerner, eating Miss Lewis's food was more than a taste of home, it was part of my education. Some years on, when I was introduced to the concept of terroir in France, it felt instantly familiar.

"What Is Southern?" did not disappoint Gourmet's editors. We felt it was so important, in fact, that we decided to build the entire January 2008 issue around the essay—a loosely patterned mosaic of the seasons as well as the food, cooks, writers, musicians, and artists of the American South. I've always had the feeling that Miss Lewis wrote it, at least in part, for her own enjoyment, weaving together memories of her childhood in Freetown, Virginia—a farming community established by freed slaves, including her grandparents—with those of the lively intellectual circles she became part of when she moved to New York City. Her observations of the world around her are infused with the ethical understanding and wisdom that come to some people when they look back on not just a lifetime but an entire way of life.

For Miss Lewis, southern was Truman Capote and Harper Lee, who were among the glamorous crowd she fed at Café Nicholson, on East Fifty-

Eighth Street. It was Tennessee Williams and Marlon Brando, who, during the Broadway run of *A Streetcar Named Desire*, would walk her home at night, stopping at bars along the way. Among the literary sensations she mentioned were some whose work was completely of the moment — Thomas Wolfe, for instance, who explored the growth of a creative genius (himself) in *Look Homeward, Angel* and its sequel, *Of Time and the River*, and Richard Wright, the son of a Mississippi sharecropper, who should be read not just with Ralph Ellison and James Baldwin but also Theodore Dreiser and Sinclair Lewis. Their work breathed life and vigor into the American experience.

"Southern is William Faulkner, *Intruder in the Dust*," Miss Lewis wrote, singling out the 1948 novel written as a response to growing racial tensions in the South. "Southern is Carson McCullers in *The Member of the Wedding*. . . . Southern is Craig Claiborne, for more than 25 years the distinguished food critic of *The New York Times*."

Claiborne, like everyone who met Miss Lewis, was struck by her insistence on using the pure, pedigreed ingredients of her southern upbringing. "What is undoubtedly the most unusual background on the New York food scene belongs to an elegant, handsome cookbook author named Edna Lewis," he wrote for the *Times* in 1979. "The community and her family were self-sustaining. They grew their own wheat, which they threshed, bundled, and took to the miller. They would return home with bags of flour. . . . They raised their own chickens and, more importantly, hogs. . . . They also ate, in season, of course, a good deal of wild game. . . . The good, free things on her family's acres also included wild strawberries, blackberries, huckleberries, wild grapes (you can smell them a mile away), elderberries, and wild, round red plums that grew along the streams."

In addition to its agrarian character, Miss Lewis's food and food writing can be best described in terms of what culinary historian William Woys Weaver, in *America Eats: Forms of Edible Folk Art*, called "connectedness." It involves several levels of meaning at the same time, he explained. Highly charged with deeply rooted emotional associations, it was the interaction of people caring for one another through food — at a hog butchering, say, when families gathered to help each other. Connectedness was also "a direct tie to one's natural surroundings: the woods, the pastures, the streams." The cook was mistress of her own food supply, he added. "She watched her corn as it grew . . . knew which hillsides had the best mountain blueberries, and which pastures had the best morels each spring." Let's pause here to think of Miss Lewis traveling by train to culinary gatherings, her luggage consisting primarily of cardboard boxes holding ingredients (including homemade baking powder) or pie dough.

Among Miss Lewis's literary strengths were her unaffected, straightforward language—she was incapable of overwriting—an unerring sense of sentence rhythm, and an overall buoyancy of tone, despite the matter-of-fact mentions of the hard work and difficulties inherent to living off the land. But it wasn't until I had waded deep into the editing of "What Is Southern?" that I realized many readers—especially those who didn't grow up in the rural South or have older relations to pass down the accumulated folk wisdom—wouldn't understand half of what she was talking about. Yes, they would be captivated and moved by her voice and the stories she had to tell, the food she described. The key to her world, however, lies in four words: *I grew up noticing.*

Her observational skills were enhanced by her capacity for utter stillness. Not many people, outside of dancers and others trained for the stage, have that sort of ability. It's invaluable, though, when you are learning how to pay attention. "Southern is an early spring morning shrouded in a thick mist. The warmth of a bright sunrise reveals shimmering jewellike dewdrops upon thicket and fence. A large spiderweb glistens, a spider trying desperately to wind its prey into the web."

That's beautiful imagery in and of itself, but Miss Lewis would have also been aware of a practical aspect: that the webs of some spider species can be used as a natural styptic, to stop bleeding—even hemorrhaging in childbirth. Much of her early life experience was informed, after all, by the customs and traditional plant-based medicines that have long been associated with the cycle of the seasons and rites of passage. And when you start looking at what Miss Lewis noticed in that context, you'll discover a sensibility that is even richer than you may have thought.

My father set out to prepare for planting corn. The first day, I walked behind him while he was plowing and singing one of his favorite hymns. For me, it was a great moment. Walking along, pressing my bare feet against the warm plowed earth. All the chickens were behind me, picking up the earthworms and bugs. He turned up the roots of sassafras bushes, which we took to the house for the next morning.

Sassafras bushes, which we took to the house for the next morning. The roots of sassafras (*Sassafras albidum*) should always be gathered before the bushes bloom; once the sap rises, they turn bitter, even poisonous, according to prevailing folk wisdom. Freshly harvested roots are cleaned of their bark, broken into pieces, and used fresh or dried to make an age-old spring tonic or year-round beverage; the early American colonists were making alcoholic "root tea," based on Native American recipes, in the eighteenth century. Today, many people think of root beer when (or if) they think of sassafras, but you won't find it on any ingredients list; in 1960, the FDA banned sassafras root bark in root beer because of its high content of safrole, a carcinogen. Happily, the ban doesn't extend to the powdered dried safrole-free sassafras leaves known as filé, a seasoning and thickener in gumbos.

I grew up among people who worked together, traded seed, borrowed setting hens if their own were late setting.

Borrowed setting hens. A setting hen is a broody hen—that is, one that's ready to set, or nest, on a clutch of eggs. The hormones causing broodiness are stimulated in the spring, with the lengthening daylight. Up until just a few decades ago, the rural population of the South was largely self-sufficient in terms of supplying its chicken and egg needs, wrote J. Dennis Lord in *Foodways*, volume 7 of *The New Encyclopedia of Southern Culture*; typically, the cash with which to buy baby chicks was extremely limited among farmers. In *The Taste of Country Cooking*, a late spring dinner revolves around skillet spring chicken with watercress. "There was always great excitement when the first chickens from spring hatching were cooked," Miss Lewis wrote. "The neighbors would announce when they expected to have their first spring chicken meal. We all reared our chickens carefully and fed them by hand, which made them especially tender and tasty. The first ones we had were usually pan-broiled."

Southern is a meal of early spring wild greens—poke sallet before it is fully uncurled, wild mustard, dandelion, lamb's-quarter, purslane, and wild watercress. . . . Served with those first wild greens, a casserole of white potatoes baked in chicken stock.

Poke sallet before it is fully uncurled. Poke sallet is a dish of the cooked young, tender leaves or shoots of the common pokeweed (*Phytolacca americana*), an opportunistic hardy perennial native to the eastern United States that now grows on every continent except Antarctica. The young leaves were eaten alone or mixed with other spring greens, and the sprouts were eaten like asparagus. The name likely derives from the Algonquian word *pocan*, referring to a plant used for dye; one alternative name for it is "inkberry." Hold that thought.

Poke, an early spring green, was harvested wild as well as cultivated in many colonial gardens. Its use as a nutritious food source eventually dwindled because of the increasing availability of frozen and canned foods and the inconvenient fact that at a point in the plant's life cycle, it becomes poisonous. The leaves and shoots should only be harvested when the plant is less than eight inches high, and they must always be cooked properly before eating. Still, it's important to remember that, in the words of renowned forensic toxicologist Alfred Swaine Taylor (1806–1880), "A poison in a small dose is a medicine." Native Americans and the early colonists used various parts of the plant in treatments for a wide range of ailments, including general aches and pains, ulcers, parasitic diseases, syphilis, and diphtheria. Pokeweed's current relevance may surprise you: scientists are using the red dye made from the plant's berries to coat efficient, low-cost fiber-based solar cells. The dye acts as an absorber, helping the fibers trap even more sunlight to convert into cheap energy—a boon to isolated rural communities or the developing world. Miss Lewis would have been delighted at this newfound resourcefulness.

White potatoes. Many southerners still refer to any baking or boiling potatoes as "white" or "Irish" potatoes to distinguish them from sweet potatoes, which aren't reserved for Thanksgiving but are another everyday vegetable.

Southern is a sun dog—something like a rainbow, or the man in the moon—on a late summer afternoon.

A sun dog. A sun dog is a bright patch of light that sometimes appears beside the sun, and in the days before widespread forecasting systems, a sun dog at sunset foretold a bad storm. The scientific term for a sun dog is *parhelion* (from the Greek word *parēlion*, meaning "beside the sun"); the origin of the colloquial term is unclear, perhaps stemming from the notion that it follows the sun like a dog follows its master. Created when sunlight refracts off plate-shaped ice crystals in cirrus clouds, a sun dog tends to be most visible when the sun is close to the horizon. It's among the most frequently observed optical phenomena, and may be observed throughout the year and anywhere in the world. Sometimes a sun dog exhibits a spectrum of colors: the area that's closest to the sun is typically red, while the parts that are farther away appear blue or green.

~~&~~

Southern is a springhouse filled with perishables kept cool by a stream running through. And a spring keeper — a salamander — is there, watching over.

And a spring keeper — a salamander — is there. Salamanders, tailed amphibians grouped with newts in the order Urodela, are called spring keepers because they're found in clean-running springs. Folk belief holds that if you kill the spring keeper, the spring will run dry. More species of salamanders exist in the southern Appalachian mountains than anywhere else in the world.

~~&~~

Southern is hunting season, a time that men take off to hunt rabbits, squirrel, opossum, deer, quail, partridge, plover, and dove. We used to trap snowbirds and enjoy a pan of them baked.

Snowbirds. These are dark-eyed juncos, a type of sparrow; in winter, they flock together in brushy clearings and open woods, where they prefer to feed on the ground.

~~&~~

Southern is the call of the whip-poor-will at midnight.

Whip-poor-will at midnight. The repetitive chanting of this nocturnal bird at dawn and dusk, and on moonlit nights, has been made famous in literature, poetry, and music. (Who can forget Hank Williams, who in 1949 wrote and recorded one of the saddest songs in existence? "Hear that lonesome whippoorwill / He sounds too blue to fly / The midnight train is whining low / I'm so lonesome I could cry.") The belief that hearing a whip-poorwill at midnight is a prophetic sign of death reaches beyond the South; in one New England version, the bird can feel a soul departing, and swoops down to capture it as it flees.

"What Is Southern?" leads us through the seasons, from spring's wild asparagus to Christmas divinity, followed by hoppin' John and greens on New Year's Day. That organizing principle works well, especially when you view the essay as a coda to *The Taste of Country Cooking*, but rereading the essay now — well, it triggered my compulsion to edit. Just the thought of fashioning it around an entirely different motif, such as the four elements — earth, air, fire, and water — is an excuse to play.

"Long before European settlers arrived, these same elements appear as clan symbology among the earliest Native Americans inhabiting the South," wrote Dorinda G. Dallmeyer in *Elemental South: An Anthology of Southern Nature Writing*. "More broadly in the world, these four elements are repeated in Chinese and Indian philosophical texts, in Celtic myth, in creation stories of the Polynesians, the Bantus, and the Australian Aborigines." Miss Lewis probably knew all this.

It wouldn't be a stretch to say that earth nourished and nurtured her physically and spiritually, from the clay pot she used for braising guinea hens with butter, fresh herbs, onions, and mushrooms to the smells after a violent thunderstorm "that tempt us to eat the soil." Earth was the bounty of the Virginia Piedmont. "Southern is weeks of canning, pickling, and preserving — cucumber pickle, artichoke pickle [made from the tubers called Jerusalem artichokes, not globe artichokes], pear pickle, tomato pickle, watermelon rind pickle, citron preserves, green tomato preserves, fig preserves, cherry preserves, grape conserve, crab apple jelly, wild blackberry jelly, fox grape jelly, quince jelly, guava jelly, wild plum jelly, wild strawberry preserves (the best)."

Air? Oh, that's even more fun, if you allow for the sky as well as the carrying of scent and sound. "Southern is Bessie Smith. Give me a pig foot and a bottle of beer. . . . Southern is Bourbon Street and Louis Armstrong. . . . Richard Wright and his 'Bright and Morning Star'. . . . Southern is fresh-made corn fritters, light and crisp enough to fly away . . . a moss rose, a camellia, a buttercup, a tea olive tree sending its fragrance through the air and into the kitchen . . . a pot of boiling coffee sending its aroma out to greet you on your way in from the barn."

With the exception of Roman candles, which ushered in Christmas before daylight, fire goes unmentioned in the essay but runs throughout it nonetheless. So much is cooked long and slow — a barbecued pig, Brunswick stew, an "assembly of greens" with cornmeal dumplings — or, like yeast rolls or deviled crabs, are best hot from the oven. Fire is what allowed Miss Lewis to turn humble ingredients—such as potatoes, butter, and chicken broth—into a casserole that is nothing short of eloquent, or a meaty ham hock, water, and green beans into a smoky, luxuriant revelation.

Last, water. It kept perishables cool, but it also fostered community and connections through "a pitcher of lemonade, filled with slices of lemon and a big piece of ice from the icehouse . . . a walk along the streams in September to find out if the fox grapes are ripening." Water, too, was the source of herring with its roe, edging out shad as "the most delicious" of the first-caught fish of spring; a turtle, washed out of the stream by a thunderstorm and destined for the soup pot; and the seafood for a heady gumbo or oyster stew. "Water—so vital to life and yet so mutable in form—reflects the simultaneous complexity and simplicity of the natural world," wrote Dallmeyer.

As did Miss Lewis. By the time "What Is Southern?" was published, this pioneer of regional southern food had become an icon and inspiration to a multitude of influential southern chefs, farmers, artisanal producers, heritage gardeners, seed savers, purveyors, food writers, and editors. "The world has changed," she wrote in the resonant final paragraph of her essay. "We are now faced with picking up the pieces and trying to put them into shape, document them so the present-day young generation can see what southern food was like. The foundation on which it rested was pure ingredients, open-pollinated seed—planted and replanted for generations—natural fertilizers. We grew the seeds of what we ate, we worked with love and care." She was passing on a legacy that she, in turn, had received from her parents and grandparents.

It is April 13, 2016, the centenary of Miss Lewis's birth. As I sit writing, the air is cool, with the sweetness of spring behind it. The cherry trees are frothy with pale blossom, the sun is pouring in on a tray of okra seedlings. And I think to myself: *We can do this.*

Jane Lear

Polished

JOE YONAN

⤙⤚

I'm ashamed to admit that I first encountered the work of Edna Lewis almost three decades after she published her masterpiece, *The Taste of Country Cooking*. I say ashamed because I was in my mid-thirties by then, a budding food writer, and in hindsight, I should have known her much better, much sooner.

It must have had something to do with living in Boston at a time long before southern food was hip; with wanting to carve out a reputation as a modern, globally minded writer and cook; and with assuming that I had no right to claim the cuisines of the South as my birthright, even though I was born in Georgia and raised in Texas. At the Cambridge School of Culinary Arts, which I attended at the turn of the millennium while working at the *Boston Globe*, we may have touched on Edna during our lecture tour of regional American cooking. But if we did, the lesson didn't stick. I was more captivated by the weeks we spent on Europe — the cassoulets, brimming with duck confit and sausages, of rural France; the true paellas, all about the rice and crusty on the bottom, of Spain; the baci di dama, sandwich cookies named for a mother's kiss, of northern Italy — than those involving anything closer to home.

It wasn't until 2003, a few years after I graduated from culinary school, and the publication of *The Gift of Southern Cooking*, the book Scott Peacock wrote with her, that I began to realize just what Edna meant to the world of food and just what it meant to be a southern cook. I know that's what Scott wanted, among other things — to introduce Edna to a generation who might not know her, or know her well, and to reintroduce her to another generation at risk of forgetting.

When *The Gift of Southern Cooking* hit my desk at the *Globe*, where I was a food writer and travel editor, I was floored at a glance. I must have stared at the cover alone for fifteen minutes before I even cracked it open.

There was Edna, her gray hair pulled back (just as it was on the covers of *The Taste of Country Cooking* and *In Pursuit of Flavor*, I would later learn), dressed in a colorful batik-print dress. And there across from her was Scott, gazing at her with what seems like a mix of awe and love as she grinned back. They were on an unmistakably southern porch, with dappled light, paint-worn railings, and greenery in the background and fore-, and on their little table for two, I could see what looks like fried chicken, black-eyed peas, big water goblets, and, was that a sweet potato pie? I could smell it all, and it seemed at once familiar and mysterious, like one of those dreams in which you're wandering through a house that doesn't quite look like yours, but somehow you know it's home. Or you want it to be.

I could sense immediately that the book would overtake me, and it did. I cooked out of it for weeks on end, or at least I think I did. (Memory is no more accurate a narrator than a dream.) I do remember corn-meal soufflés and lemon curd cakes, pan-fried chickens and catfish stews. And one recipe I ended up making for many, many years: bacon dredged in brown sugar and baked until it caramelizes and hardens. I internalized the recipe so completely that I looked at it only the first time or two, from then on making it on my own and serving it every chance I got: at brunches alongside French toast, on pickle trays that accompanied cocktails, as a topping for deviled eggs. Every time I would serve it, guests—most of them Yankees, I'm sure—would react with a raised eyebrow, then come around at first bite. The candied strips of smoky sweetness presaged the everything-is-better-with-bacon by a good decade—and not everyone was ready for them.

A few years later, I lost my first bid to become food editor of the *Washington Post* in part because, as I would later learn, one particularly old-school member of the hiring committee was repulsed when my answer to the question of what types of things I had been cooking lately included "candied bacon." (I ended up getting the job the next time it came up just a year later, in 2006, which happens to be the same year Edna died at the age of eighty-nine.)

The recipes—homey and yet surprising, full of flavor and just as ingredient-driven and technique-focused as anything I had learned in culinary school—were just part of *The Gift of Southern Cooking*'s appeal, of course. It was Scott's description of his life with "Miss Lewis," as he has always called her, and of her life before him, that pulled me in even deeper. He writes that they had been living together a few years by the time they wrote *Gift*. One photo in the front matter shows Scott with his arms wrapped around Edna from behind, an almost possessive pose. Their relationship seemed to represent a bridge between past and present, black and white, and, as I got to know Scott later, straight and gay.

I also must admit to no small amount of envy. I envied Scott for having this powerful connection to someone so obviously wise. And the more I read about his MeMaw's potato salad and Edna's wild-turtle soup, the one she learned to make in the settlement of freed slaves where she was born and raised, the more I wished my own upbringing had been nearly as tied to the rich history and cuisines of the real South—or, for that matter, to any culinary history at all. Tales of their lives filled me with a sort of phantom nostalgia, a longing to remember a life I didn't get to live.

I was born in Albany, Georgia, a three-hour drive south from Atlanta. My late father was an air force pilot, and he would tell us stories of flying home over the peanut fields of nearby Plains, birthplace of Jimmy Carter. That's about as far as my exposure to the food culture (or any culture) of my hometown goes. It would be many years before I would learn that the city had been a hotspot for civil rights protests, that it had repealed its Jim Crow laws only two years before I was born. My time there was short. My father was transferred to Goodfellow Air Force Base in San Angelo, Texas, before we celebrated my first birthday—perhaps because the air force was preparing to close up operations at the Albany base. (About the only thing I really ever got to know firsthand about Albany was the right way to pronounce it, courtesy of my oldest sister, Teri: It's "al-BEN-ee," something that, years later, I would delight in reminding those who said it like it was just like the city in New York State. That pronunciation, aided by my Texas twang, would become another way—like the candied bacon—I told the world, and I suppose myself, that I was southern.)

In San Angelo, as the youngest of seven kids, the food culture I saw was primarily limited to steakhouses, Tex-Mex joints, and Church's Fried Chicken, with a few dollops from my mother's Midwestern upbringing—broccoli cream cheese casserole and cream of mushroom meatloaf—thrown in. While I developed a fine enough affection for each, I wouldn't exactly call an enchilada my madeleine. Maybe it's because when I was growing up, I didn't feel like a Texan any more than I felt like a Georgian. My parents, after all, couldn't claim those identities, either. My mother is of mostly Irish and Scottish ancestry, and before she lived in San Angelo she followed my father from base to base throughout the South. My strongest connection to an ethnic heritage came from my father's side, as he was first-generation Assyrian immigrant, whose parents met in a farming community in Indiana after both fled massacring Turks in the Middle East in the 19-teens. From him I inherited the dark features that caused so many Mexican American neighbors and classmates in San Angelo to speak to me in Spanish — "Mita, mita!" they would say, trying to get my attention, and I would wonder, "Who is this Mita they keep calling for?" ("Oh, no, you a gringo, man?" they would say when they realized.) Was I?

Like so many children of immigrants, my father resisted talk of the "old country" where his parents were born. There was a bright line between the then and there and the here and now. He and my mother divorced when I was just a toddler, he returned to Chicago, and years later, when my sister Julie and I started making annual visits, we spent time mostly with my non-Assyrian stepmother's nieces and nephews, and less with my own grandparents, aunts, and uncles. My siblings sometimes talk about my grandmother's wonderful cooking, but I was so young that the only memory I can conjure is a hazy chicken-and-rice dish. Mostly I remember how painfully hobbled Grandma was by arthritis in her knees by the time she died. I do remember my great-aunt Ruth's koufta: rice-and-meat balls, somewhat like the filling in stuffed peppers without the peppers, or the sauce. And I can see her beaming face in my mind's eye when I think back to one dinner at her house, when she told a story about someone who got a bump on his head after a fall, or something like that. With a grin, she said, "It was as big as ... as ...," and she reached to a nearby platter, grabbed one of the meatballs in her fist, held it up and continued, ". . . as this koufta!"

But I also remember a heartbreaking scene in my grandfather's nursing home that told me all I needed to know about my father's attitude toward his own heritage. Grandpa was bedridden and pale, and to me as a child, he seemed impossibly old. He would call me by the Assyrian version of my first name, Binyami, which was also his name, Benjamin, and say in this wonderful sing-song tone, "Binyami, Binyami, such a wonderful boy." But when he tried to speak Assyrian to my father, who was apparently fluent, my father would respond harshly: "Speak English! You're in America now." I remember nothing but pain on the older man's face at the reprimand.

Julie and I visited for a month or so every summer through junior high and high school, but the amount of time we spent with our family on our father's side seemed to grow shorter and shorter with each passing year. It probably had something to do with his strained sibling relationships, which may have related to his increasing religious fundamentalism, which in turn drove a wedge between us as I started coming to terms with being gay, as a high school senior. When it was time for me to choose a college, it was between the University of Texas at Austin, a four-hour drive from San Angelo, and Northwestern University, less than an hour north of Chicago. When my father made clear he expected to see me every weekend, if not more often, and to control my social life, I knew I didn't want anything to do with his Christian, right-wing brand of oversight and went to UT instead. It wasn't until decades later that I realized that a consequence of avoiding him was the atrophying of my connections to my Assyrian family, my Assyrian-ness.

My father died in 1995, six years after I graduated from UT and moved to Boston. The next year, my stepmother gave my siblings and me each a copy of the *Assyrian Mothers' Cookbook*, published by the Assyrian Universal Alliance Foundation of Chicago, who estimated that in 1995 there were more than 70,000 Christian Assyrians in the Chicago area. By then, I was working at the *Globe* (though not yet in food), living with my sister Rebekah—an accomplished and adventurous home cook—in Boston's South End, and we decided to make use of the gift by hosting a potluck and inviting guests to bring foods of their heritage. We made khipti d'tkhuma (the same dish that my aunt Ruth called koufta), and cada, a type of dense, barely sweet cake that my stepmother used to buy in huge portions from Assyrian bakeries in Chicago and keep in the freezer, cutting off hunks and warming them for special occasions. I never liked cada as a kid, and we used to joke that, like fruitcake, perhaps there was just one huge cada in the whole world, and it just kept getting carved up and shipped out, thawed and frozen, rethawed and refrozen. But when Rebekah and I baked one for the party, it was beautiful: buttery, crisp on the outside, and creamy within. It was the first time we had tasted it the way it was meant to be, and I couldn't get enough. You'd think it would lead me to start exploring my own food roots in earnest, but in truth, although I flip through it from time to time and tell myself I should plan an Assyrian-immersion trip to Chicago, that was the last time I cooked from the book, and I haven't seen any of my father's surviving siblings since he died.

My fascination with *The Gift of Southern Cooking* led me, naturally, to Edna's other cookbooks, particularly to *The Taste of Country Cooking*, which enchanted readers with tales of Lewis's childhood in Freetown, Virginia, and recalled Sunday Revival Dinner, icehouses and cracklings, persimmon puddings and crisp biscuits, spring harvests and big breakfasts. By that point, in Boston, my best friends were those with connections far south of the Mason-Dixon Line, too—southerners up north gravitate toward one another—and they inspired me to embrace that heritage just as they had. To taste my friend Edouard's gumbo—or remoulade or grillades—was to taste the pride in his Lafayette, Louisiana, upbringing. And every time I visited my sister Teri in Florida, or she me, I got a lesson at her kitchen counter in coconut cake, tomato sandwiches, or biscuits— still the fluffiest drop biscuits I've ever tasted, and ones I've made ever since. My friends and family, along with Edna, opened my eyes to southern food, showing me that it was so much more than the fried chicken, grits, and gravy I had assumed. Teri walked me around the squares of Savannah, where her son, my nephew Brent, had moved. She showed me the two sides of southern cooking: Nita's Place, a tiny luncheonette where Juanita Dixon sang gospel songs and served up sour cream and buttermilk biscuits, crispy fried whiting, and squash casserole as rich as pudding; and the elegant, stately Elizabeth on 37th, where chef Elizabeth Terry's dishes spoke of the South, too. I remember Savannah red rice, burnt-sugar ice cream, and shad stuffed with shad roe—my first taste of either. When I was roommates with Edouard, I would come home to a pot of the most beautifully seasoned red beans on the stove, and he'd dish it out over rice. I'd watch him make gumbo, and he taught me about the trinity, and the roux. (You can't rush a roux!)

These days, there's such a fascination with southern food, credited to evangelist-chefs like Sean Brock of Charleston, Stephen Satterfield of Atlanta, and John Currence of Oxford, Mississippi, that another biscuit on another menu in Brooklyn feels like a cliché. But a fresh read of *The Taste of Country Cooking* reminds us that what is so trendy now is really nothing new. Edna's work both preceded and foreshadowed not just the future hipness of southern food but also the locavore and back-to-the-land movements ("people . . . helped each other by trading seed, setting hens, and exchanging ideas"), trends in bread baking ("this recipe requires no kneading"), even coffee snobbery ("it is of little value to grind beans unless they have been just roasted"). She was instructing readers to put up watermelon-rind pickles and Seckel pears, render lard from pork fat, concoct wine and persimmon beer, and so much more. You could pick out plenty of lines from *Taste*, plunk them into a modern context, and they wouldn't seem dated in the slightest.

Ironically, I don't think I fully understood Edna's accounts of her upbringing in Freetown until, in 2012, I spent a year in Maine, about as far from the South as you can get without leaving the East Coast. I was there to help my sister Rebekah and her husband, Peter, on the homestead where they're trying to live as close to the land as possible, something Peter has been doing since he bought the land from one of his sisters in 1976, the same year that *The Taste of Country Cooking* was published.

North Berwick isn't a community of freed slaves, of course, but in many other ways Peter and Rebekah's lives — and the life I lived when I was there — echoes Edna's Freetown. It's about a respect for the land, an intense work ethic and frugality, and cooking and sharing delicious food. My sister and her husband use limited resources in a forward-looking way that helps them meet their needs, short- and long-term. When I was there, I hauled wheelbarrows full of manure and spread them onto rows and rows of tomato plants; took countless trips to a nearby beach to collect dozens of barrels' worth of rotting seaweed for fertilizer; broke down huge piles of stones into dust for soil amendments; seemed to be constantly cleaning out the chicken coop; picked off and killed Japanese beetles by the thousands; foraged, weeded, chopped, canned, and cooked.

Freetown was more than three people trying to make the most of five acres. It was about community — but so is Rebekah and Peter's homestead. Self-sufficiency is folly, as Peter often says: smart homesteaders learn to specialize in a few things and to exchange those for help with things they don't, or can't, do. Why raise both chickens and dairy cows when you can trade eggs for milk? Many hands, from many homesteads, can help clear a plot, or build a fence.

That's why, when I returned to the pages of *The Taste of Country Cooking* recently, rereading Edna's words and cooking out of the book every weekend for a month or so, I finally felt in my bones what she meant when she wrote, "The farm was demanding, but everyone shared in the work — tending the animals, gardening, harvesting, preserving the harvest, and, every day, preparing delicious foods that seemed to celebrate the good things of each season." Every time I visit Peter and Rebekah, I jump back into work — much more eagerly and naturally now than before I spent a year there. I've always loved cooking with Rebekah (and try to schedule my visits when she might need help putting up the harvest), but I try not to stay in the kitchen. There is usually a wheelbarrow and a pile of compost with my name on it.

Something else was different when I returned to *The Taste of Country Cooking*. That phantom nostalgia I had experienced, that wistfulness for an upbringing more rooted in a cultural and culinary heritage than mine, had vanished. I still wish my father had celebrated his Assyrian upbringing with his children and that he had exposed me to more of his mother's and sisters' cooking. But I know it was my choice to not cultivate those relationships, when they were still right in front of me. I can't turn back the clock, but I have pursued other paths to culinary and cultural connection, with many more paths ahead.

Though I lived in Albany for less than a year, every time I return to the South, it feels like home. I may have been raised a Texan (and Texas isn't really the South so much as a region unto itself), but it's the southern table that calls to me. Maybe it's because I'm a proud member of the Southern Foodways Alliance, which grew out of a society Edna cofounded and which pays increasing attention to the diverse racial, ethnic, religious, and class influences on southern cuisines, past, present, and future; every year when I attend the symposium in Oxford, Mississippi, my understanding and connection to the layered complexities of southern food grows. Something about sharing in the experience of southern culinary identity at the symposium—being among a few hundred souls who hail from the South and/or revere its cooking—fills me with a sense of belonging.

My feeling of connection with Edna Lewis, I realize, may have begun out of a sense that her cultural identity was stronger than my own, but it deepened when, the more I learned about her, the more I realized just how multilayered and complicated that identity really was. Just as I am only partly defined by Albany, San Angelo, Assyria, Boston, Washington, Maine, gayness, otherness, diaspora, journalism, and cooking—or any other piece of my biography—she was only partly defined by Freetown, by slavery and freedom. Edna's heritage produced a difficult-to-categorize woman, one who became a dressmaker, newspaper worker, political activist, cookbook author, chef and cook and caterer, one who made her mark in the rural South and the urban North, who celebrated her roots but embraced her future. Her experiences didn't muddy her identity; they polished it.

Now I know: That's true of me, too. It's true of all of us.

My diet has changed since I first read Edna's (and Scott's) work. Now, as a vegetarian, I don't eat bacon, let alone candy it, and I don't agree that beans cry out for smoked and cured meat in order to correct their "dull" flavor. Revisiting Edna's recipes in *The Taste of Country Cooking* allowed me to see just what I could adopt as inspiration, keeping her principles of seasonality and flavor-building intact but meeting my own needs and desires, too—pushing the boundaries of the cuisine she described and helped define without breaking them. The following recipes are inspired by Lewis's, though some of their ingredients — pimentón and coconut cream, for example — never appeared in her own cookbooks.

Southern Baked Beans

That we automatically associate baked beans with New England shows how out of touch we are with real American regional cooking traditions. Any culture that grows beans knows that one of the best ways to cook them is to do so slowly. Unlike the sweet treatment of the North, though, Edna's bean recipe keeps them positively savory, with only a touch of sweetness coming from onion and a little tomato. My main adjustment was to take out the ubiquitous addition of pig — in this case, "streaky lean salt pork" — as the main flavoring agent. Instead, I went with a combination of coconut aminos, which give a dash of almost meaty umami, and one of my go-to spices: Spanish smoked paprika. To make this feel even more southern, seek out the beautiful smoked paprika made in Kentucky by Bourbon Barrel Foods. Serve with a green salad and crusty bread.

{MAKES 6 SERVINGS}

1 pound navy beans, soaked overnight
4 cups filtered water
1 medium onion, finely chopped
½ cup coconut aminos (I like Coconut Secret brand)
2 tablespoons tomato paste
1 teaspoon Spanish smoked paprika (pimentón)
1 teaspoon freshly cracked black pepper
1 teaspoon dry mustard
2 teaspoons kosher salt, plus more to taste

Preheat the oven to 250°.

Combine the beans and water in a heavy pot over medium-high heat, bring to a boil, then lower the heat and simmer gently for 15 minutes. Stir in the onion, aminos, tomato paste, smoked paprika, pepper, and mustard, cover, and bake until the beans are very tender and fragrant, about 3 hours. (Check the beans from time to time, and if the liquid has reduced so that it is no longer covering the beans, add hot water to barely cover and continue cooking.)

Remove the beans from the oven, stir in the salt, cover, and let sit until ready to serve.

Rye Gingerbread Cake with Coconut Cream

Edna's use of sorghum as the sole sweetener in her gingerbread in The Taste of Country Cooking is yet another example of how tastes have come back around. After long being hard to find outside limited areas of the South, sorghum has become one of those of-the-moment urban ingredients that pay tribute to southern traditions. Because Edna's original recipe calls for multiple leavening agents and oil instead of butter, I knew it could take well to veganizing. I also decided to play up the earthiness by using rye flour in addition to all-purpose, and I amped up the fresh ginger spark by adding it in crystallized form. If you'd like, you can serve this with good old-fashioned whipped cream, but the coconut cream I make here, besides being vegan, plays up the Caribbean connections to ginger.

{MAKES 8 SERVINGS}

For the cake

Solid coconut oil (chilled, if need be), for preparing the pan
1 cup all-purpose flour, plus more for preparing the pan
¼ cup chopped crystallized ginger
¾ cup safflower, canola, or another neutral vegetable oil
1 cup warm water
1 cup light rye flour
1 tablespoon baking powder
1 tablespoon ground ginger
1 teaspoon ground cinnamon
½ teaspoon fine sea salt
1½ cups sorghum syrup

For the coconut cream

2 cans whole (not low-fat) coconut milk, chilled overnight in the can
1 teaspoon confectioners' sugar
1 teaspoon vanilla extract

To make the cake, preheat the oven to 350°. Grease an 8 × 8 × 2-inch baking pan with the coconut oil, and dust with flour. Lightly oil a cooling rack with the coconut oil.

Combine the crystallized ginger and vegetable oil in the bowl of a food processor. Puree until blended, then drizzle in the water until smooth.

In a large mixing bowl, sift together the all-purpose and rye flours, baking powder, ground ginger, cinnamon, and salt. Pour in the ginger-oil mixture, and stir well to thoroughly combine. Add the sorghum syrup and stir until smooth.

Spoon the batter into the prepared pan. Bake until a toothpick inserted into the center comes out clean, 35–40 minutes. Let cool for a few minutes in the pan, then turn out onto a plate, and then invert again onto the cooling rack (so that the bottom of the cake is on the bottom).

While the cake is cooling, make the coconut cream: Open the chilled cans of coconut milk, scoop off the solidified cream from the top, and add the cream to a mixing bowl along with the sugar and vanilla. (Reserve the thin milk for another use.) Use a handheld mixer to whip the coconut cream until smooth and fluffy.

Serve the cake warm, with dollops of the coconut cream.

A Message from My Muse

TONI TIPTON-MARTIN

It's 2:30 a.m. on Friday, January 14, 1995, and Edna Lewis can't sleep. Although she is exhausted and weak from radiation, she is troubled by a conversation we've been having. She climbs out of bed, rips yellow paper from a legal pad, and then composes a three-page rant about African American food history.

A decade later, after the woman some have called the Julia Child of southern cuisine lost her battle with cancer at the age of eighty-nine, that note became a personal treasure to me. It also made me sad. Students of southern food cherished Miss Lewis's culinary talent, authentic beauty, and quiet grace. Elsewhere, she was virtually unknown.

The words she penned that night strengthened my resolve to celebrate the invisible black women who fed America.

"Every group has its own food history," Miss Lewis scribbled, with the kind of hurried penmanship that happens when thoughts are jumping out of your head and onto the page faster than you can capture them. "Our condition was different. We were brought here against our will in the millions, enslaved, and through it all established a cuisine in the South . . . the only fully developed cuisine in the country."

Her concentration strays a bit as she talks about the food of old Harlem, survival cooking, and the poetry of Langston Hughes. But she regains focus and gets back to the point:

"We developed but did not own it [southern food] because we did not own ourselves," Miss Lewis laments, "but we established a regional cuisine.

Before the arrival of this intimate letter in my office mail, ours had been an impersonal relationship, characterized by brief encounters at food events, and of course the mention of her name in a food article now and then.

It was the mid-1980s, and I was just beginning to get my footing as a budding journalist on the food staff at *The Los Angeles Times*, where rewriting news releases, generating small feature stories, and studying recipe development under the tutelage of our test kitchen director Donna Deane expanded my culinary knowledge. Fast.

I hadn't swooned over a celebrity since Elton John's rhapsodic "Don't Let the Sun Go Down on Me" melted my high school pals and me into the front row seats on the lawn at Dodgers Stadium. But there I was, at a professional meeting of registered dietitians in Los Angeles in 1985, when I noticed a small crowd in the hotel lobby buzzing around a statuesque African American woman with a magnetic smile, her gray hair swept neatly into a bun worn low at the neck—long before the U.S. Postal Service put her gorgeous face on a Forever stamp. I was young and did not yet know her, but I purchased her book, then joined the groupie gaggle clamoring for autographs the way the paparazzi scratch and claw for superstar snapshots. The regal lady leaned in close, whispered a few tender words of encouragement, then graciously signed my paperback edition of *The Edna Lewis Cookbook*, "To Toni Tipton with Best Wishes Edna Lewis."

I learned a lot from Miss Lewis after that. In time, her cookbooks mentored me quietly, passionately. I am not certain which I relished more: her recipes for delicious country cooking or her storytelling. I suppose it doesn't really matter. Miss Lewis became one of the most important forces behind my James Beard Award–winning book, *The Jemima Code: Two Centuries of African American Cookbooks*, whether she nurtured in person, posthumously, or with the pen.

For one thing, her recipes relied on "fresh ingredients of fine quality" that you grow yourself, prepare when they are at their seasonal best, and serve elegantly. She recommended herbs picked from a pot on the windowsill to give interest and distinction to mundane foods. She taught that mayonnaise laced with fresh-cut parsley or tarragon gives seafood, cold chicken, even green beans exotic taste and aroma, while butter flecked with chives makes roast rack of spring lamb unforgettable.

She put the association with black folks and fried chicken into historical perspective, explaining that the first spring chickens were pan-broiled "as they were too delicate to fry," but when they reached 1½ to 2 pounds, her family fried them as a breakfast meat or a special treat at picnics. And she disputed the myth that black people don't eat quail in a recipe that includes instructions for singeing feathers, reminding me of recipes in early twentieth-century black cookbooks for preparing slaughtered chicken for the pot.

Then there is the lovely way her cookery reflected the fusion of ethnic ingredients and great cooking methods from Africa, Europe, the Caribbean, and America's indigenous peoples and set off with accent marks, such as soufflé, vinaigrette, sauce béarnaise, and crème caramel. Babka and ratatouille helped me see the fancy and foreign names smartly attributed to her everyday farm food. In Miss Lewis's kitchen, braised meats are called ragout, stewed fruit is a compote, potatoes are whipped not mashed, and steamed rice goes to the table molded and shaped into a ring.

When *Essence* magazine celebrated 100 years of enduring black culinary traditions in a 1985 food story, Miss Lewis represented, with pride, her ancestors' creativity and ingenuity, boasting: "Many great southern cooks have been black women. Our people have been involved in cooking here since the establishment of this country." And even though an article praising updated cooking by chefs below the Mason-Dixon Line, which appeared in cook's *Magazine* that same year, ignored her, *Food and Wine* magazine acknowledged her style of local and seasonal cooking, characterizing it as old-fashioned country cooking and somewhat different than the established soul food of black folks.

Our paths crossed again in 1994 when Miss Lewis and I shared the stage at a dinner celebrating African American cuisine in Washington, D.C. I told Miss Lewis that I wanted to reclaim the reputation of professional black cooks who, like her, had championed artistic black cooking and made sophisticated, versatile, delicious food in America's middle-class homes but their contributions to southern cooking disappeared in history.

Her handwritten letter emboldened me with an exhortation: "Leave no stone unturned."

As if it was that simple. Julie, after all, had Julia. In the mid-1990s, when I embarked on my research, there just wasn't one single source conveying the rich and complicated history of America's invisible black cooks. In fact, if it had not been for exaggerated mammy stereotypes recorded in the diaries and letters of slaveholding women, their letters to friends and family, nostalgic mythology in southern literature, and prejudiced imagery in advertising and media, these tireless, talented women would have had little written history at all.

I made peace with that unfortunate reality and moved a lot of stones—boulders, really—over the next few years trying to learn more about my ancestors' unwritten history. I wore the aprons of America's black cooks, literally and figuratively—exploring everything from scholarship and literature to music lyrics and fine art for evidence of their knowledge and skills. I ran up incredible expenses traveling to historical societies. Visited special collections archives at prominent universities and the Library of Congress. Searched the census. Read city directories. Studied oral histories and slave narratives. Treaded grooves in cemeteries. And spent a chunk of my kids' college tuition on eBay in auctions of rare black cookbooks.

What emerged was a surprising alternative view of the "toothy, grin- and calico-swathed plump face" belonging to the world's best-recognized black cook, Aunt Jemima. These cooks maintained gardens. Prepared and served free-range chicken and pastured beef and pork. Practiced classic cooking techniques. Recycled. Miss Lewis wasn't the only, but she was the best-known.

Through recipes and recollections in more than 300 black cookbooks, I met cooks whose culinary skills, professional and personal values, work ethic, business sense, and passion for education and community were conspicuous and far-reaching. Like Miss Lewis, Freda DeKnight, the food editor of *Ebony* magazine, published a comprehensive recipe collection intentionally designed to help readers view African American cooks and their cuisine differently. Her 1948 cookbook, *A Date with a Dish*, featured more than 1,000 recipes for dishes being prepared and served in middle-class homes. The National Council of Negro Women also challenged the myths associated with black food and culture in 1958 in the *Historical Cookbook of the American Negro*.

Miss Lewis's cookbooks continued the tradition, portraying a style that celebrated regional southern heritage, extended the black culinary repertoire beyond plantation poverty food, and defied racial segregation, essentially destroying the old mammy monument. Her writing challenged me to reimagine, then to reclaim, things I already knew about black middle-class cooking but ignored, or suppressed. Things like: the expression of love associated with my grandmother's scratch cooking. The inherited desire to put wholesome food on the table connected to long road trips to the country, where my parents bought pastured meat. The way that the taste of processed food pales when compared to the deliciousness of freshly harvested produce from mother's urban farm. The social and environmental responsibility conveyed by the can of bacon grease on the back of the stove, the ingenuity of repurposed leftovers.

Rare cookbooks, including Miss Lewis's, helped me prove that these are values, not handicaps.

For more than 200 years, African Americans have struggled to bring their recipe collections before the book-buying public. The "something outta nuthin'" dimensions of chitlins, hoppin' John, and fish cakes pigeon-holed my ancestors as great cooks, to be sure, but their accomplishments were usually attributed to natural instinct, innate ability, voodoo magic, mystique—even love—and confined to the borders of the Old South and sorrow's kitchens. (This was especially true during the late nineteenth and early twentieth centuries, when the domestic science movement was taking shape, or in the 1960s, when the Black Power movement infused everything, from dance and music to food, with soul.)

Of course, it is true that the dishes black families ate during hard times (soul food) are heralded for their industriousness. It is also true that these delicious creations are marginalized as purely survival food, incapable of inspiring. Which is a crying shame, because our culinary flair offers more than just a few make-do dishes for budget-conscious cookery. Ask yourself: Who else has made so much money by the association with a recipe—like pancakes and cornbread? How many restaurant chains built their repu-tation on a black cook's perfectly crisp and juicy fried chicken? Whose mouth doesn't water at the mention of light and flaky biscuits like those sold in the supermarket freezer section? What trip to New Orleans would be complete without a bowlful of gumbo brewed by a Creole chef? When did anyone successfully resist a simple but decadent piece of blackberry cobbler?

Many black cookbook authors have tried and failed to tell the complete story of African American foodways, and I'm not sure I can do any better—an unfortunate that's-what-you-get outcome of arti-ficially segregating the southern food canon. In the effort to claim a space at the table of southern food history, black folks have proudly embraced the ingenious and industrious dimensions of southern cooking—soul food that limited black cooking to survival dishes made from lowly ingredients, such as unwanted pig parts, wild greens, and cornmeal. At the same time, "southern" food was a beloved regional style, known for its fried chicken, macaroni and cheese, greens, beans, decadent desserts and sweet tea, en-coded as "white." The canon became fractured.

The contributions my ancestors made were limited to their labor—working the fields where the food was grown, stirring the pot where the food was cooked, and serving the food in the homes of the elite—not their recipes, their intellectual property. Some regional cookbooks by white au-thors even used plantation language in their recipe titles, like pickaninny

Toni Tipton-Martin

cookies and mammy's muffins, or stereotyped images to distinguish black southern food from white the way Jim Crow designated public water fountains "Whites Only" or "Colored."

Which left me wondering: What shall we call the food black women cooked when resources were plentiful? Why are delicious recipes that reveal aspects of living well considered inauthentic and not really African American—whether the dishes originally were prepared for middle-class black families or white employers? Why don't we celebrate the kind of cooking that would have turned yesterday's enslaved cooks, free cooks, railroad chefs, domestic workers, cooking teachers, restaurateurs, hoteliers, vendors, and retailers into today's celebrity chefs—if they were white?

These cooks have always been with us here in the United States, hovering in the shadows as quiet culinary shepherds. For instance, a formerly enslaved woman interviewed in 1936 for the Federal Writers' Project in Texas named Mariah Robinson described hard-working black women this way: "Us has ever lived 'de useful life.'" What has begun to change is the perception of them. *The Jemima Code* introduced the world to the books black cooks like Miss Lewis wrote that validate their knowledge, skills, and creative abilities. With Miss Lewis and these authors as my muses, I intend to reframe perceptions of African American cooking by changing what we think about the people who cooked it—chronicling the transition of their skills from the villages of the African diaspora to the Caribbean and rural South and ultimately to grand displays of their talent on the dining tables and sideboards of America's elite—whether those tables were in the homes of wealthy whites or upwardly mobile blacks in the North, South, East, or West.

The late, great James Beard said that Edna Lewis made him want to go right into the kitchen and start cooking. In *The Jemima Code*, I agreed with him. But for me, she does more than just that.

Without children of her own, she wrote to pass along ideas about natural farming to future generations, sharing how things were done in the past so we might "learn firsthand from those who worked hard, loved the land, and relished the fruits of their labor." That truth—whatever it is called—inspirits confidence in my own rarely documented, often ignored middle-class culinary legacy, too. She gives me hope.

Every time I read *The Taste of Country Cooking*, I want to dig in the soil, care for baby birds, milk cows, make butter and preserves. Farm activities and menus and recipes prepared according to the time of year—sheep shearing and a spring lunch after picking wild mushrooms; an early summer lunch of the season's delicacies and a prepared-ahead summer dinner; a morning after hog butchering breakfast or a fall hunting season dinner; Christmas Eve Supper, a dinner celebrating the last of the barnyard fowl, and a dinner of chicken and dumplings and warm gingerbread—all remind me of summers spent on my grandmother's small farm in rural Southern California, where soul food staples were rare but fresh, wholesome food and culinary grace were plentiful.

I have walked in Miss Lewis's footsteps on the opulent grounds of Middleton Place and stood in the kitchen at the Fearrington House, monuments of the Old South where her chocolate soufflé is still on the menu—evidence that black women left their mark on American cuisine in the dishes they left behind. And it is here, in these sacred spaces, where her quiet voice and stories of self-reliance and creative expression help me untangle the complicated mystery of white and black Americans cooking side by side—where their cultural habits and techniques crossed boundaries of owner and enslaved, or rigid codes imposed by Jim Crow—to establish a shared cuisine.

In *A Woman's Place Is in the Kitchen*, Ann Cooper wrote that "Ms. Lewis paved the way for women into the professional kitchen, not only as one of the first women, but as a black woman as well."

I would add that as black cooks, propelled by Lewis's pilgrimage from "just another excellent cook in an apron" to "grand dame" of southern food, we also owe her our culinary freedom—liberty conferred on yellow legal paper.

Toni Tipton-Martin

Lunch with Miss Lewis

DEBORAH MADISON

—⁊⁊—

I had the pleasure of meeting Edna Lewis. Just once.

It was in 1997. I was on book tour for *Vegetarian Cooking for Everyone*, and the tour took me to Atlanta. While there I was invited to have lunch with Miss Lewis, as everyone called her, at the home of Anne Quatrano and Clifford Harrison. Anne and Clifford own the restaurant Bacchanalia, where I have had the pleasure of dining. Twice. It's my favorite restaurant in Atlanta. Also present was Scott Peacock, the longtime assistant and close friend of Miss Lewis. I don't really know how this all came about, why fortune shined on me this day, but somehow it did. I suspect Scott was the reason.

I had met Scott before, but not Miss Lewis, and I didn't really know much about her at that time. I knew her books, particularly *In Pursuit of Flavor*, which I was drawn to because of the promise on the cover that she offered "secrets of getting the best flavor from the foods available today," a subject I was extremely interested in and one I had pursued in my own vegetable-centric cooking. I looked closely at her vegetable recipes and desserts and pretty much ignored the rest. It was much later that I learned about *her*, that she had wanted to study botany, a passion I have come to embrace. Or that she was gladdened by the appearance of farmers' markets, which were just really starting to take off at that time. A few years previously I had managed our farmers' market in Santa Fe and went on to write a book about the movement of farm food to city dwellers via farmers' markets.

Miss Lewis could write and talk about eggs the way a young chef might talk about them today. I could imagine her handling food, all of it, not just vegetables, with knowledge in her hands. Although I don't think that she was particularly interested in meeting me (at least she never asked me about my own work), she was kindly and gracious, perhaps a little shy, but mostly she was quiet. I was also shy, so this was hardly a gabfest. Still, she didn't mind speaking about her cooking beliefs and the food that was being prepared for this meal. She didn't brag on it in any way, or talk about tradition or authenticity or such. She was just a very straightforward person, softly and well spoken.

When I arrived at Anne and Clifford's home in the country outside of Atlanta, Scott was icing a tall cake of many thin layers. Eleven, I believe. I remember counting them. The chocolate icing was dribbling down the sides, and there was a bowl of the most beautiful, plump raspberries that would go with the cake for dessert. Scott explained that although you could make the cake with just two layers, having many layers was considered correct for an honored guest. And I was the honored guest! Indeed, I was honored to be there in this beautiful spot with these extraordinary people.

I watched as everyone bustled around the kitchen, readying our meal. Most of it had already been cooked, so it was a matter of setting plates and platters on the kitchen table and adding finishing touches to the dishes. I offered to help, wanted to help, but was reminded that I was the guest and couldn't lift a finger. So I stood out of the way as best I could and watched as dish upon dish was set out on the long wooden table. Miss Lewis pointed out that there were many vegetables: smashed turnips wrapped in foil and a platter of big, deep red sliced tomatoes and greens stewed with tomatoes among them. There were hard-cooked eggs stuffed with their yolks made creamy with mayonnaise, but whole and standing upright, not halved and laying down, like deviled eggs. There was a cucumber pickle. A bowl of field peas. Some red beets. And there was roast chicken and gravy, the chicken carved and placed on a round platter. There may have been more dishes; I don't really remember them all, just that there were many. A discussion ensued over lunch about how, even though there was the bird, mostly there were vegetables for people to eat, and that that was Miss Lewis's way. It made such good sense: a little meat, a lot of plants. Even though I was touring a vegetarian cookbook at the time, I ate everything—the chicken, too. It was delicious, all of it.

We ate lunch leisurely, outdoors by a pool, or as leisurely as possible since I was giving a talk that evening in Atlanta and was keeping an eye on the time. During our lunch, Miss Lewis was reserved. She could have been tired. Or, again, maybe that was just her way. Scott searched for a Diet Coke in the fridge, for which he was teased. Diet Coke? Really? But that was his drink.

This meal took place more than twenty years ago, but I still keep a photograph on my office bookshelf of Miss Lewis, Scott, and me standing

Deborah Madison

near a fence, a large expanse of field bordered with very tall trees behind us. Miss Lewis is wearing a dark purple blouse and skirt, made of African cloth, and a shawl. My long hair is blowing in the breeze, and Scott is in the middle, his big arms around both of us. We are all smiling. I see this picture almost daily, and it never fails to bring me back to that moment in time, a still point in the midst of all the talk and chatter that a book tour invariably brings. And it brings me back to Miss Lewis and what I know about her now that I didn't know then.

Today, as I page through her work, there is so much I resonate with. I admire her integrity, her accumulated wisdom, her experience, and her feeling for ingredients. Above all, she was a person who had a history, and she had a special grace. For me, it was a missed opportunity. I was wrapped up in this big book I had spent seven years writing, a move to a new state, a new marriage, a new restaurant, and she probably was at an age where she really didn't need, or maybe even want, to meet more people. I was too young and too preoccupied to appreciate what Miss Lewis brought to our world in her own, very particular way. That unfolded later.

There is another photograph I especially love of Miss Lewis. She is sitting and talking with Marion Cunningham, the American cookbook author who brought *The Fannie Farmer Cookbook* up to date, who wrote her own books, and who was devoted to home cooking. In the photo, Miss Lewis is black, with her white hair pulled back into a bun. Marion is white with, as it appears in the photo, darker hair—even though she was blond—also pulled back. They are sitting opposite one another, talking, like reversed images of each other; these two elegant women, both of who were so straightforward and stately and such an important part of our culinary lives. I saw this photograph many times at Marion's house and always felt pulled toward it. Both women had this refreshing common-sense approach to food and cooking, but it was an approach that was also sensitive and tender. You could see it in the way they talked about basic things like eggs or bread or cheese, and you could feel their appreciation for the real rather than the ersatz. At the same time, you sensed their utter lack of pretension.

That lunch in Georgia so long ago was indeed special, a rare moment in time. But sadly, in some ways the timing was off. I would have loved to have known Miss Lewis better. There's so much to ask about.

Perhaps it's not surprising that that meal has stayed with me for so long. It wasn't so much about what we ate as much as the whole experience: everyone in the kitchen working or watching, then carrying our filled plates outside; the quiet congeniality at the table, the delicious food that was heartfelt and simple. This interlude was calm and so pleasant, the five of us sitting by water in the country with this culinary icon, listening to her say a few words or simply just being. Miss Lewis was indeed a true icon, but that day she was just a woman, a person, eating her own food. There was no artifice; it was a completely human moment, and that's what I valued above all.

Paying Down Debts of Pleasure

JOHN T. EDGE

—⁊ ६—

When I lived and worked in Atlanta in the early 1990s, I took cooking classes from Edna Lewis and her protégé Scott Peacock. Like many of the gambits I undertook then, I thought those classes might be good opportunities to meet girls.

Instead, gathered in a demonstration kitchen in a cookware store in the Peachtree Battle shopping center, I learned to compose an idealized country captain, pocked with golden raisins and dusted with curry powder. Later, when the classes moved to another borrowed space, hard by the interstate north of town, I practiced pulsing shrimp to make a paste that melted luxuriously over grits.

After I moved to Oxford, bent on earning a graduate degree in Southern Studies at the University of Mississippi, I interviewed Miss Lewis via telephone about the ways she bridged the Virginia of her youth and the New York of her midlife prime. I was nervous. She was cool, calm, and game to recollect. She told me, "After I moved north, my sister would can watercress and then put it in a box full of cornmeal with maybe some ham and farm fresh eggs and ship it to me in New York City. I'd open it up and have a whole southern meal. I remember that as the next best thing to going home."

That day, Miss Lewis spoke with great pride and a little wistfulness of her time in New York City. Our conversation, which offered a glimpse of Café Nicholson in its heyday, was one of the inspirations for the essay that follows.

On a summer day in 1949, ballerina Tanaquil Le Clercq, novelist Donald Windham, painter Buffie Johnson, playwright Tennessee Williams, and writer-provocateur Gore Vidal gathered at Café Nicholson, a bohemian supper club set in the back courtyard of an antique store on

49

New York City's Upper East Side. It was a heady moment. Williams had won a Pulitzer Prize the year before. Vidal had just published *The City and the Pillar*. Beneath the shade trees in proprietor Johnny Nicholson's garden, they ate and drank. They smoked and gossiped. They posed and preened, fully aware that photographer Karl Bissinger was there to capture their idyll for posterity.

In those postwar days, the café, decorated in what Nicholson described as a "fin de siècle Caribbean of Cuba style," served as a canteen for the creative class and a backdrop for fashion shoots. (Before it finally closed in 2000, the café also served an occasional movie set; Woody Allen filmed scenes from *Bullets Over Broadway* there.) Paul Robeson was a regular. So was Truman Capote, who sometimes came bursting into the kitchen looking for biscuits.

Nicholson was the Barnum of their social set, presiding with a parrot named Lolita on his shoulder. Bissinger, who served the café as an early business partner and a sometimes gardener and host, made a living curating social tableaus for magazines like *Vogue* and *Harper's Bazaar*. During the postwar years he captured everyone from a languorous Henry Miller, lighting a cigarette, to a faunal Capote, reclining in a wicker chaise. But the photograph he shot that afternoon at Café Nicholson has proved his most famous. In a *New York Times* obituary of Bissinger, William Grimes called the scene a "class picture of the young and the talented in the American arts, more than ready for their close-ups."

I first glimpsed the image on a postcard I bought at a Memphis bookstore. In that rendition, the black woman in the background was unnamed. Because I knew a bit about the history of Café Nicholson and the role that Edna Lewis, the African American cookery writer and chef, played there, and because my eyesight isn't so great, I wondered, perversely, whether the black woman ferrying what appears to be a pot of tea to the table was Lewis.

Edna Lewis was the most respected African American cookery writer of the twentieth century. Over the course of a long and varied career, she set type for the *Daily Worker* and labored as a dressmaker for high-profile clients like Marilyn Monroe. While working with Johnny Nicholson, she began to write and publish the cookbooks that earned her recognition as the grande doyenne of southern cookery. Foremost was *The Taste of Country Cooking*. Published in 1976 and re-released in 2006, it was an homage to the land and larder of Freetown, the Virginia community where she grew up. In the foreword to that thirtieth anniversary edition, Alice Waters wrote that Lewis, the granddaughter of freed slaves, was an "inspiration to all of us who are striving to protect both biodiversity and cultural diversity by cooking real food in season and honoring our heritage through the ritual of the table."

If Lewis could go unnamed in a picture that foretold the promise of America in the postwar era, I figured that image might serve as a metaphor for the lesser role Americans have long ascribed to African American contributions to the culinary arts. Telling that story might be a way for me to pay down the debts of pleasure, both culinary and other, that a privileged white son of the South like me has accrued over a lifetime.

In the spring of 2013, I attended a conference on food and immigrant life at the New School in New York City. Speakers from as close as NYU and as far away as UC Irvine talked about "gastronomic cosmopolitanism," defined "neophilia" and "neophobia," argued for the recovery of the "fragile orality of recipe exchange," and predicted that, for those of us who study food, "epistemological implosions" are on the horizon. (I'm still not sure what that last one meant.) What really walloped me was a speech by Saru Jayaraman, director of the UC Berkeley Food Labor Research Center and author of the *Behind the Kitchen Door: What Every Diner Should Know about People Who Feed Us.*

The people who put food on our tables, Jayaraman said, can't afford to put food on their own. Primary among the contemporary culprits she identified was the National Restaurant Association, which she called the "other N.R.A." When Herman Cain, the onetime Republican presidential candidate and former chief executive of Godfather's Pizza, was running the organization in the 1980s, Jayaraman said that he brokered a deal that has since kept the federal minimum wage for tipped workers like waiters and waitresses artificially deflated at $2.13 per hour.

Wages for non-tipped workers like line cooks have risen, she said, but not at the pace of other professions, nor have those workers earned benefits enjoyed by other workers, like paid sick days. Workers of color suffer the most. A $4 hourly gap separates them from white workers, she reported, citing two primary reasons: within a single restaurant, workers of color are more likely to be hired for back-of-the-house positions that pay less, like busser and runner, and they rarely get promoted from those positions. Within the industry as a whole, workers of color are more likely to get jobs in fast food, which generally pays less than fine dining jobs.

She was speaking, for the most part, about new immigrants. But listening to her talk that evening in New York City, I heard what sounded like an old southern story of the housekeepers and yardmen I knew in my Georgia youth, of the black women and men who suffered under the burden of coercive social pressures while scraping by on substandard wages and hand-me-downs, retold in this modern American moment.

Jayaraman's tales gave me a new reason to dig into the story behind Bissinger's photo and the circumstances surrounding Edna Lewis's tenure at Café Nicholson. Reading contemporary reviews of the restaurant, I learned that Lewis rose to fame there while serving simple and elegant dishes like roast chicken, which Clementine Paddleford, the reigning national critic of the day, described as "brown as a chestnut, fresh from the burr." She also favored Lewis's chocolate soufflé, which was "light as a dandelion seed in a wind."

In the *New York Times* archives, I discovered that the 1948 partnership offer from Nicholson was timely for Lewis, who grew up on a farm near Freetown, Virginia, but had no other demonstrable experience in the industry. At the time they began working together, "Edna was about to take a job as a domestic," Nicholson told a reporter.

Café Nicholson employed a conceit that presaged the reigning white tablecloth aesthetic of today. "We'll serve only one thing a day," Nicholson said to Lewis, as they schemed their first menus. "Buy the best quality and I don't see how we can go wrong." Long before farm-to-table was a marketing concept, Lewis was challenging chefs to learn "from those who worked hard, loved the land, and relished the fruits of their labor."[1]

Her approach, like her cooking, was straightforward. In a late life interview, she told Kim Severson of the *New York Times*, "As a child in Virginia, I thought all food tasted delicious. After growing up, I didn't think food tasted the same, so it has been my lifelong effort to try and recapture those good flavors of the past."

The archives at NYU, where Nicholson deposited his papers, yielded a cache of Bissinger photographs that made clear the afternoon he captured in that iconic image was not singular. More important, I discovered that I was not the only one who saw metaphorical possibilities in that 1949 black and white.

In October 2007, *Smithsonian* magazine published Gore Vidal's gauzy recollection of that moment at table on Johnny Nicholson's patio. "For me, Karl Bissinger's picture is literally historic, so evocative of a golden moment," he wrote, with the mixture of brio, ego, and privilege that was his signature. "I don't know what effect the picture has on those who now look at it, but I think it perfectly evokes an optimistic time in our history that we are not apt to see again soon."

With that dispatch, Vidal, who wrote the introduction to *The Luminous Years: Portraits at Mid-Century*, a collection of Bissinger's photographs, was finished. But *Smithsonian* wasn't. Two months after Vidal's recollection ran, the magazine published a letter to the editor by Edward Weintraut of Macon, Georgia. "I am troubled that his text does not make the slightest reference to the black waitress," wrote Weintraut, a professor at Mercer University. "I found myself wondering whether she shared Vidal's view about this time being so optimistic, whether she would welcome a revival of the society and culture in which this scene is embedded, whether she enjoyed a similar golden moment as the author and his friends did during lunches at Café Nicholson."

Over the years, I've taken a number of swipes at the "good food" movement. Because I think too many of them are surfing trends and indulging passions that will prove dalliances, instead of forging a true path toward a better-fed future, I've referred to overzealous twenty-somethings, trying to effect change in our broken food system, as agri-poseurs. After hearing Jayaraman speak, and after tracing the reception of the Bissinger photo, I recognize that my real complaint is that too much of the attention now focused on food skews toward natural resources instead of human resources and that imbalance has proved more egregious when it comes to people of color.

Recent victories, won by groups like the Coalition of Immokalee Workers, which fights for the rights of tomato pickers in Florida, watermelon harvesters in Georgia, and others, have begun to right the wrongs in the fields. But precious little work has been done to address the plight of restaurant workers. The "meal that arrives at your table when you eat out is not just a product of raw ingredients," Jayaraman wrote in *Behind the Kitchen Door*. "It's a product of the hands that chop, cook, and plate it and the people to whom those hands belong."

It's a product, too, of the men and women who serve that meal. Base wages for waiters and waitresses have not risen in more than twenty years. The notion that servers should be ill-paid conjures too easily a time when a permanent American underclass was defined by skin color. Today, the restaurant industry remains one of the last bulwarks of a system in which nameless workers of color labor out of sight, and often out of mind.

Readers with better eyesight than me probably recognized on first glance that the woman on that postcard was not the same woman who appeared on the cover of *The Taste of Country Cooking*, wearing a lilac dress, picking tomatoes in a summer field bordered with sunflowers. Virginia Reed served the crowd that day. She wasn't a metaphor. She was bone and flesh. Scott Peacock, who cowrote Lewis's fourth book, *The Gift of Southern Cooking*, published in 2003, and is now finishing a solo book about their relationship, told me that Nicholson and Lewis both called Reed a "character," which I take to mean that she was a woman with a quick wit and a bawdy humor. She was also the cook with a clock in her head, who had an uncanny ability to divine the exact moment when the Café Nicholson chocolate soufflé was ready to pull from the oven. Not much else is known about her life, which was often the case with the black workers who ran southern kitchens in the twentieth century and is now often the case with the twenty-first-century immigrants who have replaced them on the cooking line, at the dish bin, and on the dining room floor.

I'm pretty sure that Bissinger did not intend that his photograph be read as a metaphor for the exclusion of black labor from conversations about excellence in the culinary arts. Along the path of my argument, Bissinger was a fellow traveler, which is to say that he, like Lewis, had once been a member of the Communist Party, focused on workers' rights, the sort of thinker who would have owned up to a sin of omission.

But I'm a petite bourgeoisie fellow who forced this issue. To do good work in the world of southern food, I've come to believe we have to start by paying down the debts of pleasure we owe to the cooks who sustain our society. For me, that means acknowledging Virginia Reed, the woman with the glowing smile and the clock in her head who brought that pot of tea to the table in 1949. For restaurateurs of today, that means renouncing the lobbying work of the other NRA, paying employees a working wage, and as Jayaraman puts it, taking the high road to profitability.

NOTE

1. Introduction to Edna Lewis, *The Taste of Country Cooking* (New York: Knopf, 1976), xviii.

On Edna Lewis

ALICE WATERS

—⊰⊱—

My restaurant, Chez Panisse, was in its earliest years when I first read *The Taste of Country Cooking*, not long after it was published in 1976. At the time, my partners and I were trying to emulate a way of eating and a kind of hospitality that was at odds with the fast-food culture that was encroaching on us from all sides. So we aimed high and wide; our influences ranged from the haute cuisine of Escoffier and Ritz to the hospitality of goatherds in Turkey and innkeepers in the Alps, and we pursued freshness and seasonality with a single-mindedness approaching obsession. But we had a lot to learn about the convergence of contentment and community with biodiversity and sustainability, and with *The Taste of Country Cooking*, Edna Lewis became a valued teacher. She catalyzed our thinking about our responsibilities toward the land, our debt to the farmers who are its good stewards, and our accountability to our children. Under her influence, we got down to earth, literally. Our foragers set out to find and weave together a network of suppliers—fishers, farmers, orchardists, ranchers— who shared our values; and under their influence our cooking became both simpler and more complex at the same time, as we tuned our repertoire toward the unique abundance of our own particular time and place—just as the food of Miss Lewis's childhood community of Freetown was an expression of its particular southern time and place.

I had first heard about Miss Lewis's book from Marion Cunningham, a friend who was working on the first of her two revisions of *The Fannie Farmer Cookbook*. Marion and Miss Lewis shared the same editor, Judith Jones. I got a copy and read it from cover to cover, entranced; *The Taste of Country Cooking* offered up a vision of an all-American, homegrown, slow-food culture. It was fitting that the book came out in the bicentennial year of American independence; in its depiction of Freetown, the book painted a picture of an agrarian American dream. Although this dream was tied to a particular sociohistorical moment and to specific realities of geography and race, I found in it a universality that was deeply inspiring. What I read about was a world of love and work brought to life, with generosity and honesty; a world of abundance and promise where the foodways of forebears were honored and kept alive. It became my life's work to try and recreate such a world.

As it happens, I am writing this as we are preparing a menu to celebrate the anniversary of Edna Lewis's birth in Freetown, Orange County, Virginia, exactly a hundred years ago. It begins with skillet asparagus and pickled beets with chervil mayonnaise, Virginia ham, and a farm egg, followed by Dungeness crab chowder with fennel and Jerusalem artichokes. It continues with spit-roasted spring chicken with creamy morels, whipped potatoes and salsify, green peas with mint, crispy scallions, and watercress. Dessert will be rhubarb galette with nutmeg ice cream. The inspiration behind every dish came from Miss Lewis. We hope the menu evokes the heritage of the South at the same time that it serves forth the incomparable bounty of Northern California at the height of an early spring; and we hope that its execution will be true to both the letter and the spirit of Edna's bracing combination of diligence and elegance. I know we wish she could be here to enjoy it.

Dungeness Crab Chowder with Fennel, Jerusalem Artichokes, and Chives

Miss Lewis would probably have used Atlantic she-crabs full of crab roe for this soup, but our local Pacific Dungeness crabs are mighty tasty, too. The addition of Jerusalem artichokes is another nod in the direction of Freetown. In The Taste of Country Cooking, Miss Lewis recalls digging Jerusalem artichokes after the ground had begun to thaw, and how they were the first fresh spring vegetables — "a welcome change in our diet after a winter of dishes made of preserved and dried ingredients."

{MAKES 6–8 SERVINGS}

2 live Dungeness crabs
Salt
8 tablespoons (1 stick) unsalted butter
2 thyme sprigs
4 parsley sprigs
1 tablespoon coriander seeds

1 tablespoon peppercorns
1 small leek, diced
1 small fennel bulb, diced (about 1 cup)
2 cups Jerusalem artichokes, peeled and diced
1 pinch cayenne pepper
1 cup milk
1 cup cream
1 bunch chives, snipped

Bring a large pot of salted water to a boil. Use enough salt so that it tastes as salty as seawater. Add one of the crabs to the boiling water and cook for 12 minutes. Start timing from the moment the crab enters the water, and keep the heat high, so that the pot returns rapidly to a boil. Take the crab out of the pot and let it cool while you make the stock with the other crab.

Place the second crab upside-down on its back and chop it in two with a cleaver. Remove the gills and the tomalley from under the shell and discard. Chop the legs and body into large pieces of crabmeat and shell. Melt 4 tablespoons of the butter in a medium stockpot. Add the crab pieces and cook over medium heat until the shells have turned bright red and there is some browning on the bottom of the pan. Cover the crab with 6 cups of water and bring to a simmer. Add the thyme and parsley sprigs, coriander seeds, and peppercorns. Allow the stock to simmer gently for 45 minutes. Strain the stock and discard the shells.

Melt the remaining 4 tablespoons of butter in a medium soup pot. Add the diced leeks, fennel, and Jerusalem artichokes to the pot. Add 1 teaspoon of salt and a pinch of cayenne pepper. Cook the vegetables in the butter over medium-low heat until lightly softened. Pour the strained crab stock into the soup pot and bring to a simmer. Once the vegetables are tender, turn off the heat and allow the soup to cool a bit and the flavors to meld.

Pick the meat from the boiled crab.

When ready to serve the chowder, add the milk, cream, and picked crabmeat to the soup pot. Heat gently, but do not allow the chowder to come to a boil. Ladle into warm bowls and sprinkle with snipped chives.

Edna Lewis and the Black Roots of American Cooking

FRANCIS LAM

When I was assigned to write a piece on Edna Lewis's history and legacy for the *New York Times Magazine*, I'd just joined the board of the Southern Foodways Alliance (SFA). I once lived in Mississippi for a spell, but as a native of New Jersey—the northern part of it, no less—my connection to southern food and culture has always been from an outsider's perspective. Still, I'd been involved with the SFA for some years, in part because it's an organization that sees my story—an Asian American former transplant to the Gulf Coast—as a southern story. And I wanted to reciprocate a bit, to engage and learn more about the culture that welcomed that story.

I knew that Miss Lewis was among the founders of the SFA, and I certainly knew how revered and iconic she was, but I admit that I didn't actually know much more about her than that. So I thought I should leap at the opportunity to write this piece, as a way of educating myself, to better understand southernness.

When I started my reporting, searching for the thread of the story I wanted to tell, I found it challenging at first to be writing about someone who I wouldn't be able to speak with directly; my method is typically to spend most of my time with a subject, to try to get a feel for who they are. When your subject has passed, though, you are left with the people they touched, and you have to piece together a portrait based on impressions from a dozen other perspectives. I heard people talk about her importance as an advocate of seasonal, local eating; people talked about her as a powerful champion of traditional cooking; people talked about her as a mentor, a teacher, a *presence*. Over and over, though, my thoughts came back especially to the people who told me what she meant to them as a black person, as an African American culinary figure of dignity and agency, not servitude.

I went back to her own words—the books she wrote, most especially *The Taste of Country Cooking*. Lewis is often written about as a gifted chef and sweetly benevolent culinary doyenne—"People always want to talk about her like she was just some nice old lady," a friend, who knew her, said to me—but what I was struck by, upon a closer reading of her text, was how brilliant, subversive, and political a writer she was: an empowered woman who claimed the story of her people—black, rural, a generation away from enslavement—as a story of beauty whose rightful place is squarely at the center of American culture. I marveled at her language, at its beauty and evenness, even as the ideas underneath it were fierce. It's a story of dignity and resistance, and I knew then that was the story I wanted to tell.

The air around Bethel Baptist Church in Unionville, Virginia, is sweet with pine and moss. From the road, Bethel seems like any other small-town white clapboard church, though a closer look shows some wear: a few holes in the windows, spidery cracks in the vinyl siding, a plastic Christmas tree tossed into the woods behind its gravel lot, sun-bleached to a shade of blue God never intended. But the church was built to last, and it's still solid at nearly 125 years old. It sits at the corner of Marquis and Independence Roads: nobility and freedom, a fitting location for a place founded by black people who decided they weren't going to worship at the back of white churches anymore.

One of those founders was Chester Lewis, an angular man with wide, piercing eyes who spent much of his life enslaved a couple of miles down Marquis Road. After emancipation, he built a house and planted orchards with a few other families on a plot of land his former master ceded to him. He and his wife, Lucinda, were illiterate, but they welcomed Isabella Lightfoot, a black graduate of Oberlin College, to use a part of their home as a school for the fledgling community's children. They farmed, fished, and foraged all their food, threshing their own wheat, raising their own animals, and walking over to Jackson's General Store for salt, spices, vanilla, and Valentine's Day presents. They struggled but were self-reliant, relishing their freedom, and they named their settlement Freetown.

In Freetown, the people lived close to the land, cooking their harvest in wood stoves, using wells and streams to keep food cool. And they lived close to one another. Chester and Lucinda's granddaughter Edna Lewis remembered food as the center of its culture of work and community. In 1984, she told Phil Audibert, a documentarian: "If someone borrowed one cup of sugar, they would return two. If someone fell ill, the neighbors would go in and milk the cows, feed the chickens, clean the house, cook the food and come and sit with whoever was sick. I guess rural life conditioned people to cooperate with their neighbors." Their conversation was recorded a half-century after Lewis moved away, but the impression her community made on her was still profound.

Her father died in 1928, and the rest of the family, which included six children who survived into adulthood, struggled during the Depression. Lewis left Freetown by herself as a teenager, joining the Great Migration north. Eventually, the rest of the community left, too. Today, Freetown is just a stand of fruit trees, and Jackson's store has become someone's rickety machine shop, its porch greening with vines of Virginia creeper crawling through the floorboards. But nearby, there are a few gravestones behind a white fence. I read the epitaphs when I visited, arriving at the grave I had come to pay my respects to: "Dr. Edna Lewis, April 13, 1916–February 13, 2006, Grande Dame of Southern Cooking." I reached out to touch it, but then pulled back my hand; I remembered that I had the scent of cheap fried chicken on my fingers, fried chicken that I am sure Miss Lewis, as she was always known, would not have approved of.

It was tasty, that chicken, in the way that pre-fried chicken plucked out from a pile under heat lamps can be tasty: salty and greasy, slicking the lips with bird fat. But Lewis, who placed southern cooking in the pantheon of great cuisines, respected fried chicken as a special occasion food. She made hers, not by punishing it in a pot of hot grease, but by patiently turning it in a shallow pan, crisping it over time in a blend of lard, butter, and country ham, a technique that reflects something greater than the flavor of conjoined fats. When Lewis was growing up in Freetown, she learned that there was a season truly perfect for frying chickens—late spring to early summer, when the birds were the right size and had the right feed—just as there was a season for peaches and a season for blackberries. Foods, Lewis argued, are always temporal, so all good tastes are special. And when you have only a few chances every year to make something, you make it well. You use home-rendered lard to cook the bird. You brown the breasts first, then lay them on top of the sizzling legs so that they finish cooking gently in the heat above the pan. You slip in a slice of country ham to season the fat. That's how you give thanks for it.

Along the way, fried chicken has become a fraught food, somehow

Francis Lam

both universally beloved and also used in ugly stereotypes of black people. But Lewis treated all the food she prepared, perhaps all things she did, with dignity and sensitivity. You get this sense in photos of her: she always stood tall, often dressed in clothes made of African fabrics, her white hair crowning her head. Almost everyone who met her describes her as "regal." It's almost as if her parents knew, when they gave her the middle name Regina.

Lewis went on from Freetown to become a revered chef and cookbook author, a friend to literati and movie stars, and the winner of nearly every award our culinary institutions had to give. Today, her name is revered among food-world cognoscenti but less well known than your average Food Network star, and yet her championing of southern food, and cooking it close to the land, is more relevant than ever. "We weren't ready for her then," one of her acolytes, Alice Waters, says. "Now we are."

"Our mother was an excellent cook," Lewis's younger sister Ruth Lewis Smith told me recently. "Our Aunt Jennie was an excellent cook. A lot of our family went to Washington, D.C., to work as cooks. When they came home, they all learned from each other." The elite homes of Virginia, going back to the days when the colonial elite socialized with French politicians and generals during the Revolutionary War, dined on a cuisine inspired by France. It was built on local ingredients — many originally shared by Native Americans or brought by slaves from Africa — and developed by enslaved black chefs like James Hemings, who cooked for Thomas Jefferson at Monticello. Because this aristocratic strain of southern cuisine was provisioned and cooked largely by black people, it came into their communities as well, including Freetown. Smith is ninety-one and still raises chickens; a cage of quail coo in her kitchen. When I called her, she asked me to call back later because her apple butter had been on the stove for two days, and it was ready for canning.

As a girl, Lewis busied herself with gathering berries, sewing, and other home-taught skills. She watched the older women intently, learning to cook alongside them. After leaving Freetown, she made her way to New York City, where she took a job at a laundry and was fired three hours later: she'd never ironed before. She became a Communist and bristled at having to enter employers' buildings through the back door but nonetheless worked for a time as a domestic, helping to put her baby sister Naomi through art school. At one point, she became a sought-after seamstress, making dresses for Doe Avedon and Marilyn Monroe, and dressing windows for the high-end department store Bonwit Teller. Surrounded by bohemians and fashion figures, she gave dinner parties for her friends, channeling her memories of her mother and aunt at the stove.

In 1948, Johnny Nicholson, a regular at Lewis's table, was getting ready to open a café on the Upper East Side. As Nicholson used to tell it, Lewis walked by, about to take another job as a domestic, when she looked into her friend's place and said it would make a terrific restaurant. A week later, Lewis was cooking lunch at Café Nicholson. She offered a tidy menu—herbed roast chicken, filet mignon, a piece of fish, some cake, a chocolate soufflé. The restaurant was a smash. It had a dining room like a fabulist's dream: floral displays and soaring palm fronds dipping down to kiss the heads of guests like Paul Robeson, Tennessee Williams, and Gore Vidal. Truman Capote would come into the kitchen, purring at his new friend Edna for a fix of biscuits. William Faulkner once flattered Lewis by asking if she had studied cooking in Paris. But no, her sister Ruth Lewis Smith told me: she learned to make soufflés from their mother, back in Virginia. Smith, in fact, often made them herself, after the restaurant took off and she came to help out.

The restaurant critic Clementine Paddleford reviewed the restaurant in 1951 in the *New York Herald Tribune*, calling that soufflé "light as a dandelion seed in a wind" and noting a sense of pride in the chef: "We saw Edna peering in from the kitchen, just to see the effect on the guests and hear the echoes of praise." But Lewis wasn't just the chef. With Jim Crow in full effect and de facto segregation the reality in most of the North, this granddaughter of slaves had become a partner in a business that counted Eleanor Roosevelt among its favorite customers.

In 1961, Judith Jones, an editor at Knopf, ushered in an era of fascination with French cuisine by publishing an intensely detailed cookbook called *Mastering the Art of French Cooking*, written in part by a tall, warbling woman named Julia Child. A decade later, Jones was looking for someone to help America turn its sights to the glories of its own tables. One day, the chief executive of Random House, Knopf's parent company, asked Jones if she would meet his friend, a socialite named Evangeline Peterson. Peterson had taken a liking to a wonderful caterer and wanted to write down her recipes. Unsure of what the meeting would yield, Jones agreed to it. "But when Edna swept into my office, in this beautiful garb, her hair piled up, she was just such a presence that you were a little awed by her," she says.

After leaving Café Nicholson in the mid-1950s, Lewis had continued her cinematically eclectic life. She and her husband, a Communist activist named Steve Kingston, spent time as pheasant farmers in New Jersey, until all the birds died overnight from a mysterious disease. She opened and closed her own restaurant. She began catering and teaching cooking classes and took a job as a docent in the Hall of African Peoples in the American Museum of Natural History. A slip on a snowy night broke her ankle, and bored during her recovery, she accepted Peterson's invitation to write together.

They had essentially finished writing a book, *The Edna Lewis Cookbook*, that Jones thought was fashionable but characterless. But when Lewis started talking, recalling scenes of growing up in Freetown and the foods they had gathered, grown, harvested, shot, hooked, and cooked, Jones lit up. "I knew this was a voice that could teach us," she said. This was the story of American food that she had wanted to hear. Peterson graciously went home, Jones asked questions, Lewis wrote answers on yellow legal pads, and the seeds of her classic, *The Taste of Country Cooking*, were sown. Lewis would go on to write more books and to hold chef posts at esteemed landmarks like Middleton Place in South Carolina and Gage & Tollner in New York. But she will be forever remembered for writing the book that started with that meeting.

The Taste of Country Cooking, published in 1976, is revered for the way it shows the simple beauty of food honestly made in the rhythm of the seasons — the now common but at the time nearly forgotten ethos of eating farm to table — and for the way it gave a view of southern food that was refined and nuanced, going beyond grease, greens, and grits. "Until recently, we Southerners were very apologetic about our food," Lewis's friend, collaborator, and eventual caretaker Scott Peacock told me. "But she wrote about it with such reverence." She inspired generations of southern cooks to honor their own roots. Alice Waters, who is usually credited for sparking the American organic-and-local movement at Chez Panisse in California, says: "It was certainly revolutionary at that point. I was such a Francophile, but when I discovered her cookbook, it felt like a terribly good friend. By then, we were already in a fast-food world, and she showed the deep roots of gastronomy in the United States and that they were really in the South, where we grew for flavor and cooked with sophistication. I had never really considered southern food before, but I learned from her that it's completely connected to nature, totally in time and place."

The book is, in one sense, a country manual, with instructions on picking wild mushrooms and the best way to turn dandelions into wine. (It tastes like Drambuie, Lewis offers helpfully.) It's also a cookbook, because there are teaspoons and tablespoons and "cook uncovered for 10 minutes." But perhaps the truest way to describe the book is as a memoir told in recipes, where every menu, dish, and ingredient speaks to her childhood in rural Virginia and how her community made a life from the land, taking pleasure in the doing of many things.

It stands as an exemplar of American food writing, a complex, multi-layered, artistic, and even subtly subversive document. And it stands on the other side of a cruel tradition in cookbooks from the first half of the 20th century, one in which black domestic cooks often had their recipes recorded and written by their white employers, who tended not to flatter the help in the process. Toni Tipton-Martin's 2015 book *The Jemima Code*, a bibliography of African American cookbooks, collects examples of this, including one from 1937 called *Emma Jane's Souvenir Cookbook*, by Blanche Elbert Moncure. In the equivalent of blackface dialect, a servant cook, Emma Jane, ostensibly says, "I ain't no fancy cake maker but here is a re-ceet dat 'Ole Miss' taught me," then goes on to give the cake a name involving both a racial slur and an insult to her own intelligence.

Lewis is a sensitive, even-toned renderer of beauty. Her small stories in *The Taste of Country Cooking* gently urge the reader toward a life of mindfulness, a life of learning to see the details. Early in the book, she describes a spring morning: "A stream, filled from the melted snows of winter, would flow quietly by us, gurgling softly and gently pulling the leaf of a fern that hung lazily from the side of its bank. After moments of complete exhilaration we would return joyfully to the house for breakfast." As Jones once said on a panel, "You felt all through her writing that she was giving thanks for something precious."

In a passage called "Hog Killing," Lewis recalls the day each fall when her family would turn pigs into pork. It's not gruesome, but it is earthy. Today, at a time when the phrase "rock-star butchers" has occasion to exist, making us reckon with the mortal reality of meat isn't so shocking. But it's still grounding to read these lines: "My father would remove the liver and the bladder, which he would present to us. We would blow the bladders up with straws cut from reeds and hang them in the house to dry. By Christmas they would have turned transparent like beautiful balloons." Can you imagine being so intimately connected to the guts of life that you could look at a bladder, just separated from its pig, and see a balloon for your Christmas tree? Can you imagine seeing so much to love around you?

But those same hogs also point toward deeper meaning in the text. The next paragraph reads: "The following morning my brothers and sisters and I would rush out before breakfast to see the hogs hanging from the scaffolds like giant statues. The hogs looked beautiful. They were glistening white inside with their lining of fat, and their skin was almost translucent."

In November 1918, two years after Lewis was born, a black man, Charles Allie Thompson was lynched in Culpeper, a nearby town. A mob hung him from a tree after claims that he raped a white woman. He had been seen asking her to help with butchering, at hog-killing time. It's not clear whether Lewis knew this story. But she was not naïve. "She could see the ugly in the world," Peacock says. "This is someone who had street smarts." She wrote *The Taste of Country Cooking* while in her 50s, in the 1970s, after years as a political radical, after the civil rights movement, after marching for the Scottsboro Boys, nine black teenagers accused of raping two white women, who escaped being lynched in Alabama in 1931 only to be railroaded into shoddy convictions. (They were all eventually pardoned or had their convictions overturned, some posthumously.) Whether Lewis intended to imbue her hog-killing scene with such references, it became impossible for me to read *The Taste of Country Cooking* without a sense of the wider setting of her story and how she chose to tell it without terror, how she refused to let the past, her past, be defined by anyone else but her.

If someone handed you a book about a settlement of freed slaves trying to live off the land, what would you expect? A story of struggle, at least. Privation and desperation, probably. But in Lewis's telling, it is a story of peace and celebration, of receiving the gifts of the earth and hard work. The children sing at concerts in this story. The recipes are arranged by menus with formal titles as literally quotidian as "A Late Spring Dinner" or "A Cool-Evening Supper," because the very acts of cooking and serving and eating food are worthy of occasion. It is a story of refinement, not in the fine-china sense but in the sense of being meticulous and careful about the way the people of Freetown raised and grew and trapped and foraged and prepared their food, because their lives were worth that. The pleasure of that was due them.

Lewis took the story of rural black people, formerly enslaved black people, and owned it as a story of confidence and beauty. She didn't have an easy life, even in her Freetown years. Her family suffered through two stillborn children and two more who died young of pneumonia. But she chose to see, and to show us, beauty; and under the shadow of oppression and slavery, that is a political act. I spoke with Lewis's niece, her youngest sister Naomi's daughter, Nina Williams-Mbengue, who, at age 12, took her aunt's handwritten sheets of yellow legal-pad paper and typed the manuscript for *The Taste of Country Cooking*. Her aunt never said her book was meant to be political. But she often spoke of being inspired by the people and the humane, communal spirit of Freetown. Williams-Mbengue said: "She just didn't have any notion that these people were less-than because they were poor farming people. She wanted to make their lives count." And then she added: "Imagine being enslaved, then rising above that to build your own town. Aunt Edna was always amazed that one of the first things they did was to plant orchards, so that their children would see the fruit of their efforts. How could those communities have such a gift? Was it that the future had to be so bright because they knew the past that they were coming out of?"

One of the most quietly devastating passages in American literature is the opening of *Narrative of the Life of Frederick Douglass, an American Slave*: "I was born in Tuckahoe, near Hillsborough, and about twelve miles from Easton, in Talbot county, Maryland. I have no accurate knowledge of my age, never having seen any authentic record containing it." Here we find so many of slavery's psychological horrors in Douglass's two simple, measured, masterful sentences: I can tell you, in great detail, about the location of my body. But I can't tell you how long I have been here, because the system that made my body someone else's property keeps the most basic, most intimate fact of my own life away from me.

It's possible to hear the echoes of Douglass's sentences in the first lines of *The Taste of Country Cooking*: "I grew up in Freetown, Virginia, a community of farming people. It wasn't really a town. The name was adopted because the first residents had all been freed from chattel slavery and they wanted to be known as a town of Free People." You can hear the echoes in the even tone, in facts, plainly stated, that have to say no more to say so much. The message here is empowered, almost fierce: our town may not have been a town, according to the people who draw the maps and place the post offices. But it was a town, a whole world, because we, and I, say so.

"The book was this coming out," Jones says. "But she felt able and entitled to it. She was very strong in her beliefs." When they were working on the book together, Jones noticed that there wasn't a menu for Thanksgiving. She asked Lewis about it, who said, quietly: "We didn't celebrate Thanksgiving. We celebrated Emancipation Day." And so she wrote a menu for that, leaving it to the reader to figure out why.

Nearly every year, Lewis went back to Virginia, often visiting the site where Freetown had stood, even when all that remained was a stone chimney and a few houses, sagging as if molten. But she would delight in feeling the soil under her feet with her older sister Jennie, who still lived nearby. "I remember trailing along behind them, picking blackberries, the brambles getting caught in my pants and my hair," Williams-Mbengue says. "And they would be giggling, picking berries and wild greens for salads." While she was writing *The Taste of Country Cooking*, Lewis cooked with Jennie to refresh her memory of the techniques and the flavor and often called her from New York while testing the recipes. She read historic cookbooks to learn more about the cooking done by blacks in the past, how Native Americans ate, what French influences Thomas Jefferson brought to her home region. She spoke of the creativity of black women in the kitchen, how that represented some measure of freedom when they otherwise had none. "She always talked about how, in spite of these people being slaves, they created a cuisine that would become world-renowned," Williams-Mbengue says.

Lewis stood as the ambassador of that cuisine, who announced the universality of its appeal and importance and who wrote, in part, to preserve it. She feared that the departure of people from the land, and the rise of fast food and convenience foods, would change the culture of cooking. "Southern cooking is about to become extinct," she said to the *New York Times Magazine* in 1992. And she feared, too, that people would lose sight of who should be credited for that cooking. "It's mostly black," she said, more forceful in her later years, because blacks "did most of the cooking in private homes, hotels and on the railroads." She began work on, but never finished, a book about the significance of black cooks in Southern food.

Southern food has had its ups and downs in the national consciousness. In 1962, Eugene Walter of Mobile, Alabama, wrote of his culinary homesickness while traveling for *Gourmet* magazine: "It's interesting that in New York one can find authentic food of every country on earth, save of the South. What is advertised as Southern fried chicken is usually an ancient fowl encased in a cement mixture and tormented in hot grease for an eternity. Southern biscuits à la New York are pure cannon wadding. Gumbo they've not even heard of." But for the last nine years, by my calculations, two-thirds of the nominees for the James Beard Foundation's annual award for the best book on American cooking have been on the subject of southern food. Southern books have won the award all of those years but one. Yet none of those Beard award winners, or nominees, were black.

Leni Sorensen is a Virginia historian of African American cooks. "Many black people have not heard of Edna Lewis because they're urban and raised in schools to learn that farming is dirty and slavery was awful, so let's not talk about it," she told me. "There is a feeling: 'Oh, hell no, we just got *off* the farm.' And for many black people, to see any activities done under slavery now as professional is just too painful." Joe Randall, a chef of five decades and a friend of Lewis's, says: "Cooking was relegated to black folk, and when Johnson signed the Civil Rights Act, a lot of civil rights leaders said, 'We don't have to work in your restaurants anymore.'" Randall taught hospitality management at universities and says, "A lot of my students' grandparents said, 'I didn't send my baby to college to be no cook.'"

Once cooking became a profession with cultural cachet—Randall attributes this rise to the moment in 1977 when the Department of Labor began classifying chefs not as "domestics" but as "professionals"—many black chefs then became pigeonholed as "soul-food cooks." In her 2011 book *High on the Hog*, the culinary scholar Jessica B. Harris writes that in the 1960s "soul food was as much an affirmation as a diet. Eating neck-bones and chitterlings, turnip greens and fried chicken became a political statement for many." But Lewis publicly distanced herself from soul food, once saying to *Southern Living* magazine, "That's hard-times food in Harlem, not true Southern food." Adrian Miller, who wrote a book called *Soul Food*, says he understands where Lewis was coming from: "This is the food of black migrants, who were transplanting a cuisine to where they couldn't always find what they had before. So they had to find substitutes, like canned and processed ingredients. I think Lewis thought it just was something different than the scratch cooking that she made." Lewis came directly from slaves and from the land and the food that they grew and prepared for themselves. Her food wasn't a remix of food that they got from the elite; it was the same food as the elites ate, only they owned it themselves. She had no truck with the belittling mainstream idea of soul food—cheap and greasy—as the totality of black cooking, but it's easy to see how her words would fall hard on ears that still hear pride in the term.

It has been almost 10 years since Lewis died, 40 since she published *The Taste of Country Cooking.* Who carries her torch? There are many calling for seasonal, organic eating, but who else has been afforded the iconic position Lewis held, to keep showing us the rich history and influences that black cooks have had on American food? Jones found Lewis by chance. Is America looking hard enough for the next Edna Lewis?

It's a question that has weighed on Tipton-Martin for years, as she pored over hundreds of African American cookbooks to write *The Jemima Code*. She got to speak to Lewis at a food writer's event and, while still in awe of her, steeled herself to tell her that she was not the only one. "I told her that I wanted to tell the world that there were more women like her than just her," she said. A while later, Lewis sent her a letter, written on the same kind of yellow legal pad that she used to write *The Taste of Country Cooking*. "Leave no stone unturned to prove this point," she wrote. "Make sure that you do."

On Edna Lewis's
The Edna Lewis Cookbook

SUSAN REBECCA WHITE

It seems to me that there are two types of southerners: those who never leave, and those who attempt to flee the South as soon as they can. I belong to the latter category, though, like many of my kindred ex-pats, I found I could never really escape.

In the fall of 1994, I left Georgia for college in Boulder, Colorado, and then, dissatisfied with Greek life—the concept of eschewing Rush ran counter to everything I had learned at my WASP-y Atlanta prep school—I transferred to Brown, where I reinvented myself as a Northeast urban intellectual. Still, when my roommate would throw parties for her theater friends I would often appear wearing a red baseball cap, which advertised "Wayne's Feed," a company that my great-uncle R.D., who owned several grain storage units in western Tennessee, had dealings with. As the night wore on and the thespians tired of dancing, I would switch out George Michael's "Freedom" for *Alabama's Greatest Hits.* My core group of friends, Yankees all, would sing along with me to "Dixieland Delight," bless their hearts. Had I been at a southern school when this particular anthem was played I surely would have rolled my eyes and bemoaned its sentimental whitewashing. But such was my relationship to the South: I felt out of place living both in and out of it.

I returned to Atlanta briefly after college and then moved to San Francisco in 2000, where I waited tables for several years at a restaurant smack in the middle of the proudly gay Castro, marched in protest against the 2003 U.S.-led invasion of Iraq, and acquired not one but two Lodge cast iron skillets in which to prepare fried chicken and skillet cornbread, which I served to friends anytime my Jersey-born, Jewish husband and I entertained. In San Francisco my southern accent grew thicker; I used my sterling silver flatware routinely, and I prided myself on bringing pimento cheese as hostess gifts, whether the host liked the stuff or not. Far from home I was proudly reclaiming my roots, though the closest my own southern mother ever came to preparing fried chicken was to roll boneless, skinless chicken breasts in a mixture of crushed Ritz crackers and grated Parmesan, throw it in a Pyrex casserole, then bake it in the oven for an hour.

It was my mother who gave me Scott Peacock and Edna Lewis's 2003 cookbook, *The Gift of Southern Cooking*, in honor of my acceptance into a graduate writing program in Roanoke, Virginia. My mother's inscription reads: "Yeah! You are back in the South—for at least a little while." Her words were prophetic. In 2005, a week after I received my MFA, my (then) husband and I returned to San Francisco. I made certain to bring *The Gift of Southern Cooking* with me. I loved the recipes, deeply rooted in Lewis's Virginia and Peacock's Alabama, and I was intrigued by the friendship between a gay white man and a straight black woman nearly fifty years his senior. Admittedly, I was initially skeptical of the friendship—I remember looking at the photo printed on the cover of the book, beneath the jacket, which showed a pair of white hands and a pair of black hands, each stripping kernels from an ear of corn, and thinking that this was a white person's fantasy of the South: bygones becoming bygones via the glory of southern food.

Still, it was a story I very much wanted to champion, as it reinforced my own notions of progress, cross-cultural connection, and the possibility of the South leading the nation in racial reconciliation. And the more I researched Peacock and Lewis's connection, the more authentic it proved to be. It wasn't just southern food that brought them together but their shared approach to the preparing of it, which is to say meticulous, exacting, and somewhat compulsive.

A fascination with their real-life story lodged deep enough in me that I eventually wrote a novel inspired by it, *A Place at the Table*, published in 2013. The novel's storyline was invented, but I wanted the surrounding details to be as accurate as possible. In particular, I wanted to understand—as best I, a white woman, could—what Edna Lewis's life had been like when she was living in Manhattan and cooking for the artists and eccentrics who frequented Café Nicholson. And so I dug into researching Miss Lewis, which included going through the Café Nicholson archive, housed at New York University's Fales Library, and reading all four of Miss Lewis's books, as well as cooking as many recipes from them as possible.

Her first book, *The Edna Lewis Cookbook*, was out of print, so I purchased it for nearly $65 from a third-party seller. It is not the best of her books, but for me it was the most interesting, mainly because it included recipes for the sort of food she would have cooked for sophisticated New Yorkers during her Café Nicholson days, including her famous chocolate soufflé. During the writing of my novel, I prepared that soufflé several times, twice solely for myself, as my husband and I were in the process of divorcing. During that time I ate dinner alone most nights, with cloth napkin and a glass of wine, in an attempt to lift my spirits.

I wrote the following essay to explore that brief window when I was once again living outside of the South (this time in Manhattan), in my mid-thirties, in the middle of writing a novel, in the middle of a divorce, and cooking from *The Edna Lewis Cookbook*. By the time I completed the novel I had met the man who would become my second husband, and within two months of marrying him, I was pregnant with our son, Gus. There is nothing quite so grounding as having a child, and I imagine it will come as no surprise for me to say that my husband and I are raising him in Atlanta. I remain cognizant of the terrible damage that is wrought by the casual bigotry of many of my fellow Georgians, but bigotry seems to me as much an American problem as it is a southern one, and if age has taught me anything, it is that you can't outrun that which makes you uncomfortable; you have to engage with it.

Escape is a romantic notion, and I suppose I have become a realist at age forty. This is perhaps best demonstrated by comparing grocery lists between my life now and my life back when I was pretending to be some displaced southern belle living in San Francisco. Back then it was not uncommon for my list to include, say, sunchokes, leaf lard, pork shoulder, and a whole duck, which I would roast and serve with oyster dressing. Now I routinely buy pre-shredded cheese, prepared pizza dough, and rotisserie chickens. Still, every Saturday my little family and I walk the mile or so to the farmer's market at the Carter Center. My son runs from vendor to vendor while I purchase our vegetables for the week, remembering tips from Edna Lewis on how to best select and store fresh produce (she says never to store vegetables in plastic). Which is all to say: I am still profoundly influenced by Miss Lewis, though it has been several years since I last prepared her chocolate soufflé.

In my early twenties, I tried to eradicate my southern identity by moving across the country and living in San Francisco, where I would meet the man who became my first husband, a man who had no connection to the South and was eleven years my senior. During our courtship, he took me to the best restaurants in the Bay Area. I ate Kumamoto oysters, spread bone marrow on toast, bought illegally imported raw-milk cheeses from my neighborhood *fromagerie*. No longer burdened by the vexing politics and casual bigotry of my native Georgia, I felt I had found my Shangri-La.

But it did not last. In the summer of 2011, I was living alone in a Manhattan sublet, no beloved cat curled by my side at night, no familiar artwork on the walls, my husband of seven years thousands of miles away. My marriage was, in the official language of divorce, "irretrievably broken." I was shell-shocked to be on my own. I took comfort in cooking in my tiny kitchen, preparing meals for myself, which I would eat at my borrowed table, set with a single cloth napkin and a glass of wine. When not cooking, I did what I always do in crisis: immerse myself in work until the intensity of my feelings subsides.

I'd come to New York to do research for a novel inspired by the real-life story of Edna Lewis, long considered the godmother of seasonal southern cuisine. Born in 1916 and raised in a farming community founded by freed slaves in Virginia—her grandfather was one of "Freetown's" first settlers—Lewis grew up with a mother who was supremely adept at preparing the bounty they hunted, caught, and harvested. During the Depression, Lewis moved to New York, where she joined the Communist Party and held an assortment of jobs—some menial, some creative—including helping her friend Johnny Nicholson dress windows for department stores. Among her comrades, she earned a reputation as an excellent cook.

In the late 1940s, Nicholson, an avid traveler, decided to open a coffee house in the spirit of Rome's Caffè Greco, the centuries-old bar known as a haunt for writers, artists, and people of influence. The day his Sutton Place café was to open, Lewis happened to stop by. She suggested the space would be perfect for a restaurant. Nicholson offered a deal: if she cooked, he'd give her half ownership. Their Café Nicholson would become a preferred venue of New York's literati, attracting luminaries such as Truman Capote, Tennessee Williams, Gore Vidal, and Tanaquil Le Clercq.

Nicholson outfitted the café with white marble statues, Tiffany lamps, objets d'art, and a parrot named Lolita. Located in the shadow of the Queensboro Bridge, it was a meeting place for the stars of Broadway, the bohemians of Greenwich Village, and the socialites of the Upper East Side. Actors, writers, artists, and "ladies who lunch" all flocked there. Nicholson owned a silver Rolls-Royce and offered chauffeur service to guests who lived within a sixty-block radius of the restaurant. Miss Lewis served a limited but delicious menu: diners had the choice of roast chicken with herbs or steak with béarnaise sauce, and more, for dessert, bittersweet chocolate soufflé or a ripe pear with Stilton. Capote, delighted to find a fellow southerner in the kitchen, would beg Lewis to fix him biscuits. She refused.

The more I studied Edna Lewis and her days at the Café Nicholson, the more I yearned to have a place that was stylish and discreet where I could while away the afternoon. I wanted a place where I would *not* think about my impending divorce. I wanted to be consumed instead by thoughts of Lewis's food. Everything I read, both by and about her, highlighted the meticulous care with which she prepared her meals. She paid attention to the sounds of cakes cooking; she tested recipes again and again, relying on her memory of how good everything had tasted when she was a girl living on the farm. I wanted to experience her memories made incarnate, to be offered something warm, nourishing, and filling, prepared by her. I imagined that to eat Lewis's food was to experience a secular form of Communion, something I craved during that summer that I felt so very alone.

Both Lewis and the café she helped found have passed from this world. But I found consolation: I could taste her food by cooking her recipes. Her most famous cookbooks, the ones upon which her reputation rests, focus on the regional cuisine of the South, but recipes from the café can be found in *The Edna Lewis Cookbook*, her first effort, and the only one that is out of print.

The Edna Lewis Cookbook is arranged by seasonal menus, starting in spring and ending with a Christmas buffet. Its first menu begins with cold poached lobster with "special sauce" (a blend of ketchup, sherry, lemon juice, and Tabasco). Baba au rhum finishes the meal, and in between, roast rack of spring lamb with herb butter is served. Sautéed potato balls and asparagus with browned breadcrumbs accompany the meat. Though there are a few southern recipes included (corn on the cob, yellow cake with caramel frosting), the book was aimed at sophisticated New Yorkers. Many of the dishes have a European influence and listed in the back are "Some Favorite Shops," including Bloomingdale's Delicacies Shop, Zabar's, the Schapira Coffee Co. on West Tenth, and Zito's on Bleecker.

With the publication of her second book, *The Taste of Country Cooking*, Lewis became primarily associated with southern food. Not the sort of deep-fried everything that is often used to caricature southern cuisine, but food that is native to the South or to Africa, harvested seasonally, and prepared simply yet with attention paid to coaxing out its best flavor. Think crispy biscuits with butter and strawberry preserves, pork-flavored green beans, sweet potato casserole, boiled Virginia ham, and caramel pie.

Susan Rebecca White

Her meticulous approach to cooking is a constant through all four of her published books, but *The Edna Lewis Cookbook* is the only one in which the recipes mark a distinct cultural moment in our nation's history when fine dining meant looking across the pond for inspiration. Included in the book are recipes for coquilles St.-Jacques, braised leeks, poulet à la crème, cheese soufflé, crêpes Suzette, and profiteroles filled with whipped cream and custard. Did Lewis feel that if she were to serve southern food at an eastside restaurant she would be revealed as a rube? Or maybe, like so many of us, it wasn't until she planted herself in unfamiliar soil that she was able to more fully embrace where she came from.

When living in San Francisco, I'd begun to miss the tastes of the South. I wanted to go to a party where someone offered homemade cheese straws made with sharp cheddar and cayenne, instead of the ubiquitous fifty-dollar cheese stray served with thin slices of walnut bread. I wanted real pit-smoked barbeque, not the ersatz stuff they served at the hokey barbeque place in the Haight, where the South was reduced to caricature. I wanted tall, moist layer cakes, made even taller by a swirly coating of sweet, creamy frosting, not some flourless chocolate thing, slightly sunken in its center, with only a dusting of confectioner's sugar for garnish. I was like Truman Capote, begging for biscuits when presented with soufflé. For Capote and for me, it was biscuits we really wanted, biscuits we craved.

I am now back in Atlanta, married to a local fellow, about to have my first child, settling once again in Georgia's sticky red clay. Though my New York summer is over, my divorce finalized, and my novel completed, my relationship with *The Edna Lewis Cookbook* continues. Within Lewis are both the traditions of the South and the promise of the North, and I suppose I, too, will always live with a sense of dual identity, knowing that I am as shaped by my escape from my birthplace as I am by the fact that, in the end, the South pulled me home.

And so I continue to look to Lewis for guidance. She tells me that when I think a cake is finished baking, I should take it out of the oven and hold it close to my ear. If I still hear tiny popping sounds, the cake needs a few more minutes. She tells me to cook corn in a tall pot of water, dropping the ears in when the water is still cold, cutting off the flame as soon as it comes to a boil. She tells me to slightly underbake my chocolate soufflé, just as she did when cooking at the Café Nicholson so that the dessert would continue to rise as the waitress rushed it to the table, where it would arrive fragrant and tall. And then a spoon would be pushed into its center, and the dessert would collapse around it, its towering moment now past.

How to Talk about Miss Lewis?

Home Cook. Writer. Icon. One Young Black Woman's Act of Remembering.

CAROLINE RANDALL WILLIAMS

My mother and I have been talking about Edna Lewis for more than twenty-seven years. I am only twenty-eight years old. Mama began the conversation before I could talk.

And before I could walk I became part of a posse chasing after Miss Lewis through the Union Square farmers' market. I like to imagine her the way my mama tells it; Lewis on foot, alone, a shopping bag gripped tightly in one hand, the other free to finger the late fall produce. I was being toted, grocerylike in a hippy rigged denim sack; my godmother, Mimi, at my mother's side.

It was 1987. I was a Nashville-born baby girl, whisked off after three weeks in music city to live in Manhattan, to sleep in a handwoven southern Moses cradle in a duplexed brownstone just down the block from the Empire Diner and around the corner from the Chelsea Hotel. At that point in the neighborhood's history, buppies with puppies—bougie black couples with babies—were not living in Chelsea.

Except we were, and it had everything to do with Miss Lewis.

My mother had been on bed rest in Tennessee for months of her pregnancy. That put her more than 8,000 miles away from my father, who was serving as a State Department officer in Manila. It put her more than 800 miles from most of her friends working in law firms, banks, and publishing companies in New York City. Most important, it put her in Nashville, under the care of Alberta Bontemps, my (then) eighty-year-old great-grandmother, widow of Harlem Renaissance poet Arna.

Grandma regaled my mother with stories of Harlem during the Renaissance, the private life of Zora Neale Hurston, and tales of Edna Lewis holding court at the Café Nicholson. My mother was intoxicated by the idea of the city, of the writing life, of the figure Miss Lewis cut in Grandma's narrative.

My mother spent her confinement helping cook in Grandma's kitchen and reading in Arna's library. I love imagining the moment when she discovered a tiny *New York Times* ad for a duplex apartment with a walled garden—she did not wait to act. She dialed the number from Arna's old rotary dial phone, which sat right as he'd left it, next to his manual typewriter. When the owner told her the walled garden had an apple tree that bore fruit 'til Thanksgiving, Mama rented the apartment sight unseen. When my father balked at the rent—$3,000 a month—my mother turned, perhaps for the first time, to Edna Lewis, who had the answer. "An apple orchard is a basic part of every homestead," Mama quoted.

Actually, my mother misquoted Lewis. In her second and most famous cookbook, *The Taste of Country Cooking*, Lewis writes, "An apple orchard *was* a basic part of every homestead. It supplied all of the fruit used. The orchard was also a kind of nursery . . . and a haven for birds, especially bluebirds and robins. The little bluebird always made its nest only in the hollow of an apple tree." Lewis was writing about a past that was lost and distant when she published *Taste* in the bicentennial summer of 1976. Eleven years later, my mother was determined to find and give me what was lost to her and much of black America: food eaten in season, cooked by loving hands at home, eaten in the peace of sheltering nature, eclipsing the trauma of lynching trees.

Edna Lewis looked at and cooked for the world with the eyes and hands of a nature poet. She knew the preciousness of good, ripe things, of things that grow from the earth and that remain familiar to their earthy and earthly colors, looks, and flavors. I think of her sometimes in conversation with Zora Neale Hurston that way; they both created worlds that revel in a kind of unrestrained joy of blackness, pockets of comfort in the hard truths of the black South; they knew about "Diddy Wah Diddy" and the new life you can find from sitting under a fruit tree.

To this day, my mother considers that garden with its apple tree one of the great extravagances of her life, and she regrets it not at all. She felt inspired and sanctioned by Miss Lewis. She imagined and then enacted nursing her daughter—me—in the outdoors, sheltered by the dappled light filtered through a one-tree orchard.

Back then, my mother only dreamed of making Lewis's applesauce with nutmeg for me, wondering, in the contrary and inquisitive way that I've inherited, whether the last apples of the season would make for more interesting sauce than the early season apples that were Ms. Lewis's prefer-ence. Eventually, Mama followed her Edna Lewis applesauce dreams into the kitchen, and she took me with her. Even now, one of her most trea-sured dishes is a crêpe stack cake filled with layers of Lewis's applesauce and topped with sprigs of rosemary.

The fourth character in our Union Square adventures, my godmother, Mimi Oka, is still my mother's best friend, and almost her exact opposite. Mimi is an investment banker turned chef, then food performance artist, and she is given to radical understatement. At Harvard in the seventies they founded a short-lived organization called Harvard Friends of Food. The black girl from Detroit, Alabama, and the Japanese girl from Lon-don cooked blini, beef Wellington, coulibiac, salmon mousse, flan, and any number of other complexities in their dormitory kitchens. The organiza-tion was so popular it had to disband when they couldn't decide how to decide who could be invited to the too-popular dinners.

Because of my mother's gift for romantic remembrance and my god-mother's commitment to subtlety, their eyewitness accounts of the exact same event can differ dramatically.

One of the few trips they describe in much the same way, though, is that first venture to the Union Square market. Mimi was looking out at the world. Mama was cooing at me. Mimi spotted Dame Edna and sug-gested that they follow her from stall to stall and see what she bought. As Mimi foraged, informed by Lewis's discernment, buying what Miss Lewis bought, my mother told me a truncated and translated version of *The Taste of Country Cooking*, one that she'd tell me again and again, until it eked its way into my living memory, transforming the cookbook into a fairy tale with a beautiful black princess who lived, ate, and cooked in a magical kingdom called Freetown.

Later she would talk to me, young woman to grown woman, about Edna moving to New York, Edna joining the Communist Party, Edna cooking at Café Nicholson, with its small but perfect menu. It was clear from the beginning that my mother didn't much relish that part of the Edna Lewis story; at the time I didn't understand why she rushed through the politics and that fine dining room. I think I understand better now, but more on that later.

My mother loves the Judith Jones chapter of Miss Lewis's life, and with good reason — Mrs. Jones encouraged the writer in Miss Lewis, and we got from their friendship *The Taste of Country Cooking*, a book that in my mother's telling was a perfect cross between *Their Eyes Were Watching*

Caroline Randall Williams

God and *Mastering the Art of French Cooking*. It is a sojourn into a prelapsarian black Eden.

❧ Now a strange thing about my mother is that she told this story much the same way from the beginning. She doesn't talk down to children or talk slow for people who think at normal speeds. She speeds, and you hold on to what you can. What I got from the very beginning was that Edna Lewis was a very important person and a very important writer. I got that she was choosy and that it was good to be choosy. I got that timing is everything, particularly when it comes to cooking. And I got to experience the pages of her magical cookbook come alive on my tongue as my mother cooked and I tasted Lewis's recipes cooked for me by my mama.

My godmother—ever precise, ever interested in global context—told me about the other cookbooks Judith Jones had edited. When I was living alone in my first little house in Greenwood, Mississippi, Mimi sent me Jones's own late-life cookbook, *The Pleasures of Cooking for One*.

But that would come later. First would come me in a diaper able to talk and walk but not yet two years old, sitting on the dining room table with fresh washed hands helping Mama and Mimi make turkey dressing. My job was to tear baguettes into large, irregular pieces that they would toast to make white bread croutons that would be mixed with cornbread. But first would come eating Lewis's thin-sliced cucumbers and white vinegar dressing, her green bean salad with sliced tomatoes.

Miss Lewis has said, "My first memory of who I was was food." I don't think I could say it truer than that. I don't remember my parents married. My mother became a single mother, and Edna Lewis helped her raise me. Mama wrote screenplays that got produced, songs that got recorded, and novels that got published. The food I remember her fixing during those busy days? The simple Lewis side dishes she could make ahead and serve chilled.

❧ I owned my own set of Edna Lewis cookbooks well before I could understand how much she mattered, and I owe that to my nana, Joan Bontemps. My grandmother died in 1998, and I inherited her cookbook collection. I have written about this collection in other places, so I won't say much about it here, except that I was eleven years old when I came to own more than 2,000 cookbooks purchased by a black woman who supported herself, her husband, her family, and then much of the civil rights movement in Nashville working as a university librarian. My grand-

mother Joan was a committed eater. Cookbook reading was a central pleasure of her life. New books came into the house weekly by the time I knew
her. Of course, her collection included *The Taste of Country Cooking* and
In Pursuit of Flavor—but these were books I had already seen, these were
books in my mother's comparatively tiny cookbook collection. But there
was an earlier book in the collection, *The Edna Lewis Cookbook*, written
with Evangeline Peterson. This was a book I did not know.

And this is the book no one talks about. The one she wrote with Dr.
Peterson, a psychoanalyst. The one that might be my favorite, should I
find myself forced to pick. The recipes I love from that cookbook include
Crème Caramel Filled with Whipped Cream and Topped with Pistachio
Nuts, Crisp Roast Duck Garnished with Kumquats, and Apple Brown
Betty with Custard Sauce. This cookbook is fancy. But it is fancy home
cooking. It is the kind of food I cooked for myself when, after years of
watching and "helping" in the kitchens of women I loved, I finally started
cooking for myself, by myself, as an undergraduate abroad in Oxford.

This is the book that speaks most deeply to the wonderful truth that
Miss Lewis lived; the black feminine is elegant, international, inviting, and
intellectual. She is as at home (if not more!) before the psychoanalyst as
she is before a hearth. She is not exotic. She is elemental. She is elegant.

The Edna Lewis Cookbook is a book with pretensions, and it is a book
with roots. It is glamorous and fabulous, and it is intimate. It is the food I
suspect Edna Lewis served to her friends and to herself when she was eating alone. It is certainly the Edna I fell in love with, an Edna who claimed
her own pleasure, a worldly pleasure, a black cosmopolitan—in many ways
a pleasure that belied the trauma of the South by turning away from the
South.

The Edna Lewis Cookbook is a cookbook of escape and self-creation. It
is a cookbook of earned appropriation. Of trying on and casting off. It is
a cookbook of refusing to stay in one's lane, a cookbook of refusing to be
placed. It is a cookbook that says I can do what you can do—cook, say, coquilles St.-Jacques—and I can do what you cannot do—fry chicken with
knowledge and care, toss a pie in my hand just so. The book is swaggering
and convivial. And it is discreet. It is the only one of her cookbooks that
doesn't have a picture of her face on its cover. Her name is on the cover
twice, in a way that for me announces: this is a woman of significance, a
woman to be valued for her ideas and her words, not the labor of her hands
or the heart promised in her big smile. It is a cover that resists fetishization.

Judith Jones, who is most certainly a cookbook expert, has said that the

Caroline Randall Williams

first cookbook hid Edna's voice. And I cannot disagree with that. I do, however, take issue with any reading of that observation as a criticism of *The Edna Lewis Cookbook*. I believe that the absence of a distinctly Lewis-esque voice reveals a particular audacity. As a black woman reader, I find the book less confined in its neutrality. It defies any inclination to impose caricature or stereotype. It is not willing to be received as a culinary authority only in a particular, segregated, black, and country realm of cooking.

The book is a manual, not an old-fashioned song and dance. It is, to me, beyond reproach. I respect the fact that the recipes work. I respect the way she refused to cook and write to the expected type. Edna Lewis doesn't exercise an authority she was given in *The Edna Lewis Cookbook*; she claimed and asserted her authority without permission. I respect that.

My mother began teaching a course at Vanderbilt University, "Soul Food in Text as Text," and she taught three of the Lewis books. *The Taste of Country Cooking, In Pursuit of Flavor,* and *The Gift of Southern Cooking*. Of course, before she taught her students she taught me, and so we began to talk about the ways in which *Taste* truly functioned as a fairy tale, presenting a never existing early twentieth-century South, where the Klan wasn't ever present, and poverty wasn't bitter. By this time I had read *Spoonbread and Strawberry Wine* (published in 1978), and it was amazing to me that the Darden sisters, Norma Jean and Carole, who had much more sheltered lives, were way more overtly political than Edna Lewis. They talked about lynching, they talked about white presidents sexually engaged with slaves they owned—they told it all, the terror and the terroir. I read Vertamae Smart-Grosvenor: who could be a teenage cook and not swoon in the throes of her hippy-trippy recipes? I wanted to vibrate when I cooked. For a long while Edna was all but forgotten.

Then I moved to Mississippi and started teaching in a ragged and rural place, the Delta. I taught in Moorhead, crossroads of the Southern and "Yellow Dog" Railroads, and then in Ruleville, Fannie Lou Hamer's hometown. I passed one of Robert Johnson's grave markers daily. My commute to work was on a road lined with catfish ponds. It was the road on which Emmett Till had been dragged to death.

I was a long way from home but closer in many ways to that hip-slung baby following Edna in New York than I'd been in twenty years. I started thinking about food in new ways. The students I taught were living on soda and chips. Dialysis, amputations, diabetes, strokes, and heart attacks were facts of everyday life. Surrounded by the richest soil on earth, my students and their families ate out of gas stations, not out of gardens. I started foraging in Walmart and started to write a cookbook that my students could use and afford to create healthy, delicious meals on their table.

If you are me and you start to write a cookbook, you reread your Edna Lewis. I started with *In Pursuit of Flavor.* I noted in this reading the undertone of inadmissibility. Over and over Lewis suggests to her readers, to her would-be cooks, that they will not be able to taste the food as she tasted it, if you did not live on the farm she lived on. She has a robust and righteous pride. Her project includes making the argument for a superior black table that thrived in a mythical past—a kind of Xanadu or Camelot, Pompeii or Babylon, or my favorite, Diddy-Wah-Diddy—that cannot be evaluated because it no longer exists. This got me thinking and talking with my mother about other forgotten black foodways.

We started researching black fishing culture in the rural South before the Civil War and in the urban North after the Second World War.

The Gift of Southern Cooking is a book Mama and I have talked about as a scrapbook or an idealized southern family album from a postracial South that has never existed except in misty-eyed dreams. Reparations? Exploitation? Honoring? Code switching? It's all going on here. Scott Peacock, Lewis's protégé and coauthor, is clearly about giving Edna her due, reverencing her capacity to cook with skill and precision, and her right to sit at the table as well as to serve at the table. But one wonders how many buy the book and entertain from the book who never sit down to eat in their own homes with people who do not look like them. It is hard to gift what has been stolen.

This brings me back, for a moment, to the Café Nicholson days. The days I romanticized in my teens and early twenties because I imagined Edna at the light, bright center of the New York literati; she was Josephine Baker and Ada Bricktop in 1920s Paris. She was captivating, and lively, and free. And then I reread Clementine Paddleford's *New York Herald Tribune* review, in which the well-meaning Paddleford writes, "roast chicken cooked with herbs. It comes brown as autumn chestnuts. We saw Edna peering in from the kitchen, just to see the effect on the guests and hear the echoes of praise." Calling her by her first name. Gazing at her from the dining room, the view of the nice black girl in the kitchen. The idea that all she got were "echoes of praise," and even that she had to claim, clandestinely, for herself.

Café Nicholson is an important chapter in the Edna Lewis story, but it is one she left behind with intention, and I am glad to leave it behind, too.

I want to turn back to Miss Lewis the writer, Miss Lewis the home cook, Miss Lewis the living icon who shopped for greens in Union Square.

This way of remembering Miss Lewis—from the vantage of a black baby girl in northeastern city following the magnificent black woman writer of southern food—is a testament to the complex nature of the intersections inhabited by southern food. With all due respect to Miss Lewis's title, the harder truth (and one I believe she knew) is that southern cooking is not always a gift; it is a collaboration sometimes forced. It is a magnificence. It is something beautiful and sustaining that rises out of some of the ugliest and most destructive acres and times in the history of man. "The Strange Magnificence of Southern Cooking" would be a better title for the Lewis-Peacock volume. For it is a strange magnificence that rises over the most trying of times and geographies to celebrate the human pleasure of eating.

For me, this is the genius of Edna Lewis—she celebrates herself by telling us, not how she cooked, but how she ate, how her tongue discerned. And she celebrates herself by writing about food rather than cooking food. Though she cooked. Significantly. Beautifully. But she also wrote. Significantly. Beautifully. And the writing is a less fleeting monument and a less fleeting inspiration. I don't remember my grandmother cooking me Edna's food. I do remember seeing her handwritten notes in the pages of one of Edna's books.

For me, cooking my way through her pages, I found my own authority in the kitchen, courage to attempt to be a published cookbook author, and a way back to the farm.

According to popular mythology, black American women learned to cook watching their mothers or other family members. I learned to cook taught by the cookbook collection I inherited and experimenting alone an ocean away. Miss Lewis was a primary teacher.

Many black women find their way to writing cookbooks by first working as domestic servants or working in restaurants, their own or someone else's. I've written of the ways in which I have been both drawn to and repelled by Edna Lewis's work at Café Nicholson. I continue to grapple with the cost of being a black woman dishing up food for white people, whether they be strangers or loved ones. For Miss Lewis that already ponderous challenge was layered; she fed southerners displaced in Manhattan. I have to wonder, how comfortable were the black writers in Café Nicholson, sharing space with the likes of Truman Capote demanding hot biscuits? I loved the idea of Lewis being in charge in the restaurant, curating her tiny, just right menu — doing her thing, and having that thing be something surprising — but I couldn't escape the sense that her cooking there was a performance of servitude as well as glamour.

Her writing, particularly *The Taste of Country Cooking*, was something else altogether. It was centered in her black and brilliant self. Whites could visit, but they didn't get the best seats while she stood over a hot stove.

By the time I was born, Le Bernardin was the fancy restaurant Mama dragged me out to for her first postbaby meal, Quatorze was the closest cool bistro to our Chelsea townhouse, Lutèce was about to close, and no one talked about Café Nicholson.

It was Edna Lewis the author, Edna Lewis the rooted home cook, whom we chased around the Union Square market. It was not Edna Lewis the chef. And so it was, by having her second career as a cookbook author so thoroughly eclipse her career as a chef, that Edna Lewis became our Julia Child and *not* our Alice Waters.

I don't believe I would have been able to be a black woman publishing a cookbook without ever having a restaurant or a catering shop or working in someone else's kitchen if it hadn't been for Dame Edna.

And so I followed her footsteps and wrote a cookbook inspired by, and talking back to, all four of her cookbooks. Edna Lewis cooked with her mother. I wrote with mine. We talked about kitchen rape and lynching and how that changed the way my Alabama family saw trees. This was all talking back.

My most significant inspiration from Lewis does not appear in my cookbook, *Soul Food Love*. Joining Miss Lewis in the world of cookbook writing galvanized me to go in on a sweet potato farm in Alabama. Rereading *The Taste of Country Cooking*, I found my way back to the farm that terrified my grandmother. I borrowed her memories and her lies and her dreams, and I braided them to the Emmett Till Highway and the field-after-cotton-filled-field and decided that one of the things I was going to do to make a difference in this world was return to the soil. I joined forces with a cousin. Our family, the Johnson family, has been farming in Alabama since before the Civil War. His part of the family has maintained the farming knowledge. We are working together. I have new recipes for sweet potatoes. He has organic sweet potato slips. I am steps closer to my true taste of country cooking, and Edna Lewis keeps lighting the way.

I wrote earlier that one of my favorite recipes of Edna Lewis's is one for crisp duck garnished with kumquats. One of my closest college friends, after meeting my mother, stated, "The kumquat doesn't fall too far from the tree." That friend is Nigerian and owns a large yam farm. We're in discussions right now about making it the first organic yam farm in Nigeria. More unexpected echoes of Edna.

What I came to love best about *The Taste of Country Cooking* is the way in which Lewis creates an all-black world much in the way Hurston did in *Their Eyes Were Watching God*, a black world that is whole, resonant, independent, lovely, significant, beyond trauma, and does not use the white world as a defining point of reference.

Lewis became a reference for the white world. She moved out of the kitchen and lived on the page, lived in the farmers' markets, lived beyond restaurant service to others, lived situated in feeding her worthy self with worthy food that tied her to nature and to the earth, not to particular politics.

And with those particular choices she planted seeds in one brown daughter that would grow into a passionate food politics rooted in the field, on the page, and savored on the tongue.

My mother followed Edna to an apple tree in Chelsea; I followed her to a sweet potato field in Alabama, then on to Nigeria. Edna Lewis doesn't make me pine for the past. She makes me want to fight for the future.

PART TWO

Miss Lewis Standing in Culinary History

Eu Tenho um Pé na Cozinha

Put(ting) Your Foot in It

SCOTT ALVES BARTON

—❧❧—

My essay is in three acts. It serves to honor the life's work of Edna Lewis, contextualize her as a culinary icon of the African diaspora, recognize her as an important U.S. chef, and honor the hand of black women at the stove. Although today my métier is culinary scholarship, I previously spent decades as a working chef and consultant in New York City, Colorado, and San Francisco. My research focuses on northeastern Brazilian African diaspora foodways that are inscribed as both secular and sacred cultural traditions. Edna Lewis is a throughline, an entrepôt on the map of diaspora culinary heritage. Yes, she is an exemplar of Freetown, Orange County, Virginia. Yet she also reflects Salvador da Bahia, Paris, and Port-au-Prince, Lagos, Charleston, and New Orleans. My conceptualization of chef Edna Lewis, the locus of her culinary knowledge and her contributions to American cookery, is a result of having passed through several crossroads across my career.

AT A WALKAROUND

In the 1980s I ascended from line cook to executive sous-chef for chef Patrick Clark. I worked with Patrick in the heydays of the Odeon, at Cafe Luxembourg and at Metro. There were only a few African American chefs of note at the time and few if any events dedicated to African American culinary professionals or their heritage. Occasionally causes and organizations, such as Meals on Wheels or the James Beard Foundation, invited African American chefs to cook alongside the French and Italian standard-bearers. Aside from Joe Randall's *Taste of Heritage* and later the annual charity affair hosted by the 100 Black Men of Sonoma County, though, there were no culinary organizations or fraternal groups honoring African American or Latin chefs. Inclusion into the elite French "boy's culinary club" necessitated the involvement of talent, politics, collegial respect and support, and the need to leverage race as a fulcrum to better solicit charity funds for underserved populations in New York City.

I first encountered Edna Lewis when Patrick cooked alongside her in the 1980s at New York City charity events. In those moments I remember her standing tall, proud, hair—more gray than black—pulled back and tied in a bun. She had a glowing smile and a humble countenance, and she was keenly aware of the scene at large. Once she donned a monogrammed chef's coat. On another occasion, she wore a dashiki-style knee-length tunic. In the West African cloth she held court, added sprigs of fresh herbs for garnish, more than she stirred the pot. Those few of us in attendance who were black and, like Patrick, disciples of nouvelle cuisine and infatuated with French gastronomy were befuddled at seeing her prepare and serve what we saw as "home food," such as a black-eyed pea and roast pepper salad that I remember in particular.

With Miss Lewis, Patrick was always humble and respectful, offering her a cook to help plate her food, a cold drink, or simply his infectious good humor. The first time Miss Lewis and I crossed paths, I asked Patrick who she was. "Edna Lewis is an important chef, and you should go and introduce yourself to her," Patrick replied. He instilled in me and the other cooks present the awareness that we needed to hold her in high esteem.

In many ways Lewis was one of Patrick's culinary forebears. Patrick, a Brooklyn native, was the son of institutional chef Melvin Clark. Patrick had some roots in the South—one needed only sample his take on collards, liberally seasoned with smoked hocks, applewood-smoked bacon lardons, and shoulder meat, and finished with vinegar and chili peppers, to taste it. Stewed greens never appeared on his restaurant menus, though: only in those discreet moments when Patrick cooked a snack for staff, or for one of his family's social events, was that particular southern staple brought to table. In such instances I saw a glimmer of the dishes I saw on Edna Lewis's banquet tables in that era.

Professionally, Patrick had wholeheartedly embraced French haute cuisine, having apprenticed with the nouvelle cuisine pioneer Michel Guérard in southwestern France. But despite being a consummate Francophile, Patrick always counseled me to cook from my heritage. Naively, I did not

Scott Alves Barton

envision my family's home foods as being viable or credible on the culinary scene. My mother had aspired to be a chef. Yet in pre–World War II New York City, a woman—and a black woman at that—would never have attained that dream. Instead, she became a dietician, then a special education teacher. Her cooking reflected the need to balance nutrition against the challenges of two working parents with finicky young sons, as well as to incorporate her West Indian roots, my father's Fall River, Massachusetts, love of fish, and his Tennessee bloodlines, and the telegenic influence Julia Child had bestowed on her holiday fare. Back then, I was enamored with vol-au-vents, foie gras terrines, pâte à choux, and the like. Black-eyed peas appeared at picnics and home dinners, not in restaurants. It would be years before I would fully understand the significance of Lewis's contributions and the necessary inclusion of her food and persona at these events. If Patrick represented the front line of African American chefs, Lewis spoke to our heritage as cooks, chefs, and culinary cultural workers.

Much later, when I read *The Edna Lewis Cookbook*, I realized that Lewis's cooking was also deeply intertwined with French cuisine. That first book of hers does not belie race or region. With recipes that included Yorkshire pudding, lobster à l'Américaine, gazpacho, babka, and sweet biscuits, Lewis cannot be pigeonholed, thus claiming the mantle of urbanized global chef. Two particular recipes, though—Gravy for Southern Fried Chicken (a Sunday supper dish) and Peanut Sauce—recall her roots. The peanut sauce recipe in particular speaks directly to West Africa in its blend of peanut butter and hot peppers, even though it recommends the then relatively unknown sambal oelek, or Indonesian chili paste, and ketjap benteng asin, or Indonesian sweet soy sauce (via Holland, per the recipe's postscript).

I may have been ignorant of the depth and breadth of Miss Lewis's culinary acumen in my initial experiences of her, but I adored the benne seed wafers that she offered at one event. She schooled me on how the word *benne*, for sesame seeds, derived from West Africa. *Benne*, from the Mandinka branch of the Senegambian Wolof language family, is also a foodstuff that survived the Middle Passage. I finally found a recipe for those wafers years later in the cookbook she wrote with Scott Peacock, *The Gift of Southern Cooking: Recipes and Revelations from Two Great American Cooks* (2003). I have since served them on numerous restaurant menus, at the James Beard House, and for family dinners.

My Riff on Miss Lewis's Benne Seed Wafers

{MAKES 4 DOZEN}

1 cup sesame seeds (5 ounces)
3 cups unbleached all-purpose flour
1 teaspoon cream of tartar
½ teaspoon baking soda[1]
2 teaspoons sea or kosher salt
Freshly ground black pepper to taste
½ cup frozen duck fat
1 tablespoon toasted sesame oil
⅔ cup cold milk

Preheat the oven to 425°. Toast the sesame seeds in a dry skillet in the oven for 4 minutes, stirring occasionally, until deep golden. Transfer to a plate and let cool. Grind half of the toasted seeds to a coarse meal with a mortar and pestle.

In a large bowl, sift the flour with the cream of tartar, baking soda, and 1 teaspoon of the salt. Cut in the duck fat until the mixture resembles coarse meal. Stir in the sesame seeds, sesame oil, and milk. Mix the dough until blended.

Turn the dough out onto a lightly floured surface and knead briefly. Chill 20 minutes. Divide the dough in half. Roll out 1 piece of dough as thinly as possible (at most ⅛ inch thick). Prick the dough all over with a fork and stamp out 2-inch rounds. Transfer the rounds to a large baking sheet and sprinkle with the remaining salt. Bake for 10–14 minutes, or until deep golden brown. Let cool slightly, then transfer to a rack. Repeat with the remaining dough. Serve the wafers warm or at room temperature.

EU TENHO UM PÉ

The Negro is a born cook. He could neither read nor write, and therefore he could not learn from books. He was simply inspired; the god of the spit and the saucepan had breathed life into him; that was enough.
— *Charles Gayarré,* Harper's Magazine, *1880*

Louisiana historian Charles Gayarré's statement, which opens Jessica Harris's foundational scholarship on diaspora cooking, *Iron Pots and Wooden*

Scott Alves Barton

Spoons: Africa's Gifts to New World Cooking (1989), relates directly to two expressions, one Afro-Brazilian and one African American. The first is "Eu tenho um pé na cozinha" (I have a foot in the kitchen). This archaic Brazilian colloquialism subtly identifies race, African ancestry, and a possible self-reflexive interpretation of pride or personal shame. Any speaker of this phrase is acknowledging his or her links to West African ancestry, since black Africans were long presumed to be the best cooks in Brazil. "Eu tenho um pé na cozinha—I have a foot in the kitchen—I have black blood inside me—We are all or partially African," supports the Brazilian identity politics of a mythic racial democracy. This premise ostensibly validates an imagined African Brazilian nation-state.

Former president Fernando Henrique Cardoso's use of the phrase to garner black votes in his 1994 election campaign exemplifies the pervasiveness of the saying. Cardoso revisited this expression to acknowledge his awareness of and attention to racial discrimination and inequalities while speaking to a largely African Brazilian audience in Rio de Janeiro accompanied by visiting president of South Africa Thabo Mbeki in 2000.

On a day-to-day level, various older Brazilian women that I have observed cooking or being interviewed in Bahia (the province in northeastern Brazil widely considered to be the beating heart of Afro-Brazilian culture) have used the phrase in conversation. They often toss off the quotation as a self-evident reality, since clearly they are racially black. "Branco no Brasil é um conceito relative. . . . O Brasil gosta de ser misturado, a despeito de tudo. . . . Também eu tenho um pé na cozinha. Eu não tenho preconceito— não (Being white in Brazil is a relative concept. . . . In spite of everything, Brazil sees itself as being mixed. . . . I also have a foot in the kitchen. I have no prejudice—none)."[2]

The identification with food and cooking as a gendered African Brazilian space, as well as a location of racial identity marked by the acquisition of certain technical skills, ingenuity, and a capability to create and evaluate relative qualities of taste are joined to the aforementioned quotes as a pseudo valuation and respect for black identity. Peter Fry's comparative analysis of food and culture, "Feijoada é 'Soul Food'" (Feijoada is "soul food"), opens by drawing cultural parallels between Alabaman soul food cookery and the production of the slave stew, feijoada, the Brazilian national dish, as products of a collective African diaspora culture. In both cases, prepared dishes are lauded by a privileged elite group, which elevates aspects of cultural identity while continuing to marginalize of diaspora populations. For marginalized peoples facing a paucity of economic options, food becomes a site of both recreational entertainment and essential nourishment, satisfying hungers both physical and spiritual while stimulating the palate.[3]

And so I return to our subject, Miss Lewis. Where her first book, *The Edna Lewis Cookbook*, has a sliver of racial or cultural context, *The Taste of Country Cooking* opens with Miss Lewis recounting how her enslaved grandmother, trained as a briskmason, was forced to leave her children unattended in their cribs from morning until past nightfall. The legacy of that trauma caused her to carry a lit kerosene lamp upstairs in their Freetown home to check in on her then grown progeny, "a measure of the pain she bore." Lewis's affinity to her grandmother's hardscrabble life and her solidarity with her Freetown community indelibly marks that book. The vignette is not about cooking per se, but *it has her grandmother's foot all in it*. African Americans declare proud ownership of an event or a well-prepared meal when they state, "I put my foot in it."

Miss Lewis "put her foot in" her first book by exhibiting exemplary technique.[4] In contrast, *The Taste of Country Cooking* more intimately marries her devotion to good cooking with her racial identity, her Freetown, Virginia, heritage, and the cycles of seasonal agriculture. Harnessing necessity, ingenuity, and skill she embodies the savoir-faire of a chef. (It could be argued that Judith Jones privileged Lewis's racial identity to add dynamism to the text.) Lewis illustrates her culinary acumen and authorial voice in *Taste*, for example, in her reference to the seasonality of fried chicken as a specialty decades before the farm-to-table movement came into vogue, writing, "Produced only once a year from late spring through early summer . . . hand-raised and specially fed—producing the most delicious-flavored chicken. We fried them in sweet, home-rendered lard, churned butter, and a sliced piece of smoked ham for added flavor." The chickens of Lewis's youth bear no relation to the ubiquitous industrial chickens that moisten most lips today. The seasonality of fried chicken was also noted in *The Edna Lewis Cookbook*.[5]

Here the inclusion of ancillary contextual narratives drives home the need to savor and make use of seasonal bounty. Miss Lewis wrote of the deliciousness of corn pone, a distant relative to the ashcakes "legendary in our history." Sealing the bond, she cites Paul Laurence Dunbar's poem "When de Co'n Pone's Hot," putting both of her feet squarely in the pot.[6]

When you set down at de table,
Kin' o' weary lak an' sad,

Scott Alves Barton

An' you 'se jes' a little tiahed
An' purhaps a little mad;
How yo' gloom tu'ns into gladness,
How yo' joy drives out de doubt
When de oven do' is opened,
An' de smell comes po'in' out;
Why, de 'lectric light o' Heaven
Seems to settle on de spot,
When yo' mammy says de blessin'
An' de co'n pone's hot.

When de cabbage pot is steamin'
An' de bacon good an' fat,
When de chittlins is a-sputter'n'
So's to show you whah dey's at;
Tek away yo' sody biscuit,
Tek away yo' cake an' pie,
Fu' de glory time is comin',
An' it's 'proachin' mighty nigh,
An' you want to jump an' hollah,
Dough you know you'd bettah not,
When yo' mammy says de blessin'
An' de co'n pone's hot.

"I put my foot in it" is the analog in American black English. As with
"Um pé," it relates to culinary expertise and black identity. Orally and gus-
tatorily, these affirmations of embodied expertise valorize the black hand
in our food, and the black women who cook it. How, then, do we define
the contribution and power of African American influences to American
culinary culture? Foods such as black-eyed peas and okra can provide one
lens or point of entry. Russell and Cherie Hamilton have written a geneal-
ogy of caruru, calalu, and gumbo, all emblematic diaspora dishes based on
okra. Psyche Williams-Forson's foreword to the 2011 reprinting of Vertamae Smart-Grosvenor's *Vibration Cooking: or, The Travel Notes of a Geechee
Girl* heralds the book as a touchstone that stressed the importance of our
culinary foremothers, foodways traditions, and heritage practices to shape
lives, thus revealing diasporic epistemologies and valorizing Africans in
the Americas. In cookbooks, literature, and scholarly texts, numerous authors have identified the importance and often the invisibility of African
influences in the Americas' cookery. In *If I Can Cook / You Know God Can*,

Ntozake Shange notes, "At Candace Hill-Montgomery's *Art on the Beach* installation on the sands approaching the Hudson River in the middle of virtually nothing stood throngs of refrigerators, different models, years, some vintage, all filled with collard greens and not one more thing. No doors to afford privacy. All we got to eat this day was some unseasoned greens with nary a stove in sight. . . . I remembered our mothers and grandmothers tending mustards and collards. . . . I thought about slavery."[7]

In the colonial era the evidence of the black hand was deliciously felt on the tongue, as a delicate caress of a pending dinner's perfume wafted into one's nostrils or echoed by a sizzle or a contented hum from the cook—whether seated at "big house" tables or contemplating steaming hoecakes. The verbal resonance occurred in dialogues, call-and-response conversations between slave cook and plantation mistress. One read, suggested, insisted, implored, or demanded; the other listened, pondered, memorized, calculated, improvised, and produced. These unique authorial culinary voices satisfied the grateful tongues of those who ate the fruits of black mammies' or slave cooks' labor even as they remained largely nameless.

Until the advent of the era of civil rights and civil disobedience in the mid-twentieth century, this white mistress–black servile relationship remained largely unchanged. But at the same time, we have the culinary legacies of Hercules, James Hemings, Samuel Fraunces, Edith Fossett, Fanny Hern, Dolly Johnson, and Nat Fuller, men and women who ran kitchens, worked as chefs, owned restaurants, and catered to or cooked for presidents.[8] African American servants and chefs published books that captured and enshrined the black voice—at the stove, as the household manager, and as a global citizen. Early exemplars of this tradition are Robert Roberts's *House Servant's Directory: or, A Monitor for Private Families* (1827), Tunis Campbell's *Never Let People Be Kept Waiting: A Textbook on Hotel Management* (1848), Malinda Russell's *Domestic Cookbook: Containing a Careful Selection of Useful Receipts for the Kitchen* (1866), Abby Fisher's *What Mrs. Fisher Knows about Old Southern Cooking, Soups, Pickles, Preserves, Etc.* (1881), and Rufus Estes's *Good Things to Eat as Suggested by Rufus* (1911). These books asserted the accumulated skill, training, and command of all aspects of the kitchen, dining room, or household management by people who were born enslaved, were recently manumitted, served as state senators, ran railroad dining cars, owned and managed boardinghouses, or were employed by political elites such as the ancestors of former vice president Albert Alfred Gore Jr.

Scott Alves Barton

Russell and Fisher reveal not only their culinary acumen but also a perspective of who they were as self-determined women. These books, unknown to a wide audience until recently, challenge arguments that the black contribution to southern or U.S. cooking was grounded solely in poverty and improvisatory ingenuity. The texts illustrate the skills, knowledge, and agency of African Americans through the distinct voice of servitude, entrepreneurship, and passion. Edna Lewis also exhibited such solidarity as a proud, free, and self-identified black woman in her cookbooks. Where *The Edna Lewis Cookbook* is spare in explanatory narratives, *The Taste of Country Cooking* is abundant.

For example, in Ham in Heavy Cream Sauce, Lewis writes: "Ham in heavy cream sauce was the most delicious combination one could ever hope to taste in leftovers. After carving away all the nice slices, the base of the ham was left with a lot of rough pieces." Lewis instructs the cook to dice the meat and cover it with heavy cream skimmed from a crock of milk, drawn a few days earlier from the family cow. This cream, she says, is heavier and superior to machine extractions, which tend to separate. The saucepan full of the ham and cream mixture is simmered on the back of the stove until the sauce has thickened and has a requisite "hammy" taste. This preparation is ready to be spooned over hot freshly baked biscuits. Lewis's final note recommends that, if one is using Virginia ham, the bottom should not be used because it is usually dry and stringy. Also, "I don't think any other type of ham is any good. They just don't have the same flavor."[9]

What may not be readily apparent to the reader is that her recommendations in the headnote are apparently written for someone cooking on a wood-fired stove, with access to fresh cow's milk that has sufficiently aged to have begun to clot, or ferment. The waning fire of the wood fire will allow the ham-cream concoction to simmer slowly until the right level of flavor and unctuous texture is achieved. Visual cues and not time are the gauges of doneness. The written recipe below the note appears to be a revised text geared to a modern stove. The cream is scalded before the chopped ham is added. The mixture is simmered for thirty minutes, and served hot.

This recipe is truly a set of twins—fraternal, not identical—illustrating what Lewis did over a wood fired stove as a child versus what can be done (indeed, what she *did*) on a gas or electric stove as an adult. Her subtle gradations, the type and portion of the ham, the quality and age of the cream (connoting the ferment toward crème fraîche), and the level of the heat under the pot at the back of the stove demonstrate her expertise and thoughtful attentiveness as a chef.

CONVERGING WORDS AND ROADS

Delta legend says that originary bluesman Robert Johnson sold his soul to the devil at the crossroads. That meeting with the trickster change-agent Exu—Eleggua lying in wait at that intersection—gave Johnson the gift of playing the blues. Bets were laid where those roads converged, gifts were given, barters were made, and debts had to be paid. The price of the ticket may have had an attendant penalty, and also a hidden perk.

The harsh limitations of adversity bring a resultant necessity to be as resourceful as possible with one's meager resources. The manner in which we analyze the results of that price may yield a benefit. The virtuous balance of expression and restraint of a blues, or the tension between a caramel cake's feathery crumb to maintain a dialogue with its bittersweet mantle, may be just that reward. The ingenuity, skill, and presence of an adept practitioner attuned to the particularity of his or her métier is evidenced by the ability to embody its form and function in spite of any limitations. Such restrictions may similarly harness nostalgia and sense memory to elevate a meager repast into a feast. A steaming yam on a wintery Harlem avenue thus understudies a groaning board at a Sunday southern supper in Ralph Ellison's prose:

> Then far down at the corner I saw an old man warming his hands against the sides of an odd-looking wagon, from which a stovepipe reeled off a thin spiral of smoke that drifted the odor of baking yams slowly to me, bringing a stab of swift nostalgia. . . .
>
> "Here you are, suh," he said, starting to put the yam into a bag.
>
> "Never mind the bag, I'm going to eat it. Here . . ."
>
> "Thanks." He took the dime. "If that ain't a sweet one, I'll give you another one free of charge."
>
> I knew that it was sweet before I broke it; bubbles of brown syrup had burst the skin.
>
> "Go ahead and break it," the old man said. "Break it and I'll give you some butter since you gon' eat it right here. Lots of folks takes 'em home. They got their own butter at home."
>
> I broke it, seeing the sugary pulp steaming in the cold. . . .
>
> "Give me two more," I said.

Scott Alves Barton

"Sho, all you want, long as I got 'em. I can see you a serious yam eater, young fellow. You eating them right away?"

"As soon as you give them to me," I said.

"You want 'em buttered?"

"Please."

"Sho, that way you can get the most out of 'em. Yessuh," he said, handing over the yams, "I can see you one of these old-fashioned yam eaters."

"They're my birthmark," I said. "I yam what I am!"

"Then you must be from South Car'lina," he said with a grin.

"South Carolina nothing, where I come from we really go for yams."[10]

Yams are a substitute for Carolina and a life lost in migration. Ellison's *Invisible Man* needs to move beyond adversity and realize some personal power and his desire for equality. Neither option presented itself to him. Nostalgia briefly assuaged his alienation and hunger. After the Great Migration, shifting geographies of black bodies altered perceptions of blacks and their cultural expression and sense of self, as reflected in literature, media, politics and culinary aesthetics; by the mid-twentieth century, southern food proudly became soul food for some and a vestige of slavery and degradation for others.

In the wake of the civil rights era, more attention began to be focused on who cooked, served, and ate "our" foods. The power of food memory in LeRoi Jones's essay "Soul Food" highlights the proud celebration of blackness and the simple gustatory pleasure of cow stomachs, pork intestines and sweet potato pie mimicking Ellison's poetics of yams: "Maws are things ofays seldom get to peck, nor are you likely ever to hear about Charlie eating a chitterling. Sweet potato pies, a good friend of mine asked recently, 'Do they taste anything like pumpkin?' Negative. They taste more like memory, if you're not uptown."[11]

In both texts food signifies taste, place, and a longing for a life left behind. Food conjures subsistence, but also nurturing domestic scene of southern living—family time, country, home, a world apart from segregation and northern migration. As the 1970s sociopolitical climate caught fire, two unique female authorial culinary voices arose: Edna Lewis and Vertamae Smart-Grosvenor. Both had been raised on wood-fired stoves that demanded keen sensitivity in one's cooking. Each held court in distinct iterations of high society. Predominantly in New York, Lewis fêted

Marlon Brando, Marlene Dietrich, Greta Garbo, Tennessee Williams, Salvador Dalí, Eleanor Roosevelt, and Truman Capote. Twenty years Lewis's junior, Grosvenor's global salon included her best friends, Maya Angelou and Nina Simone, her husband, artist Robert Grosvenor, and comrades such as renamed poet Amiri Baraka, Sun Ra, Archie Shepp, Muhammad Ali, Bob Thompson, Alan Lomax, and Larry Neal.

In 1970, journalist, actress, griot, and Lowcountry native Vertamae Smart-Grosvenor published both her manifesto "The Kitchen Crisis" in Toni Cade Bambara's anthology *The Black Woman* and her book *Vibration Cooking: or, The Traveling Notes of a Geechee Girl*, modeled after *The Alice B. Toklas Cookbook*. In these works Grosvenor reframed the dialogue of identity politics for black Americans into one focused on their membership in the African diaspora and as key contributors to U.S. culture. Using foodways and commensality as her interlocutors, Grosvenor articulated a multivectored, cross-fertilized cultural landscape that reframed hierarchies of power and inclusion for people of African descent. Both her life — engaged as Grosvenor was in performance, political action, and child-rearing — and her cooking reflect active motion across the Afro-Atlantic continuum. At its core, *Vibration Cooking* highlights her Geechee heritage and role in the black arts movement, as typified by the final chapter and some of its subheadings: "Mixed Bag: 'Poultices and Home Remedies,' 'Aphrodisiacal Foods,' 'White Folks and Fried Chicken,' and 'The Jet Set and Beautiful People.'"

Edna Lewis was first defined by her time as chef at Café Nicholson. In her first two cookbooks, Miss Lewis's voice was as measured and assured as Grosvenor's was improvisatory and strident. Her books were closely tied to the land and finely attuned to local seasonality. They could almost be titled *Edna's City* and *Edna's Virginia Country Cooking*, respectively. The first book is quite French — er, Continental — and the second nearly wholly southern. Both her voice and her food spoke of elegance, tradition, and fine, if sometimes simple, dining. There is a deeply ephemeral tone to her cooking, tied to the particularity of the ingredients, chosen at the apex of their ripeness, and the finesse associated with cooking foods over wood-fueled stoves. She forthrightly argues for southern food to be considered a cuisine seated alongside the world's noteworthy cuisines. Subtly, her work was quite political. If southern cuisine is deemed a global cuisine and enslaved Africans are foundational influencers of

Scott Alves Barton

southern cuisine, then the cultural value and identity of the African diaspora increase exponentially.

Nearly a decade after *The Taste of Country Cooking* was published, sociologist Jack Goody argued that Africa lacks haute or a stratified cuisine owing to a lack of a highly differentiated socioeconomic class structure. If we accept this perspective (which, I admit, I only partially do), then the southern plantocracy provided the hyperelite analogous to royalty or gentry counterbalancing the proletariat and the enslaved. Within this frame, Miss Lewis—without thunder, but with quiet fire—carefully constructed a nuanced southern cuisine with aspects of both the haute and the provincial; importantly, hers was available to any and all, not solely the gentry.[12]

Both Lewis and Grosvenor wrote and cooked deeply from the roots of an African American culture that had not previously been granted a place at the culinary pulpit. Arising from distinctly different regions and origins, the two women descended from plantation cooks, country folk, and West African culinary traditions. Their recipes reflect a bygone era when directions were precisely written for a skilled cook, were ostensibly open to interpretation, but in fact belied tacit knowledge in method and the varied vocabularies of cooking.

Lewis's and Grosvenor's recipes and words followed in the footsteps of subaltern slave women like Maum Sarah, rendered barely visible in plantation era southern receipt books such as Sarah Rutledge's *Carolina Housewife: or, House and Home* (1847) and Mrs. Samuel G. Stoney's *Carolina Rice Cook Book* (1901). In deliberately titling their receipts with a slave's name—Maum Sarah's Dirty Rice, for example—elite white mistresses implicitly validated their slave women cooks.[13]

Toni Morrison's work of literacy criticism *Playing in the Dark: Whiteness and the Literary Imagination* accurately interprets these references of blackness as a means of naming whiteness through sublimation of the black character, rendering black individuals invisible while concurrently inflating white dominance. Ultimately, these unheralded women are given voice and identity despite their status as chattel. Grosvenor's and Lewis's recipes, stories, and fabled social events effectively communicate the agency that they had within black communities in Virginia, the Lowcountry, Harlem, or Paris. They compel their readers to engage more directly with African American culture, reframing the narrative that bell hooks adroitly defined as *Eating the Other*, a deeply sexualized metaphor reacting to rape and enslaved subjugation, to one of respect, admiration, and praise.[14]

Honoring iconic ingredients and cultural tradition becomes a culinary praise song. Grosvenor opens *Vibration Cooking* by introducing us to the legendary diaspora composed rice dish hoppin' John, often attributed to slave cooks. Grosvenor instructs the cook to cook the peas, then add rice to the pot and cook until the rice is tender, adjust seasoning, and "you got it." "And speaking of rice. I was sixteen years old before I knew that everyone didn't eat rice everyday. Us being geechees, we had rice everyday. When you said what you were eating for dinner, you always assumed the rice was there."[15]

She continues with a detailed description of how to cook rice properly. For Lewis, in comparison, those same peas are an exemplar of the season, a boon for conditioning the soil, and an exponent from Africa by way of Thomas Jefferson's botanical experiments: "Purée of Green Black-Eyed Peas": "Black-eyed peas were popular in the late summer and fall. They were not planted in the garden but were planted by farmers as a green manure crop. Before the sowing of wheat, when in full foliage, they were chopped into the soil. A week before, everyone was welcome to gather the green pods before the crop was chopped under."[16]

In neither recipe are amounts given. Before the late twentieth century, savvy southern women cooks—both black and white—who prepared food daily knew how to cook black-eyed peas, whether freshly picked or dried. Those details become superfluous. I disagree with Miss Lewis regarding the origin of the black-eyed pea. She orients them to Jefferson's importation of European seed stocks and his botanical experiments. In fact, they are West African. Jefferson may have popularized them as one of his agricultural experiments, but enslaved Africans introduced them via and throughout the diaspora. They are both a sacred and a secular food; their mythic New Year's Day luck associated with Grosvenor's Hopping John may in fact be tied to their role as an offertory Yoruba food for the preeminent warrior deity, Ogum, god of iron and technology. Honoring the *orixá* merited praise. In contrast to the narrative similarities in their black-eyed pea recipes, compare these women's quail dishes.

Miss Lewis's (which begins, "Quail are small birds and we usually added other game near the end of cooking, sometimes a squab chicken") is an elaborate execution involving a delicate stuffing of milk-soaked crustless bread laced with the bird's livers, butter, and sage. Once stuffed, the quail's cavities are sewn shut with a needle and thread. She notes that the stitches will be removed before serving and that the game should be wiped and not washed, lest one remove the "flavor peculiar to game." Then between two heavy iron or enamel casseroles, first sear the seasoned squab chicken in foaming butter and "place it skin side down"—one assumes breast down—with bacon slices strewn around it. Quickly sear the quail. Then place the quail overtop of the chicken, as though they were roosting. Season the birds with salt, pepper, and thyme.[17]

When the birds are almost done, heat the other pan, add butter, and sauté sliced mushrooms over a high flame, stirring. Remove the birds to a heated platter and scatter the cooked mushrooms around this pseudo-barnyard scene. To finish, "Squeeze ¼ cup of juice from the grapes and pour it into the pan the quail was cooked in. Loosen all particles on bottom and sides, blend well, and season to taste. Then pour this hot sauce around the quail. Serve hot. Six quail and one squab chicken will serve 4 to 5."[18]

Grosvenor, in contrast, commands the cook to keep it simple. "Clean and wipe and dry your quail. Then salt and pepper it. Brush with a mixture of melted butter and peanut oil and place in a shallow pan in a very hot oven and bake until tender. Brush often with the butter and oil mixture." Her quail and its pan drippings are served over cornmeal mush, which is seasoned with salt and cooked in a double boiler. The mush is cooked for "about" 45 minutes. The quail's cooking time is a guesstimate.[19]

Miss Lewis crafted a chef's recipe, precise and measured, despite the archaic timing for cooking game birds. She carefully plotted her dish to highlight the flavor of the birds, nesting quail overtop of the squab and bacon to shield the smaller birds from the oven's wrath. Her denouement is a riff on Escoffier's Sole Veronique; she enhances a fricassee of mushrooms with the juice and the just-warmed fruit of white grapes. Both Grosvenor and Lewis wish to maintain the funky aura of the quail—wipe them, don't wash them. Grosvenor's recipe is not truly grilled but roasted like Lewis's dish. Where Lewis luxuriates her quail in a surfeit of butter and other ingredients, Grosvenor's bird is spare, yet apparently also scrumptious; hers simply relies on the contrasting texture of the bronzed, crisp skin on her roasted and basted quail against the unctuous cornmeal porridge. She times by look, feel, and estimation in contrast to Lewis's meticulous precision. Although Lewis's dish is a feature of her *Taste of Country Cooking* classic, which was decidedly reflective of and geared toward home cooks, this quail dish appears to be restaurant ready, or at least company-coming-for-dinner fare. Grosvenor's, on the other hand, reads as delicious comfort food.

I do not intend to preference one of these foundational African American chefs over the other. They are both iconic. Placing them in dialogue elevates both chefs and the overall station of black women as cooks and chefs. Their shared legacies have moved our culture, its cooking, prestige, and identity, far forward. In spite of their age difference, both women became consecrated as change agents in the same era of sociocultural unrest. Their lives, work, and cooking need to live on in mind, body, and memory to carry us home.

Postscript. Although both this essay and the book are dedicated to Miss Edna Lewis, I would like to also honor the work and memory of Vertamae Smart-Grosvenor, who departed us Saturday, September 3, 2016.[20]

NOTES

1. Miss Lewis was adamant about the primacy and necessity of handmade leaveners to do their job properly without leaving the metallic aftertaste of commercial baking powder. Her blend of cream of tartar and baking soda solves that challenge, as elucidated on page 259 of *The Taste of Country Cooking*.

2. Emanuel Neri, "FHC se diz mulato com 'um pé na cozinha," *Folha de São Paulo*, May 31, 1994, http://www1.folha.uol.com.br/fsp/1994/5/31/brasil/18.html; Daniela Nahass, "'Branco no Brasil é um conceito relativo,' diz presidente ao homenagear colega sul-africano, em Florianópolis: FHC se define novamente como mestiço," *Folha de São Paulo*, Dec. 14, 2000, http://www1.folha.uol.com.br/fsp/brasil/fc1412200022.htm.

3. The essay appears in Fry's *Para inglês ver: Identidade e política na cultura brasileira* (For the English to see: Identity and politics in Brazilian culture). The title phrase *"Para inglês ver"* is drawn from the postindependence regency period, 1830–40, during the formation of the independent nation of Brazil, when England pressured Brazil to enact laws to halt the Atlantic slave trade. Brazil created laws that weren't enforced, solely "for the English to see." Peter Fry, *"Feijoada é 'Soul Food': Notas sobre a manipulação de símbolos étnicos e nacionais,"* in *Para inglês ver: Identidade e política na cultura brasileira* (Rio de Janeiro: Zahar, 1977).

4. See, e.g., Tracy Morgan's appearance on the Sept. 6, 2016, episode of *The View*, in which Morgan remarked repeatedly how his wife "put her foot in her cooking."

5. Lewis and Peterson, *Edna Lewis Cookbook*, 51.

6. Paul Laurence Dunbar, "When the Co'n Pone's Hot," in *The Complete Poems of Paul Laurence Dunbar* (New York: Dodd, Mead, 1913).

7. Russell G. Hamilton and Cherie Y. Hamilton, "Caruru and Calulu, Etymologically and Socio-Gastronomically: Brazil, Angola, and São Tomé Príncipe," *Callaloo* 30, no. 1 (2007): 338–44; Vertamae Smart-Grosvenor, *Vibration Cooking: Or, The Travel Notes of a Geechee Girl* (1970; Athens: University of Georgia Press, 2011); Ntozake Shange, *If I Can Cook / You Know God Can* (Boston: Beacon, 1998), 1.

8. White House cooks Edith Hern Fossett and Fanny Hern were trained by James Hemings, Sally Hemings's brother. Samuel Fraunces owned and operated Fraunces

Scott Alves Barton

Tavern in New York. He opened his doors to revolutionary rebels, including George Washington. He is said to have saved the future president's life from attempted poisoning. President Benjamin Harrison chose Laura "Dolly" Johnson over the French chef he had previously installed in the White House. Nat Fuller was a Charleston chef and restaurateur who owned Bachelor's Retreat. See Chelsea Lenhart, "Hercules," *Digital Encyclopedia of George Washington*, http://www.mountvernon.org/digital-encyclopedia/article/hercules/; Ashbell McElveen, "James Hemings, Slave and Chef for Thomas Jefferson," *New York Times*, Feb. 4, 2016; Jesse Rhodes, "Meet Edith and Fanny, Thomas Jefferson's Enslaved Master Chefs," *Smithsonian*, July 9, 2012; Adrian Miller, "African American Cooks in the White House: Hiding in Plain Sight," *Washington Post*, June 3, 2014; and "Nat Fuller's Feast: The Life and Legacy of an Enslaved Cook in Charleston," Low Country Digital History Archive, http://ldhi.library.cofc.edu/exhibits/show/nat_fuller/bachelors-retreat-civil-war.

9. Lewis, *Taste of Country Cooking*, 54.

10. Ralph Ellison, *Invisible Man* (New York: Random House, 1952), 201–6.

11. LeRoi Jones (Amiri Baraka), "Soul Food," in *Home: Social Essays* (New York: William Morrow, 1966), 101–4.

12. Jack Goody, *Cooking, Cuisine and Class: A Study in Comparative Sociology* (Cambridge: Cambridge University Press, 1982); Steven P. Sangren, "Dialectics in Comparative Sociology: Reflections on Jack Goody's *Cooking, Cuisine and Class*," *Food and Foodways* 3, no. 3 (1989): 197–202.

13. The *Carolina Rice Cook Book* is reproduced in Karen Hess's book *The Carolina Rice Kitchen*. For examples of recipes with slave names, see Karen Hess, *The Carolina Rice Kitchen: The African Connection* (Columbia: University of South Carolina Press, 1992), 25, 41, 57, 130, 135, 142, 155. See also Pierre Bourdieu, *Distinction: A Social Critique of the Judgment of Taste* (Cambridge, Mass.: Harvard University Press, 1984), 205, 222, 314–15, 483.

14. Toni Morrison, *Playing in the Dark: Whiteness and the Literary Imagination* (Cambridge, Mass.: Harvard University Press, 1992); bell hooks, "Eating the Other," in *Feminist Approaches to Theory and Methodology: An Interdisciplinary Reader*, ed. Sharlene Hesse-Biber, Christina Gilmartin, and Robin Lydenberg (New York: Oxford University Press, 1999), 153–215.

15. Smart-Grosvenor, *Vibration Cooking*, xvi.

16. Lewis, *Taste of Country Cooking*, 174.

17. Ibid., 172–73 (squab chicken refers to young chickens, 1–1¼ pounds in size, suitable as a single serving).

18. Ibid.

19. Smart-Grosvenor, *Vibration Cooking*, 6.

20. Anita Gates, "Vertamae Smart-Grosvenor Dies at 79, Celebrated Food and Culture," *New York Times*, September 6, 2016.

Edna Lewis

African American Cultural Historian

MEGAN ELIAS

$\rightarrow$ $\in$

In 1972, *Ebony*, a popular monthly magazine for an African American audience, published a travel guide titled "Do Yourself Proud: Discover Black History." Alongside a map identifying important African American historical sites, the editors advised, "They punctuate the countryside as stubborn reminders of the richness and diversity of black American history." These were the "scenes of long ago battles and explorations, sites of political and judicial debates; enduring reminders of black achievement in science, technology, education, literature and many other areas of national development." The message to the magazine's African American audience was to make themselves acquainted with black history and to feel proud of their place in it. Honor the ancestors at sites like Sojourner Truth's grave, but also take pictures of themselves in these places and bring their children to see the sites as a way to reinforce understanding of, and connection to, the black past. This was a subtle but powerful call to claim a nation that had never really encouraged African Americans to consider it their native home.[1]

When she published *The Taste of Country Cooking* in 1976, the chef and cookbook writer Edna Lewis took up this call and contributed to the work of reclamation by identifying a black food history. Her work stood on its own but could also supplement the tourist's experience in the sensorial realm of cooking and eating. Lewis wrote about her family's foodways, material that took her beyond simply recording their recipes. In focusing on the agricultural practices and mores around food and meanings associated with foods in her community's history, she ventured into writing African American history and helped to provide black Americans with a usable, as well as edible, past. Although she may not have seen herself as a historian, the attention she paid to the historical suggests that she believed in the importance of context in writing about food.

The year 1976, when *The Taste of Country Cooking* was published, was not only the nation's bicentennial year but also the year Alex Haley's *Roots*, a chronicle of African American history from slavery to the present, was published. In 1976, too, John Hope Franklin, the nation's most respected African American historian published *Racial Equality in America,* a collection of lectures on the history of racial discrimination. It was a moment for national reflection on the legacies of the past that extended deeper than the fireworks and tall ship displays. While Anglo-Americans might focus on the triumph of the Revolution, Lewis and Haley celebrated the longer, more formative social transformation that was still under way.

Lewis's book also contributed to a new trend in nostalgia for the same American cuisine that food writers, both American and European, had been deriding for half a century. Among her peers in this work of resurrection were Judith Jones, her husband, Evan Jones, and the food journalist Raymond Sokolov. Jones published *American Food: The Gastronomic Story* in 1975, and Sokolov published his collection *Fading Feast* in 1979. Sokolov's subtitle, *A Compendium of Disappearing American Regional Foods,* took a conservationist's view of the culinary scene. Edna Lewis shared Sokolov's wistfulness for vanishing foodways. She noted, for example, that "the fur has been bred out of peaches today, as well as most of the flavor." At the same time, her own career as a chef showed that these food memories could be a point of departure into contemporary cuisine.[2]

Lewis can be seen as part of the renaissance in American cooking that began in the late 1970s, but she also had a different agenda from many of the other chefs who became famous in this era. While chefs like Marc Forgione and Mark Miller were reinventing American fine dining by borrowing broadly from American folk traditions and applying their own French-style culinary training, Lewis remained true to one particular foodways — that of early twentieth-century rural America. Her goal, especially in *The Taste of Country Cooking,* was not particularly to turn American elites away from France and toward their own shores but instead to valorize African American cooking as both elegant and bountiful. In this pursuit, she was to some extent writing against the new proponents of soul food while her colleagues were writing against an older generation devoted to the cult of French haute cuisine. Because cosmopolitan Americans bowed to the perceived supremacy of French cuisine at the time, Lewis reported that customers at Café Nicholson often assumed that she had trained in

France. Her soufflés, learned in a Virginia kitchen, did not fit with popular conceptions of American food.[3]

The most fascinating of these interactions came when fellow southerner William Faulkner stopped by the kitchen to ask if she had lived in France. Ironically, Faulkner had not recognized that Lewis was (regional differences between Virginia and Mississippi notwithstanding) feeding him his own home cooking. Lewis surmised that the assumption derived from unrecognized similarities between all rural peoples' approach to cooking and eating.[4]

From the very beginning, *The Taste of Country Cooking* is emphatic in its singularity; it is not *a* taste of country cooking but *the* taste. Lewis's title stakes her claim to the archetypal flavors of rural America, and in this it is quietly radical. When white food writers wrote about African American food, which was seldom, they wrote about African-flavored contributions to southern elite cuisine. African American cooks were seen to influence white foodways but not to belong to those traditions themselves. Lewis represented African American food as the national culinary heritage, not tangential to it.

Her book's dedication introduced the work as memorial as well as culinary: "This book is dedicated to the memory of the people of Freetown and to Judith B. Jones, with many thanks for her deep understanding." The first half of the dedication is a historical statement—that the people of Freetown exist in memory and deserve honoring. Jones is thanked for her understanding, not guidance—her reception of the work, rather than any hand in its making. The work stands on its own but simultaneously with Lewis's people.[5]

Lewis's acknowledgments helped to establish the book's provenance and at the same time identified Lewis as a person who bridged cultures. She possessed and could share with others her ancestral community's rural history, but she was also a member of a multicultural urban social set, in which she and Jones had met and collaborated on the book. Lewis first identified her family as the foundation for her work, with thanks to her sister for "her invaluable help and very fine recipes, and for spending many hours over the hot stove cooking, canning, and preserving to refresh our memories." Together the siblings made memory physical and edible, performing work of historical reenactment in order to understand and convey the truth. A few lines later, Lewis also thanked "Mrs. Grace Saran, a young organic enthusiast and an expert in the knowledge of edible wild mushrooms." Here Lewis aligned herself with a new movement in American food that had its apotheosis in restaurateur and culinary activist Alice Waters.[6]

Interest in organic farming and in foraging were popularly associated with, but not necessarily driven by, the 1960s and 1970s counterculture and the back-to-the-land movement. Small-scale family farmers like those in Lewis's community had of course long practiced organic farming, and after her time at Café Nicholson, Lewis operated a short-lived organic farm herself. Public proponents of the organic farming movement tended to be Anglo-American and urban, framing their commitment to the natural in opposition to modern city life. For restaurateurs and chefs who are typically tied to urban markets, this new interest meant making connections with growers and foragers in the nearest nonurban space. The year 1976 was the year in which Waters's restaurant Chez Panisse first offered an American-themed menu, having previously always focused on French food. The ingredients for this menu were gathered locally in Northern California, including Tomales Bay oysters and California geese. Waters and Chez Panisse's chef Jeremiah Towers considered this moment a watershed in the restaurant's history, the moment when they began to look to their natural surroundings for material and to find America edible.

The wild mushrooms that Lewis mentioned in her brief acknowledgments had been a kind of totemic food of self-styled American gourmets since the 1930s and gained new cachet with the interest in organic and American ingredients. Alice Waters had an arrangement with a local forager to supply her restaurant with wild mushrooms. By referencing the mushrooms, as she would do again later in the book, Edna Lewis identified herself with the food intelligentsia and revealed a kind of culinary pedigree.

In noting her connection to these worlds of food connoisseurship and cultural experimentation in the same space in which she established herself as authentic in an African American context, Lewis commanded her readers to drop their preconceptions of what was and wasn't black. Throughout the book, in her recipes and in her vignettes, Lewis challenged those mainstream expectations of what was properly considered African American food and culture, revealing a culinary world beyond the fried chicken, hoecakes, and gumbo that white American cookbook writers typically associated with black home cooking.

For the most part Lewis's recipes could have been found in any European American cookbook from the early twentieth century, the era of her childhood. They were dishes like lemon pie, chicken with dumplings, scalloped potatoes, corn fritters, and oyster stew, which graced the tables of Americans from the Atlantic Coast and across the Midwest. Lewis's menus ranged into the upper middle class with dishes like blancmange, beef à la mode, and roast pheasant. In the case of each of these, she confronted what she assumed were her readers' class assumptions. As preface to her pheasant recipe, for example, Lewis noted, "While many city dwellers may seem to think pheasant is only served under glass, for country folk it was a way of life." Lewis briefly attempted to make a living off of her knowledge of the game bird when she and her husband tried their hand at raising pheasants on a New Jersey farm in the mid-1970s. In her book, Lewis challenged stereotypes about both African American and rural life, offering a careful historical corrective.[7]

Edna Lewis's description of her family's life on a farm would have been distinctly familiar to many European Americans of her generation who read it. If the reader had grown up in the country, then he or she had shared with Lewis most of the experiences she related. From the intense awareness of seasonal shifts to the spirit of community, Lewis implicitly argued, rural Americans are all formed by the same forces, no matter their ancestors' origins.

The book began in an autobiographical mode but quickly turned to the history of a place and people. Lewis opened with the explanation, "I grew up in Freetown, Virginia, a community of farming people. It wasn't really a town." In these two sentences there is much that is calculated to interest and to tell a tale. The contradiction is intriguing on its own. It suggests people with a pretension to something, an interest in representing themselves as more than others think they are. That Lewis identified her people as "farming people" rather than by their racial ancestry was a significant move on her part. She placed her people among the mythological agrarian forebears of the nation. Their connection to the land was their essential defining quality. Importantly, the people of Freetown were farmers, not sharecroppers, not tenant farmers. "Farming people" implies land ownership, which was not traditionally associated with African American involvement in agriculture. Telling her family's story to what she must have known would be primarily a white audience, Lewis overwrote cultural notions of African Americans as landless and at the mercy of whites.

Careful to balance the particular against the general, Lewis explained her origins: "The name was adopted because the first residents had all been freed from chattel slavery and they wanted to be known as a town of Free

People." The capitalization indicates the importance of the concept to her ancestors. Use of the word "chattel" to describe their previously unfree condition emphasized its dehumanization and the importance of freedom that made them, and later Lewis herself, want to capitalize Free People.

Among those Free People, Lewis explained, her own grandfather was an important person—one of the first settlers and the person around whom all others built their houses. To establish a black man as important in his own community gave him a dignity not often accorded to black men in writing by white Americans, historical and otherwise. Though readers might want to know what made him such a special figure, Lewis left this unexplained and turned instead to her grandmother's story. This fascinating account offers a powerful message of the dignity of labor. Lewis began, "My grandmother had been a brickmason as a slave." This version of history jars with white assumptions of what women's work is—housework and caring for children—and made the important point, especially significant in 1976, in the midst of second-wave feminism, that ideas about work and women's roles that apply in white communities have seldom been true for women of color.

Lewis recounted that her grandmother, a skilled person had been "purchased for the sum of $950 by a rich landowner" who wanted to build two houses. One of the houses had been destroyed in the war, but the other still stood when Lewis wrote. As a testament to the quality of her grandmother's work, she noted that it was "owned and restored by a college professor." This might make a reader wonder if the professor (who was most likely white and male, given the times) knew who made the bricks and built his house. And it further urged the reader to consider how much of America was built by hands who labored in bondage but nonetheless with remarkable skill. Subtly, Lewis reminded her readers that the wealth of the nation was built on slave labor.

And then, as the reader reflected admiringly on the artisanship of her grandmother, Lewis reminded them of the cost of this labor: "It was a job that caused my grandmother great anguish because she would have to go off all day to work on the big house, leaving her babies in their cribs." She was not able to come home to cook for them until late at night. This hardship had lasting effects: "Years later, after her children had grown up and were living in Freetown, she would still take her kerosene lamp and go upstairs to make sure they were there and all right." This watchfulness, Lewis argued, was "a measure of the pain she bore." This was a pain that Lewis wanted her readers to witness, a pain that freedom never took away because it was so deep. Lewis stayed with this theme even as she described the family home. It had been built large enough, surely at her grandmother's instigation, to keep everyone in the family together, and had become the center of community life. This was the kind of private detail of the impact of slavery that few contemporary professional historians were able to summon. Even those who quote from interviews with formerly enslaved people can seldom claim a personal connection to the emotional life of slavery and freedom.

None of this rich and fascinating detail has anything to do with food. Most other food writers would have set the table for us immediately. Raymond Sokolov has his readers enjoying fried chicken (vicariously) within two pages. Evan Jones, for his part, began by denouncing American "public food" as "pretentious and derivative, or vulgarized like hot dogs and hamburgers oozing with spicy-sweet sauces." He may not have wanted us to eat, but he put the food on our plates.[8]

Instead of feeding her readers at once, however, Lewis instead drew them into family history, into the history of slavery and African American survival. Was this her way of letting readers know where her food and she herself came from? Or perhaps it was a broader argument that food is a way to learn the past, as legitimate as any other kind of history?

Lewis's chronicle is striking because of its sensitivity to the quotidian, more aware of the meaning inherent in everyday details, indeed, than most social history of any kind in the era. In American social history, it would not be until Laurel Thatcher Ulrich's classic and Pulitzer Prize–winning history, *A Midwife's Tale*, that a historian would so carefully consider how people in the past made meaning through their everyday activities.

Lewis's depiction of the role of food in her family's life fills in some elements missing in *Roll, Jordan, Roll*, Eugene Genovese's well-regarded 1974 portrayal of African American life during the era of slavery, particularly on the subject of cooking. Genovese made the mistake of not recognizing two distinct but intimately linked foodways in the slaveholding South. Traditionally, historians of African American foodways, like Jessica Harris, identify the foodways that African American cooks performed for slaveholders as markedly different from the foodways they practiced among their own family and friends. Differences in resources and time separated the two cuisines, but there is also the hard-to-trace matter of taste. In the slaveholder's kitchen, flavors and textures and preparations in general had to align with Anglo-American ideas of correct comestibles. In the quarters, these expectations did not apply; those who cooked were able, as far as time and resources allowed, to please their own palates. They could carry on African food traditions and employ personal creativity.

Black cooks, of course, also brought both African and personal influences into their work in the kitchens of the big houses, but there creativity had to be exercised within the boundaries of existing taste conventions, whereas in slaves' own kitchens, the only limits were imposed by available resources. Genovese elided these distinctions when he wrote, "However much soul food may be despised by today's Black Muslims, as an ugly cuisine imposed from above, it represented the culinary despotism of the quarters over the Big House in antebellum times." Genovese seems to have collapsed home cooking and professional cooking into one set of foodways here, which misses much of the complexity of food in slavery.[9]

Edna Lewis wrote against that version of history in which African American cuisine makes the best of master's rations. She instead portrayed a culinary tradition that is distinctly chosen—hunted, foraged, and grown. Food that is, to use the old phrase, "high on the hog," which is essential to understanding antebellum southern foodways. Indeed, one of Lewis's most detailed sections is about hog butchering. The food of Freetown was not a *cucina povera*, even as it made the most of local wild plants and animals, but much more like the *cuisine bourgeoise* that American connoisseurs had begun to celebrate in the 1920s and had fully sanctified by the 1960s and the success of Julia Child, Judith Jones's first culinary star. Lewis's roasts, cakes, pies, puddings, and vegetables, not to mention her pickles and preserves, would have been at home on any thriving farm community's table in the nation in the early twentieth century.[10]

Lewis's portrait of Freetown challenged stereotypes of rural people, and rural African American people in particular, as unsophisticated when she recounted both her community's reverence for education and its dedication to cultural expression. Freetown's first school, supported by the community, was held in Lewis's family home. The teacher was an Oberlin graduate, Oberlin having been one of the first colleges to integrate in the antebellum era. Most contemporary rural white communities, such as those depicted in Laura Ingalls Wilder's widely read *Little House on the Prairie* series, were content to hire high school graduates with teaching certificates. Freetown's families, in contrast, chose a college graduate.

Lewis recalled that the teacher, whom she does not identify by gender, settled in Freetown and helped to fund a school building that the community constructed later. We can't know the teacher's reasons for staying, but it seems likely that the decision stemmed in part from the community's commitment to education. This respect for higher education was also evidenced in Lewis's story of her aunt: "One of the biggest achievements was when my youngest aunt went away to a boarding school in Manassas, Virginia; her brothers had all worked and raised the money to send her." Lewis portrays this as a community achievement, rather than just a family matter.

The effect of the teacher on the school spread beyond the schoolhouse, as Lewis remembered, and "soon Freetown became a lively place, with poetry readings, singing quartets, and productions of plays put on by the young people." Literate and culturally in tune with the rest of the nation, Lewis's Freetown challenges popular representations of black life as unsophisticated and somehow foreign to mainstream American ways. Part of the power of Lewis's chronicle is that she never makes these comparisons or arguments herself but instead lets her readers absorb what she is saying as a new, more accurate reality to replace what they may have ignorantly assumed. Where two other black cookbook writers of the era, Ruth Gaskins and Vertamae Smart-Grosvenor, celebrated African American culinary traditions as both distinct from white foodways and kept private from whites themselves, Lewis posits a more national food culture.[11]

At the same time, Lewis was not assimilationist. Moments throughout the book reminded the reader of the legacies of slavery and the ways in which African American culture developed internal supports to protect against discrimination and the persistent threat of violence. She drew particular attention to two community celebrations: Revival Week and Emancipation Day, standout events among "various other feasts that punctuated our farm year." The first two were holidays that her white readers would not know about or have personal experience with, so these provided moments of distancing, even as she drew reader and writer close together again by referring to the farming-cycle feasts that are also part of European American traditions.

Lewis's assertion of an alternate calendar was a declaration of an African American history that runs parallel to, while often overlapping with, Euro-American history. The differences were sometimes noted in pain — her grandmother's suffering — and sometimes in pleasures like these holidays that are thoroughly American but not accessible to many of those who would consider themselves American.

Lewis's tone is especially pastoralist, almost reminiscent of Willa Cather, here: "The spirit of pride in community and of cooperation in the work of farming is what made Freetown a very wonderful place to grow up in. . . . The farm was demanding but everyone shared in the work — tending

Megan Elias

the animals, gardening, harvesting, preserving the harvest, and, every day, preparing delicious foods that seemed to celebrate the good things of each season." She offered a moving and also familiar portrait of a people whose lives were shaped by agricultural labor and its rewards. It was this tone that the food writer M. F. K. Fisher responded to in a note to Lewis's editor, Judith Jones, about *The Taste of Country Cooking*. Fisher praised Lewis's work as "In the best sense *American*, with an innate dignity and freedom from prejudice and hatred." The comment is revealing of what white audiences perhaps feared they would find in an African American cookbook in the age of Black Power. It is also reflective of Lewis's choice to represent her people's history as American rather than as a side narrative.[12]

In moments when she summoned up unique characteristics of African American culture, Lewis did so in a restrained but powerful way. Writing about the Revival Day, she explained, "Memories of slavery lingered with us still, and Revival was in a way a kind of Thanksgiving. There was real rejoicing: the fruits of our hard labor were now our own, we were free to come and go, and to gather together for this week of reunion and celebration." Because Lewis's book does not include a menu for the mainstream Thanksgiving holiday in November, her statement about Revival Week is all the more important. In leaving out the popular American holiday, Lewis may remind readers of Frederick Douglass's famous 1852 speech about another national holiday, in which he asked the crucial question, "What, to the American slave, is your 4th of July?" By leaving out Thanksgiving, Lewis obliquely asks her readers just what African Americans would have to be thankful for in a holiday that celebrates English settlement in New England and, more broadly, the birth of nation that, in the words of African American abolitionist David Walker, had "got so fat on our blood and groans"? It is worth noting, too, that Lewis did not offer a menu for July Fourth either, especially notable in a book about American food published in 1976, the country's bicentennial year.[13]

Instead of offering thanks for the Plymouth Pilgrims' beginning, Lewis offered thanks for something else—the freedom that came with the end of slavery, another kind of beginning to take the place of the colonial narrative celebrated in Thanksgiving. In her explanation of the meaning of Revival Week, Lewis offered an appreciation of the difficulty that families dispersed by slave sales found in reuniting even for brief visits. Travel between slaveholders' properties typically required a pass, which depended entirely on the master's whim. Even if a pass could be obtained, some family members lived too far apart for travel to be feasible, particularly since it almost always had to be accomplished on foot. The persistent maintenance of family ties in the face of these restrictions is one of the most remarkable elements in the history of American families. Lewis invited her readers to consider how much sweeter, given that history, African American family reunions might be.

Lewis's explanation also recalled how much her community could relish the freedom to take time from work to celebrate together. Because the essence of slavery is that one's time is not one's own, the opportunity to linger communally away from labor had a deeper meaning for the first generation out of slavery than it could for any other people in America. Her reminders were subtle but also pointed; reader who thought they were going to be reading about a church supper in this chapter found themselves confronted with the extraordinary restrictions of the enslaved life and the long reach of its impact. Lewis's implicit argument here was something that other historians of slavery had acknowledged: religious practice in African American communities was imbued with a different history and thus a different meaning than white Christianity. While revivals certainly had social aspects in white communities, too, Lewis pointed to their special role in the lives of the enslaved.

Revivals enabled the oppressed to gather as a mutually supportive community. For this reason, enslaved Christians frequently met in hidden places, known as brush arbors and hush arbors. Free African Americans during the era of slavery suffered great hostility from whites toward their religious institutions. The best-known example of this hostility was the harassment of members of the African Methodist Episcopal Church that contributed to Denmark Vesey's plans for a rebellion in Charleston in 1822 and the subsequent destruction of the church as white revenge for Vesey's plot. In the story of Denmark Vesey we learn the importance of churches to free and enslaved black communities as sites of self-determination, even within the confines of organized religion. In *The Taste of Country Cooking* we learn that freedom of association remained a kind of sacrament associated with church events after Emancipation and passage of the Thirteenth Amendment.

Although she emphasized the historical context of Revival Week, Lewis downplayed the religious content of the festival time, perhaps because she wished to appeal to a white urban audience who might be uncomfortable with discussions of intense Christianity. As Eugene Genovese remarked in his discussion of Christianity in slavery, "In this secular, not to say cynical age, few tasks present greater difficulty than that of compelling the well-educated to take religion seriously."[14]

For Lewis, what mattered, always, was the food. To celebrate Revival Week and the freedom of association, the people of Freetown feasted on a cornucopia of dishes, some primarily southern, some less tied to region. Among the quintessentially southern dishes were baked Virginia ham, southern fried chicken, sweet potato casserole, corn pudding, green beans with pork, biscuits, sweet potato pie, Tyler pie (a simple egg custard pie), caramel cake, and iced tea. Less markedly southern were braised leg of mutton, sliced tomatoes with "special seasoning" (sugar, black pepper and salt), spiced Seckel pears, yeast rolls, and apple pie, that supposedly all-American favorite.

Lewis's description of Emancipation Day, the other distinctly African American holiday mentioned in her book, does not include any particular activities or characters associated with the date in her community, as she describes for other seasonal events. But her menu choices directly address the theme of origins. In giving her recipe for Guinea Fowl in Casserole, Lewis noted, "The guinea fowl has its origin in West Africa and their African link was passed on generation to generation by African-Americans." Here Lewis revealed that black Americans celebrate their African heritage and have done so for many generations. For white readers, this might come as some surprise, partly because then-prominent historian Stanley Elkins had claimed that African culture was stripped away in the trauma of the Middle Passage, and partly because white culture had itself based its discrimination against black Americans on this heritage. Lewis's readers might have been aware of Afrocentrism in the contemporary Black Power movement, but they likely had no knowledge of its deeper roots. Lewis's simple statement, then, packs an unexpected punch of correction to common white misreadings of her culture.[15]

One implicit theme of the Emancipation Day dinner was foraged foods. These were foods that the enslaved, in the era of slavery, could gather for themselves and so thus represent independence from the slaveholder and the tyranny of monotonous rations. One example of foraged foods is the guinea fowl itself, which Lewis said, "had to be shot, as they lived in trees and roamed the countryside." Another example is the watercress that her family served with the guinea fowl and the wild rice they served as a side dish.[16]

In American cookbooks of the time, wild rice was typically associated with Native American foodways as an indigenous American food. Lewis noted that her family did not bother to gather the rice themselves, but that her mother's turkeys ate the rice, which made them especially delicious.

Lewis adds that "since then" she had "become interested in wild rice and various ideas about how to cook it." This interest perhaps stemmed from her time in New York, where wild rice was prized among urban food connoisseurs. The recipe mixed notions of indigeneity with a new approach to American cooking. Lewis wrote African Americans into national food history but also its future.[17]

Alongside other foraged elements in the Emancipation Day menu Lewis included grape jelly, recalling that "among the flurry of fall activities was the hunt for wild grapes," used for jelly making. Two other native, though domesticated ingredients, green beans and tomatoes, and two markedly European American recipes, Parker House Rolls and Purple Plum Tart, also graced the table. The tart, incidentally, appears to be the very same recipe that became the *New York Times*'s most requested recipe. Originally known as Pflammenkuchen, the dish had origins in western Europe.[18]

Parker House rolls, associated as they were with a famous American hotel, were emblematic of mainstream middle-class culture. Defying stereotypes that associated African American cooks, and the South more generally, with biscuits and corn pone, Lewis declared that "the cooks of Freetown loved making yeast bread" and that they formed rolls into all sorts of shapes. Her note carries a message embedded in what seems like a mundane detail. While quick breads like biscuits and cornmeal hoecakes were typically associated with the enslaved cook who lacked time, ovens, and fuel, Lewis showed her readers another history of African American foodways in which time and ovens are in plentiful supply. Her reference to Parker House rolls also reflected an early twentieth-century trend across the South toward yeast breads—particularly packaged breads made with refined wheat flour and away from homemade cornmeal breads.[19]

By focusing attention on the theme of origins, Lewis associated Emancipation Day with African American roots but also with change since the time of slavery. Where once foraging had offered a route to culinary self-expression within the confines of slavery, African American home cooks had moved beyond this to claim the culinary heritage of their nation. Even as they feasted on the guinea hen as a symbol of their unwilling migration from Africa, they dressed the bird with a stuffing connected to a North American native as well as European American heritage. Lewis's Emancipation menu celebrated freedom from culinary constraints in concert with respect for traditions.

Lewis returned to the theme of time as a luxury in her memory of the custom of family visiting during the winter. Freed from their ties to the land for a season, her neighbors and ancestors traveled to stay with one another for stretches as long as a few weeks. Among her grandfather's peer group, these visits followed a regular pattern. While homemade cakes and homemade wines were served and a fire roared in the fireplace, "there would be lively conversations, with the aged men doing most of the talking and the young adults of my father's age group listening." As a child, she enjoyed sitting with the old men and listening to them talk, but "I was too young then to understand why so much time was spent in discussion." Only in later years did she understand that "they were still awed by the experience of chattel slavery fifty years ago, and of having become freedmen." Having experienced one of the most profound social transitions in world history, "It was something that they never tired of talking about." A song they liked to sing together expressed their amazement: "My Soul Look Back and Wonder How I Got Over." One couplet in the lyrics to this song asks, "Tell me how we got over Lord / Had a mighty hard time coming on over."[20]

The Taste of Country Cooking is Edna Lewis's own version of those long talks among family and friends, retelling collective histories for a new audience—her mostly white readers. In using her cookbook as a vehicle for African American history, Lewis invited her readers in to wonder with her at how the soul "got over" and to recognize that crossing as an essential thread in the American story. By drawing our attention to the legacy of both slavery and emancipation and to the formative importance of the first generation who lived in the transitional time, she presented an archetypal American story to parallel that of the founding fathers who were being so lavishly celebrated in the bicentennial year. They, too, after all, had got over. Lewis left her readers to wonder for themselves at how much there was still left to get over before all Americans could celebrate equality.

NOTES

1. *Ebony*, June 1972, 176.

2. Edna Lewis, *The Taste of Country Cooking* (New York: Knopf, 1976), 62.

3. For more on this theme, see Doris Witt, *Black Hunger* (Minneapolis: University of Minnesota Press, 1999), 183–84.

4. Edna Lewis and Evangeline Peterson, *The Edna Lewis Cookbook* (New York: Bobbs-Merrill Company, 1972), xii.

5. Lewis, *Taste of Country Cooking*, v. Unless otherwise noted, all quotations in this essay are from the Introduction to *The Taste of Country Cooking*. In a later edition (2006),

prefaces by Alice Waters and Judith Jones were added to the text, but in this essay I wish to focus on the book as it was originally published, with only Lewis's version of herself and her history. Both Waters's and Jones's statements are interesting as artifacts of culinary history, but my interest here is in Lewis's work as a historian.

6. I have been unable to learn anything else about Grace Saran than what we find here.

7. Ibid., 150.

8. Evan Jones, *American Food: The Gastronomic Story* (New York: E. P. Dutton, 1975), 1. It is also interesting to note about Jones that he did not mention African Americans at all in his chapter about colonial era cooking.

9. Eugene Genovese, *Roll, Jordan, Roll: The World the Slaves Made* (New York: Vintage Books, 1972), 543. Genovese also quotes an African American chef, Bob Jeffries, who does identify soul food exclusively with cooking done for the enslaved by the enslaved: "Soul food cooking is an example of how really good southern Negro cooks cooked with what they had available to them, such as chickens from their own backyard and collard greens they grew themselves, as well as home cured ham and bakin' powder biscuits, chit'lins, and dubie [berry cobbler]."

10. Because European Americans considered the parts of a pig found higher off the ground to be the tastiest, leaving lower parts like the feet for the enslaved, "high on the hog" has come to represent good, even luxurious eating.

11. See Ruth Gaskins, *A Good Heart and a Light Hand* (New York: Simon and Schuster, 1968); and Vertamae Smart-Grosvenor, *Vibration Cooking: or, The Travel Notes of a Geechee Girl* (New York: Doubleday, 1970).

12. Judith Jones, *The Tenth Muse* (New York: Anchor Books, 2007), 119.

13. Lewis, *Taste of Country Cooking*, 117; Frederick Douglass, "The Meaning of July Fourth for the Negro," speech at Rochester, N.Y., July 5, 1852; David Walker, *Appeal to the Colored Citizens of the World* (Boston, 1829).

14. Genovese, *Roll, Jordan, Roll*, 161.

15. Lewis, *Taste of Country Cooking*, 159.

16. Ibid.

17. For example, Charlotte Turgeon identified wild rice as both a luxury and a food that "the Indians knew long before the arrival of the white men." Charlotte Turgeon, *The Saturday Evening Post All-American Cookbook* (Nashville, Tenn.: Thomas Nelson, 1976), 195.

18. Lewis, *Taste of Country Cooking*, 162. Amanda Hesser notes in her *Essential New York Times Cook Book* that the *Times*'s recipe for purple plum torte was "both the most often published and the most requested recipe in the *Times* archives." Amanda Hesser, *The Essential New York Times Cook Book* (New York: New York Times, 2010), 763.

19. Lewis, *Taste of Country Cooking*, 163.

20. Lewis, *Taste of Country Cooking*, 227.

The African Virginian Roots of Edna Lewis

MICHAEL W. TWITTY

Miss Edna Lewis is venerated as a southern cook and cultural icon. Her classic cookbook *The Taste of Country Cooking* defined her approach to traditional southern food and amplified the importance of her gustatory memories in shaping her development as a self-taught chef. The work draws us into her childhood and spells out the seasons and labors on a small central Virginia farm in the early twentieth century. It sets the tone for her career as an advocate for going back to the resources of the southern countryside. *The Taste of Country Cooking*, published in 1976, America's bicentennial year and the year that Alex Haley's *Roots* debuted, provided a record of an African American—but more accurately African Virginian— culinary microcosm in transition from the nineteenth to the twentieth centuries, and this pivotal work provided a glimpse of a new kind of African American cookbook. It honored her childhood and gave a Norman Rockwell–like portrait, I venture to say, of a black farming community. It also placed the food enjoyed by the residents of Freetown, Virginia, within seasons and cycles of labor.

Beyond Lewis's legendary persona—which has only grown in stature since her passing—the context of her origins has scarcely been interrogated beyond the notion that she came from a small, rural Virginia community—Freetown—founded by former enslaved peoples after the Civil War. What is most remarkable about Miss Lewis is the position she eventually arrived at and the influence she wrought in the world; few black female chefs of her generation had the kind of connections or influence that she had. Many were confined to the role of a domestic who cooked for white families or worked on African American kitchen staffs at hotels and establishments where they themselves could not take meals. We don't have much recorded knowledge about the world that many of these cooks came from, because their memories were passed down orally, scattered across family members and generations. Few narratives exist that center on the upbringing and food-voices of African Americans in the South on the verge of the Great Migration, or of the bridges those individuals had to the world of slavery. Lewis's is a rare firsthand voice in a field of relative quiet.

My purpose here is to look at the life of chef Lewis as a continuum of a specific culinary and cultural legacy rooted in a particular regional and familial past. This essay seeks to demonstrate the ways in which Edna Lewis might have reflected many southern stories, but she was not pan-southern. She was the product of a specific South with a specific African Virginian culinary heritage, and as a cook she was the product of many forces — historical, genealogical, ecological, culinary, and sociopolitical — that shaped her journey as a cook who was too often perceived as having supposedly "simple" roots.

Reading Edna Lewis's works as cultural texts or ethnographic documents, we are exposed to her not merely as a cook with a country pedigree but as the memory keeper of a community — indeed many communities — that represented the flow of human beings that found themselves participants in some of American history's largest migration patterns. Miss Lewis's ancestors were likely part of the more than 280,000 Africans brought in the eighteenth century to what would become the United States, as part of the trans-Atlantic slave trade, the largest forced migration in human history. Those 280,000-odd enslaved Africans were also part of the largest trans-Atlantic bloc to cross from the Old World to the New, the Americas. More enslaved Africans would cross the Atlantic than Europeans before 1800. From 1619 to 1774, Virginia was where roughly half of those enslaved Africans were brought. Virginia, the mother of presidents, became the leading slave society in mainland North America; more "African Americans" would be born there from 1619 to just after the Civil War than any other state or colony. By the 1750s, the majority of African Virginians were Afri-Creoles, the bridge generation born in North America rather than Africa but not fully assimilated.

Edna's colonial ancestors were a people whose cultural structure was a mix of colonial European American informed by West and Central African lifeways, the harsh reality of enslavement, and reactions to European and Native American influences. Cooking was one of the more powerful and sustainable connections to African and Afri-Creole heritages, and en-

Michael W. Twitty

slaved people created a food culture that the historian Charles Joyner once described as an "African culinary grammar," in which "methods of cooking and spicing, remembered foods, [and] ancestral tastes" merged with a largely northern European (in the case of Virginia, British, German, and French) vocabulary of ingredients. On the way, African and Africanized items (guinea fowl, peanuts, tomatoes, hot peppers, sorghum, eggplant, sweet potatoes, rice, black-eyed peas, and more) found their way into the larder, but the translation of all of these pieces into a cohesive and specific culinary narrative was what made the African Virginian table exemplary.

EDNA LEWIS'S PLACE

A cook is built, in part, by his or her landscape. As someone who helped define what southern means today, it is important to understand what South Miss Lewis came from. The people of her part of the South — where they came from, their landscape, the climate and what it permitted them to grow, and the seasons that defined the agricultural year — influenced what she put on her plate. In addition to this were the human narratives that led to the historical circumstances she was heir to. All of these elements combine to define Miss Lewis's "place."

First there is the notion of "the South" to be addressed. The reality — one that is often forgotten in popular narratives that foreground images from the Old South of sweeping plantations, southern belles, and groaning sideboards — is that there are many Souths. It is perhaps most important first to recognize that Miss Lewis's South was not the Deep South — no pecans, cotton fields, sugarcane, alligators, live oaks, or Spanish moss or a host of other signifying stereotypes. Orange County was not a land studded in Greek revival plantations and sprawling estates. The optimal number of enslaved workers on a Virginia wheat farm was small compared to the plantations of the Deep South, requiring only about fifteen to twenty, so essentially two to three extended black families — if that — might belong to a slaveholder of modest but successful means. Central Virginia plantations were no *Gone with the Wind* Taras. Clapboard houses and whitewashed log cabins with additions were the usual big houses, and cooks on these smaller farms and plantations often worked alongside other enslaved people at harvest while cooking for both the white and black communities on a property. Upon emancipation, settlements like Freetown — Lewis's hometown — were modeled after enslaved quarter communities, with homes built in an almost African compound style, encircling the home of a founder. In Edna's case, the dwelling of her own grandfather, a community elder, sat at the center of the community.

The American region that Edna's ancestors came to was part of a secondary tier of settlement in the eighteenth century. Just beyond the fall line and the Virginia Tidewater but before the Blue Ridge, Orange County and adjacent Albemarle, Louisa, Madison, Greene, Spotsylvania, Culpepper, Fluvanna, and Goochland Counties formed the core of a central Virginia heartland where King Tobacco once reigned. The region was largely populated by enslaved Africans brought from present-day Senegal, Gambia, and southeastern Nigeria and their descendants, with a few Africans from what is now Ghana and historic Kongo-Angola. In Virginia's heart — the Black Belt — diverse cultures such as the Malinke, Fula (Fulani, Fulbe), Wolof, Serer, Igbo, Ibibio, Efik, and Moko forged new cultures and new cuisines as they coped with new realities and limitations. Skilled in growing tobacco and maize, raising tubers like the sweet potato, and cultivating corn and other grains, these ethnic groups were considered prime field hands. However, they were also skilled artisans, proficient in blacksmithing, woodworking, animal husbandry, gardening, cooking, hunting, and fishing. These early African Virginians used much of their experience from home to forge new identities as they came into contact with alien cultures.

When Orange County, where Lewis grew up, was founded in 1734, it was tobacco country planted in the Orinoco variety, which was mostly used for snuff. What was once the colony's western frontier became, in a short period, part of the tradition of patrician Virginia. Blessed with a milder version of the region's humid subtropical climate, Orange and the surrounding counties had climatic and geographic advantages. This, combined with the slaveholders' search for power and property, created a unique meeting of minds and a local culinary scene in the nineteenth century that existed in the shadow of Virginia's greatest tables. As I wrote in an essay on Edna Lewis in *Icons of American Cooking* (Greenwood, 2011):

> Orange County and with it, north-central Virginia holds a special place in American food history. Orange and the neighboring counties were the seats of the Madisons, the Monroes, the Jeffersons and the Randolphs — founding families with gourmet tastes and an appreciation for the fertility and bounty of the land. The influence of these families, their enslaved communities and the dishes for which their plantation kitchens were lauded could

be felt in the tastes and flavors of local cooking. Whether it was the fine tables of Montpelier or close-by Monticello, the legacy of Mary Randolph—cousin to the Jeffersons and author of *The Virginia Housewife*—the first Southern cookbook, or the cooking of the African American women who formed the "waiter-carriers" of Gordonsville, famous for their fried chicken and hot rolls served at train side; this little county was a crossroads of culinary influences that would make a significant mark on American cuisine. Even after years of intensive cultivation in tobacco, wheat and corn, the rolling hills and fields of Edna Lewis's home produced stellar produce, wild plant foods, orchard fruit, and richly flavored wild game and grass and corn fed livestock.

As the colonies approached the War of Independence, tobacco's hungry nature sucked all the nutrients out of the land and the tobacco market shrank. As a result, prices for the colony's primary cash crop fell. Slavery in Orange shifted from King Tobacco to grains like wheat and maize in the late eighteenth and early nineteenth centuries, with "the vile weed" still maintaining stubborn hooks in the economy as in other areas of the Virginia Piedmont. After emancipation, with the loss of enslaved laborers, the Virginia farming economy downsized from large tobacco and wheat plantations to orchards, livestock, and dairy.

Orange County was in the Upper South—a place with cultural and culinary connections that in some ways made it closer to the eastern midlands than those of the southern seaboard. Edna's world was a crossroads where multiple cultures left their mark on the cuisine; the region was home for hundreds of years to the Siouan-speaking Manahoac people who were displaced by German, Welsh, English, and Scotch-Irish immigrants and forced migrants in the form of enslaved Africans. The cooking of the small farms—a European facet of the region's heritage—is easily traced to the places from whence the settlers came, from the charcuterie and sauerkraut of Westphalia in Germany to the fruit preserves and baking traditions of Wales, Bristol and southeastern England, the surrounding counties around London, and further southwest to Kent up over to Northern Ireland. The settlers maintained contact with family and businesses in small Virginia cities like Fredericksburg and Richmond, but also with places farther afield, such as Georgetown, Annapolis, Baltimore, and even Philadelphia, thus expanding Orange County residents' access to cookbooks, ingredients, and ideas about food in much more cosmopolitan spaces.

This is significant, given that tobacco's depletion of the land could have easily pushed Miss Lewis's ancestors westward to where Virginia's enslaved often ended up once profits fell short in "Old Virginny." Luck and circumstance, combined, allowed them to stay. The *domestic* slave trade was the largest forced migration in American history, moving approximately a million enslaved blacks from the Upper South states to the Lower South as tobacco land became infertile. Shifting crop cultivation obviated the need for a large year-round workforce, whereas the expanding southern cotton industry demanded a huge influx of black workers. It was Virginia's founding fathers themselves who brokered the deal cutting off legal importations of Africans from abroad in the first decade of the nineteenth century, thus ensuring the Commonwealth a new cash crop to sell that surpassed the value of Orinoco and sweet-scented tobacco—the black body and its labor.

Edna's great-great grandparents were probably born in the late eighteenth century. Before them, her ancestors were most likely a mixture of new African immigrants and those who had been born in Virginia. The African Virginian population was perhaps the most important demographic in the colonial and antebellum South. Although 40 percent of all enslaved Africans brought to North America entered through the port of Charleston, Virginia was responsible for the importation of almost 100,000 enslaved Africans, and most of them survived. The colonial Chesapeake, for all of its epidemics and the perils caused by the violence of slavery, was still one of the healthiest places for an enslaved African to arrive. By 1740, the black population there did something it did nowhere else—self-reproduce to the point where black children born in North America outpaced the numbers of Africans brought ashore.

Edna Lewis's grandfather Chester was born in May, sometime between 1835 and 1837, to John Lewis and Sarah Smith, born in Louisa and Orange Counties, respectively. Chester was likely enslaved on or near the plantation of Claiborn R. Mason, the man who "gave" some of his land to his former chattel to found Freetown. Chester's wife, Lucinda, a brick maker purchased for $950, was born in about 1836 in November. Such uncertain birthdates were common for the generations of slaves for whom no birthdate can be found unless they were one of the few to have their birth recorded in a Bible record kept by their slaveholder or, worse, a "stud book."

Charles was recorded on the early census as a mulatto, but most probably his skin color and appearance reflected his almost inevitable mixed

Michael W. Twitty

ancestry; among African American males, almost 30 percent had a white father or grandfather. The cultural blending that we have come to blindly explain away as part of the "melting pot" idea of American civilization was not the product of an easy and effortless diffusion. Slavery was brutal, violent, uncomfortably intimate, and intrusive, and it affected the blood, bone, manners, and habits of all who were within its grasp, enslaved, enslavers, and all who encountered them. The vines of food, slavery, southern cooking, and African American peoplehood were, and are, inextricably tangled and complex.

Although Miss Lewis's family stayed in eastern Virginia, many African Virginians would not remain in the places they had landed on arriving in the colonies. Thousands of enslaved African Americans from the Chesapeake, Tidewater, and Piedmont of the Upper South, and the Lowcountry and Sea Islands of the Lower South, were sold into the newly acquired "Southwest," including current-day Kentucky, Tennessee, Alabama, western Georgia, and Mississippi, and eventually Louisiana, Missouri, Arkansas, and Texas. Within a century, an African American family that had rooted in Old Virginia could have grandchildren born in Tennessee or Kentucky and great-grandchildren born in Texas or Mississippi. Others seeking their own path to freedom would carry their foodways into the Northeast — Philadelphia and Boston, for example — and as far as Canada and the urban Midwest. Even though the domestic slave trade and freedom-seeking separated thousands of blacks from their family members, Virginia would remain the largest slaveholding territory until full emancipation at the end of the Civil War, predominantly because of the slave-breeding complex.

African Virginian foodways traveled with people of African descent as they left for other parts of the country after emancipation. From 1865 to 1910 and then from 1915 to 1940, African Virginians took part in the different phases of the Great Migration. Miss Lewis and other family members picked up and left the segregated world of Virginia looking north for better opportunities. Some migrated no farther than Washington, D.C., and Baltimore, both segregated but exciting, with economic opportunities and links to other cities along the Atlantic Seaboard. Black Virginians also went to the cities of Ohio, Pennsylvania, New York, and Massachusetts. They joined previously established black communities in Cincinnati and Dayton, Pittsburgh and Philadelphia, New York, Buffalo, and Boston. Miss Lewis herself went to Washington and, later, New York. The Great Migration, the largest *voluntary* movement of Americans in our nation's history, spread southerners and, with them, African Virginian culture; Edna Lewis certainly was not rare in following the patterns of such mass movement, but she became one of its most prominent carriers.

INTERPRETING LEWIS'S LARDER
THROUGH AN AFRICAN VIRGINIAN LENS

The secret is in the ingredients, if you don't put Southern
ingredients in, it's not Southern cooking. . . . Some think the
ingredients are too heavy or out of date, but I don't think we should
throw away our culture because of some fad or new ideas.
—Edna Lewis, "What Is Southern?" (2008)

We can read, in the textual record left by Miss Lewis, a clear connection to the generations who preceded her. Her work is, in many ways, an extension of the slave narratives of Virginia. Most of the food or food production that Miss Lewis writes of could just as well be from a hundred years before her birth or more, with the caveat that few enslaved African Virginians would have enjoyed the full variety of foods as expressed in her work (particularly *The Taste of Country Cooking*), although as cooks in Big Houses, many may have prepared similar recipes for their slaveholders. However, most of the scenarios she details—gathering, fishing, hunting, the capture of injured rabbits and small game during the gathering of wheat, the making of hominy, and the preservation of meat—all harken back to the days of slavery.

Miss Lewis's work reflects two enjoined, yet distinct, foodways: the simple country cooking of the southern midlands that spread across the Upper South, eventually becoming the dominant cooking style of African Americans before the Civil War, and the products and cooking of the majority of the enslaved people of Greater Virginia. Lewis's food was not just a comfortable reminder of the care and love put into food in some distant past; it was the sum total, the accumulation of multiple histories and narratives, giving a culinary-historical layer-cake geology quality to her work. It was also part of a wider tradition that had disseminated from the Upper South over many generations that spanned nearly two centuries.

One of the many cultural shifts resulting from slavery was in the role of gender. Traditional West and Central African society relegated men to field crop production and women to gardening; men to the roasting, smoking, and preservation of meat and fish and women to domestic cookery. In early America, black men as well as black women often found themselves as the heads of colonial kitchens, and black women often slaughtered and processed livestock for smoking. Black males became gardeners for both the planters and themselves, and their provision grounds became a matter of survival in a system where the old guarantees of familial stability were not a priority.

Tastes, too, changed among enslaved Africans and their descendants as they navigated assimilation, appropriation, influence and material realities. A fundamental shift in what this cuisine looked and tasted like probably occurred about the same time that the majority of enslaved blacks in the colony became Virginia born—a shift that occurred between 1740 and 1760. Foods that appealed to, say, a woman arriving from what is now southeastern Nigeria in the 1720s might not be appealing to her great-granddaughter born in southeastern Virginia in the 1760s.

In the New World, both Creole-born Africans and Europeans living in the Americas would come to greater cultivation and appreciation of their sweet tooth. The traditional African palette favored more hot, bitter, spicy, and oily dishes rather than sweet ones. In the Americas, however, Africans would not only cut cane but embrace the confections of the societies that enslaved them. The soothing nature of sucrose was one of the few comforts known to bondspeople. Great-grandmother was a stranger to sweet, but great-granddaughter would be fond of jumbles, biscuits, cakes, sweet bread, jams, and other delights.

Forced immigration required shifts in venues and modes of cooking as well. In southeastern Nigeria, as in other regions of Western and Central Africa, a kitchen hearth was an outdoor or separate building with a fire pit that held three supporting stones, on which a variety of clay or iron trade pots could be placed. Wooden spoons, bush knives, mortars and pestles, brush whisks, baskets, grinding stones, and gourds used as bowls were the primary cooking equipment. Contrast this world of simple hearth, clay, wood, reed, and gourd husk cookery with the brick hearth and predominantly metal and utensil-rich cooking environment that great-granddaughter might cook in at the home of a prominent Virginia planter. The latter kitchen, born in northern Europe, and the culture that surrounded it would introduce many African-born Virginians to baking, as neither wheat flour nor long baking was traditional to West Africa.

When Mary Randolph penned her famed *Virginia Housewife* in 1824, she drew extensively on the cooking of enslaved people. Usually supplied with only a pot or Dutch oven, a spider skillet, and a few spoons, enslaved Africans made earthenware vessels that they cooked in, and they cooked over pits and on open fires as they had in their homelands, traditions we still see in the cooking of their descendants today. The colonial Virginian diet, based on quick breads, one-pot soups and stews, and fried, roasted, and grilled foods inspired Lewis's inclusion of a number of Virginia favorites in her cookbooks. Dishes such as okra soup (using the Igbo-sourced name for the plant), turnip greens cooked "Virginia style" with country ham, sweet potatoes roasted or stewed with chicken, herbs, and pepper, fried chicken, okra and tomatoes, boiled okra, black-eyed peas, and fried cakes made with black-eyed peas, pepper vinegar, and barbecued shoat all drew in part on the tastes and traditions of the Africans who surrounded Randolph at her home plantation. Native, African, and European tastes mixed and recombined as a southern diet was being formed on the edges of strict adherence to old traditions. Possums roasted with sweet potatoes came from cutting grass rat stewed with yam. There were groundnut stews. People used collard leaves to wrap and roast food, and roasted corn on the cob, as they had done across the Atlantic. There were probably many more dishes that were improvised and have since been lost, meaningful only in the moment of their creation.

A number of gastronomical links to West and Central African heritage remained through the turn of the twentieth century. This African culinary grammar was what helped define the cooking of the greater Chesapeake and southern midlands, including Freetown. Black-eyed peas, peanuts, sweet potatoes, watermelons, eggplant (also known as "guinea squash"), red peppers, leafy greens, and okra were grown in the gardens of African Virginians from the late seventeenth century onward, and African influences were further reflected in sorghum cane grown in Orange County and the black-and-white-speckled guinea fowl that served as alarm clocks, pest control, and game birds.

In addition to cultivated crops, a number of wild edibles noted in Lewis's work have links to West and Central Africa. Botanical cognates to plants from across the Atlantic were also a part of the African Virginian diet into the early twentieth century. Most notable was the American persimmon (*Diospyros virginiana*), cousin to a similar species from West Africa (*D. mespiliformis*), which, much as in West Africa, was used to brew a liquor and to make sweets and confections. There were others, such as edible greens like purslane (*Portulaca* spp.), pokeweed (*Phytolacca*), and lamb's quarter (*Chenopodium*), that infested fields and had to be weeded out, and were enjoyed on both sides of the ocean. Another wild crop, berries (*Rubus* spp.) were gathered by children in both tropical Africa and temper-

Michael W. Twitty

ate America. A plethora of African wild nuts and a variety of wild fruit unknown in North America were replaced by indigenous and Eurasian nuts, tubers, and fruits, among them black walnuts, plums, gooseberry, elderberries, Albemarle Pippins and Stayman Winesaps, quinces, peaches, Kieffer pears, and Muscadine grapes. Edible immature gourds in West Africa were replaced by cucurbits indigenous to the Americas, including cymling squashes (White Bush scallop pattypans) and pumpkins. The dozens of cultivated species of amaranth and other leafy greens native to tropical Africa were supplanted in the New World by cabbages, collards, beet tops, kale, rape greens, turnip tops, and watercress.

In 1866, John Dennet described a black garden to the southwest near Lynchburg in which "a fence of palings, or of pickets interwoven with brushwood, enclose a small patch of garden ground, planted with cabbages, string-beans and tomatoes[;] nearby is a bush or two of red peppers, much used by these people in medicine and cookery." We can imagine the garden of early Freetown bearing a strong resemblance to this depiction. The other vegetables mentioned in Miss Lewis's work reflect the common produce of the Atlantic world—tomatoes, potatoes, green beans, onions, and cucumbers. Many of these New World and Eurasian crops had come to West and Central Africa early on and were adapted because of their similarity to indigenous produce and their high productivity. These were also crops that came to define the new nature of food in the colonial era, which revolutionized the eating habits of the Americas, Africa, and Europe.

Turnips, parsnips, beets, cresses, carrots, and salsify, all noted in Lewis's text, were common to Orange County's Scotch-Irish, English, and German settlers; all became endemic in the gardens of Virginia's plantations and small farms, and slowly assimilated into African Virginian gardens. The herb patches of Lewis's youth included tarragon, thyme, chives, horseradish, chervil, garlic, parsley, mint, sage, and purple basil. Of these, garlic, mint, sage, thyme, and basil were known in both West Africa and Western Europe by the eighteenth century, reinforcing their importance in early African American foodways.

Owing to the Native American contribution passed down from the Manahoac, corn, beans, squash, pumpkins, and Jerusalem artichoke were central to the Virginia kitchen, and hominy, corn pone, spoon bread, succotash, cornbread, fried corn, grits, corn on the cob, and corn pudding, as well as ashcake and hoecake—the hardtack of the plantation workforce—grew out of the interplay of cultures working with this indigenous staple.

Hominy, something Edna Lewis said her Aunt Jenny Hailstalk was famous for making, was one of many important reasons for African Virginian reproductive success. Eaten along with legumes and leafy greens, hominy formed the basis of a nutritious diet. Elsewhere in the New World, enslaved Africans suffered from malnutrition from consuming a diet that was vitamin poor and lacking in essential amino acids like lysine, which hominy gained when the corn was nixtamalized using lye made by dripping water through ashes. Having a diversity of ecosystems from which to draw sustenance also helped ensure that many African Virginians were eating a varied rather than monotonous diet, improving both their overall health and quality of life.

The protein sources of enslaved Virginians and their descendants in Freetown illustrated patterns that drew on the African heritage and the plantation experience. Preserved pork graced the Lewis table, just as their holidays, like those of the enslaved, began with the bursting of hog bladder balloons by the fireside. Smoked hams, shoulders, bacon, cracklings, and sausage—which had been largely unavailable to enslaved Virginians—were sure signs of freedom to the generations that followed in Freetown. Beef and lamb or mutton were close behind as domestic meats, consumed, according to plantation custom, when an animal was sick, old, or butchered for a special occasion. Both bear some significance as preferred protein to Lewis's Senegambian ancestors—some of whom would have been Muslim or influenced by Islam. From the scant evidence we have, it is known that Islamic dietary laws and food preferences did continue among some enslaved people well into the nineteenth century.

In slavery, poultry yards provided meat, feathers, and eggs for barter or sale to the Big House, the town market, or passersby. Turkeys, Muscovy ducks, and guinea fowl joined chicken in colorful, squawking communities around the cabins. The people of Freetown were expert trappers and hunters, as their ancestors had been. Squirrel, rabbit, quail, plover, snipe, woodcock, wild turkey—and likely raccoon, deer, and opossum as well—were caught in traps, shot, and culled after accidental wounding in the field. The streams, millponds, rivers, and the like provided springtime herring and shad, eels, catfish, and trout, depending on the season. Turtles washed up from the creeks and were made into soup. It is easy to envision enslaved communities following similar subsistence patterns. Oysters were brought from the Chesapeake Bay just as they had been a century before in the days of Jefferson, Madison, and Monroe.

Those forced to leave the Old Dominion during the domestic slave trade often waxed nostalgic about the "good vittles" of their old home, Virginia, as displayed in the words of Joseph Holmes, a formerly enslaved man sold to Texas from Henry County, Virginia, interviewed by an employee of the Works Progress Administration: "Lord honey, Virginny is the best place on earth for good eating and good white folks. You wouldn't believe the fruit us did have. Such as apples, cherries, quinces, peaches, and pears. It makes my mouth water to think about them. Cheese apples that was yellow like gold, and them Abraham apples, the likes of which ain't no to be had. And those cherry trees bit as these oaks, with long limbs and Big Sugar and Sweetheart and Black Heart Cherries. Then there was another kind of cherry called the Gorilla that was round and growed as big as the yellow plums down way."

In sum, the food world of Edna Lewis, as reflected in her cookbooks, was not crafted in the quaint desire to embrace the simple rustic country life. Rather, it was shaped by traditions rooted in the foodways of enslaved African Virginians and the plantation culture that surrounded them. In this world, transitioning from slavery to freedom, Lewis's community translated their past into the heritage we read in her narratives. Of the thousands who lived nourished by African Virginia's food heritage, it was Edna Lewis who went on to live an extraordinary life in Manhattan and to bring this exemplary cuisine to a wide audience. Because she did, we have the opportunity to learn more about what remained the same, what changed, and what persists from the world of Virginia slavery and emancipation. *The Taste of Country Cooking* captures more than just a community; it captures a moment when a people chose the gastronomic luggage they would take with them out of a dark and troubled past.

CODA

In our contemporary world the meaning of "southern" is debated, argued, and constantly redefined. The same can be said for southern food. If we see Edna Lewis as emblematic of the South and of southern food, it is critical to ask which South she emerged from and what that South's significance is. Delving into the particularities that shaped her life and experience helps us practice raising questions that can help to trouble stereotypes and generalizations.

Edna Lewis's particular South — Freetown — was an insular black community born of emancipation in the South's largest bloc of enslaved people, one whose roots went back to the beginnings of British North America's engagement with the transatlantic slave trade. While Edna Lewis certainly saw herself as southern, more than a few people in the South would wince at north-central Virginia as representing their entire region today.

In addition, Edna Lewis is viewed as an archetypal black southern cook even though she spent many formative years in New York City as a southern expatriate of sorts—driven from her homeland by oppression, lack of opportunity, and misfortune. Her food and her memories reflect that. Perhaps the details of a geographic and cultural history such this book will help readers and explorers of Lewis's life and work to delve deeper into where her South came from and what it ultimately meant in the formation of her particular cooking and writings; that hers wasn't a generic South, or one that could be transposed just anywhere on the southern map, is vitally important to beginning to understand the myriad cultural and geographical Souths that emerged in the wake of the colonial period.

Edna Lewis's South was beef à la mode, blancmange, briskets, and brioche, not meat and threes, Cheerwine, moon pies, collard greens, and fried okra. Yes, there was hominy, chicken fried with ham in the skillet, poke salad, and spoonbread, but these were old-time, almost regional variations on southern food, important to the Upper South but also to the state of Virginia and the wider Chesapeake region as a whole.

Why, then, has Lewis been placed in the cultural box of generic southernness when nothing in her life—as a migrant, as a celebrity, as a chef, and as part of a community that rarely gets to determine southern (read: black southerners)—reflects that? Why has Edna Lewis so rarely been associated with the culinary world of the Madisons, Jeffersons, and Randolphs that surrounded her community? She clearly was—not only because dishes such as blancmange and damson preserves made it into Lewis's family's seasonal routine of enjoying good, self-produced fare but because it was the enslaved people in her cultural sphere who cooked for the patrician class.

We locate Edna Lewis's genius in her cooking, when the truth is that many women from the same world cooked in similar ways. There were many undiscovered Edna Lewises from her generation, but few made their culinary journey in such a way that the world would know them.

Perhaps we would do well to begin by relocating Lewis in history and memory. Here is my start to that project: I position Edna Lewis as the daughter of the first generation outside of slavery living in a village founded by her grandparents, born into slavery in the South's Old Dominion. They were the descendants of Africans and African Americans who founded and closed the chapters on American slavery. Edna's family was most likely

Michael W. Twitty

taken from specific parts of West Africa, and these places inevitably made an impact on the heritage that came down to her through Edna's mother's kitchen. Lewis's culinary heritage is not without the scars of slavery, nor is it without the empowerment of emancipation and freedom. Rather, it is a layered journey that is meaningless if we do not acknowledge the history that preceded it. Miss Lewis left us a reflection on the proud family compound she had to leave behind but never could truly leave.

Edna Lewis: Selected Portraits

JOHN T. HILL

Church reunion, Bethel Baptist Church, Orange County, Virginia, 1971.

Garden behind Ellerslie Plantation, Lahore, Virginia, 1975.

Judith Jones and Edna Lewis, Central Park, New York City, 1974.

*Edna Lewis, Duane Park,
New York City, 1983.*

Edna Lewis and the
Melancholia of Country Cooking

LILY KELTING

꙳

I don't remember how I first learned about Edna Lewis — only that once I heard her name, she was everywhere. Like a word you learn and then hear on the radio the next day. Like an echo. My curiosity to learn more about her grew into something like hunger. But traces of Edna Lewis in the public record were hard to come by. When the local public library didn't have her books, I bought them secondhand. I read them many times before I started to cook from them. I started feeling that Edna Lewis was something like my friend. And stranger still — other people, even those who never knew her — seemed to feel the same way. This essay traces my friendship with a woman I have never met, indeed will never know. It asks what I have been asking myself for six years now: What is it about Edna Lewis that renders her always partially out of view, hard to get a hold of and harder still to let go?

Specific attempts to contain or represent Edna Lewis — from the 2014 U.S. Postal Service commemorative stamp to archival materials to a one-woman show based on her life — raise broader questions about the role of the experiential within the historical record. Ultimately, I reconsider the way in which chefs — especially women of color like Lewis — are celebrated after their deaths, given that, as I show in this essay, such commemorations can serve, paradoxically, as sites of erasure. Yet Lewis remains. And so this essay concludes with a meditation on the nature of the grieved-but-not-gone, filling the gaps between my own imaginative investments in Miss Lewis and her absence from most forms of public recognition.

A goal of this maneuver is to reevaluate the status of culinary evidence altogether. As Heather Dubrow writes on the way in which ephemera is undervalued within academia, "Those who write and praise criticism that courts the label *solid* pride themselves that such works, unlike concoctions from French ovens, will not collapse for years after it is prepared and cannot, under any circumstances, be described as light or flaky." Instead of these "solid" commemorative practices that threaten to speak over Lewis, unwrite her from the archive, or crop her from the frame, I write, instead, in favor of the flaky piecrust, the crackle of guinea skin, the fleeting but triumphant puff of a hot soufflé.

BETWEEN AFFECT AND ARCHIVE

All of which is to say that there is tension at work between affect and the archive, between recorded history and embodied sensations. This is probably true for any attempt to agglomerate, sediment, or otherwise fix the realm of experience within the historical archive, but it is certainly true of my attempts to write about Lewis. On the one hand, being inscribed in the public record is a big deal for those who lie outside of it. Historically, writing cookbooks and recipes has been a mode of writing autobiography and cultural memory for women not usually afforded the opportunity (as importantly argued by academics working on this theme, such as Anne Bower and Susan Leonardi).

All the more for black women. The relationship between African Americans and written history is fraught for the obvious reason that slave era barriers to literacy have implications up to the present day. As Lewis herself notes in her posthumously published essay, "What Is Southern?": "It is also interesting to note that the South developed the only cuisine in this country. Living in a rural setting is inspiring: Birds, the quiet, flowers, trees, gardens, fields, music, love, sunshine, rain, and the smells of the earth all play a part in the world of creativity. It has nothing to do with reading or writing. Many of those cooks could not read or write."

And so—on the other hand—a revisionist history merely including the excluded from the annals of history does little to challenge the fundamental problem that archives are, by nature, exclusionary. That is, when discussing black American culinary icons, then, one must create new models of history that move outside dominant modes of reading and writing to which many cooks—those who taught Lewis included—did not have access. This context is not incidental to Lewis's history but rather central. *The Taste of Country Cooking* is dedicated to the "memory of the people of Freetown." The cookbook begins, "I grew up in Freetown, Virginia. . . . The name was adopted because the first residents of the town had all been freed from chattel slavery and they wanted to be known as a town of Free People." Lewis continues, mincing no words on the matter—"My grandmother had been a brickmason as a slave. She was purchased for $950."

Community knowledge and involvement are at the heart of several of Lewis's recipes: "Freetown was a beehive of activity, with everyone . . . gathering dandelions and setting them to wine." To commemorate Lewis can and should be to commemorate Freetown and its Free People, its dandelion wine, the mothers and aunts and cousins who appear throughout Lewis's writing. This essay is an attempt to revalue Lewis's own undervalued contributions to American food culture without resorting to dominant modes of writing history.

The academic field of performance studies uses the term *scriptocentrism* as shorthand for this fallback concept—that by turning the world into a text to be read and analyzed, as many academics do, much is lost. It's a simple concept that speaks well to the challenges of memorializing Lewis. So much of what inspired Lewis's cooking lies outside of language, "birds, . . . love, sunshine, . . . the smells of the earth." Yet so often, and in academia in particular, there is a deep cultural bias toward that which can be found in print, in writing. This bias strikes at the very heart of a discipline like food studies; as American studies scholar Marcie Cohen Ferris quips in *The Edible South*, "The challenge of food studies remains food itself." In other words, those who work with food have long understood the importance of challenging a world-as-text model but struggle with food's ephemeral nature, its entanglement with the slippery stuff of senses and memory. Lisa Heldke's succinct advice to pickle-makers, offered in Sandor Katz's *Art of Fermentation*, could double as a banner for those looking to reclaim sensory or embodied histories: "Life's truths cannot always be reduced to 12-point Times Roman." In short, the written record and the icon, both traditional modes of remembrance, are an imperfect fit for both southern food and Lewis; an affective history, which I gesture toward here, might be a more fitting replacement.

French theorist Michel de Certeau writes of Western (read: white) society, "Here only what is written is understood."[1] This worldview's strictures leave much out. As performance studies scholar Dwight Conquergood notes in his essay "Performance Studies: Interventions and Radical Research," he or she who only understands what is written is "not attuned to meanings that are masked, camouflaged, indirect, embedded, or hidden in context." We must remain so attuned. The challenges of memorializing Edna Lewis show us why. In practice, though, it is often simply harder to evaluate that which is ephemeral or in the body. How do we take feelings seriously?

Here's an even knottier question: How do we take seriously feelings that aren't even discrete emotions, but instead a more nebulous *arrangement* of feelings that occur through the senses and in the body? And furthermore, how do we square the inchoate feelings we have about Miss Lewis or her recipes with histories of racism that are all too concrete? All of these very real concerns about how to attune to sensory or embodied meanings lead to the central polemic of this essay—the necessity of writing a culinary history based, not on archival writings or visual iconicity, but on food itself, its visceral intensities. I don't complete this task—and maybe it's not even possible. Conquergood continues sarcastically, "Between objective knowledge that is consolidated in texts, and local know-how that circulates on the ground within a community of memory and practice, there is no contest. It is a choice between science and 'old wives' tales.'" But it's worth a try.

Edna Lewis's work consists precisely of the kind of experience-based, sensory knowledge—"local know-how"—that has been historically undervalued both within academia and even in the increasingly professionalized culinary industry. Lewis's cookbooks don't have slick photographs. Lewis's culinary knowledge, indeed, often sounds like Conquergood's "old wives' tales," as when she writes, "It was said that the seed that blossomed should be planted when the moon was light, whereas vegetables grown underground should be planted in the dark of the moon." Even less mystical examples underscore the ways in which Freetown cooking, now celebrated through Lewis's recipes, relies on sensory and embodied knowledge that is not—indeed, *cannot* be rendered—codified or objective. For example, "All the grownups had their own way of measuring, be it on a dime, nickel, teacup, or sifter, and their cakes were perfect." It is precisely this kind of intuitive and experiential knowledge that falls outside most recorded history.

Of course, oral historians, public historians, and even a growing crew of sensory historians work hard to write versions of history that recenter communal, embodied, or experiential knowledges. Gender and Africana studies scholar Tina Marie Campt writes: "The monumental is rooted in minute questions of the local, the 'little' details of the everyday, or what I will call the monumental minutiae of everyday lives. . . . We are often able to apprehend larger monumental social, political, and discursive systems of organization only through an examination of the minutia of the everyday and the local." Campt is talking about the importance of Afro-German testimony in understanding the Third Reich, but the same could be said for Lewis's importance in understanding the Reconstruction South, the Great Migration, American foodways, and all the rest. The tastes and smells of country cooking might not be minutiae but rather monuments.

A FEW WORDS ABOUT A STAMP

That Edna Lewis was, indeed, the most famous chef nobody had ever heard of was confirmed for me in 2014, when the U.S. Postal Service released a stamp in her honor, under the rubric of "Celebrity Chefs." The collection pairs Julia Child and James Beard with Joyce Chen and Felipe Rojas-Lombardi, a motley crew that smacks of tokenism even as it suggests a genuine attempt to celebrate the nation's multifaceted food cultures. Suddenly, my private pastime of rhapsodizing to unwitting friends and strangers about Lewis and her writing became a public project. But it felt like a step too far, "celebrity" an ill-fitting label for someone unassociated with the trappings of the celebrity chef, even those of her day. She was no Julia Child, with her television show and her consistently best-selling cookbooks.

To call Lewis a celebrity is, in some sense, an attempt to tidily resolve that which cannot be resolved—a tension between a Lewis who lingers and one who is lost, between a singular chef and the community of Freetown, between the Freetown of *The Taste of Country Cooking* and the Postal Service's stereotypical euphemism "down home." The stamp slips Lewis from chef to visual icon. Let me be clear: it is not that the celebrity status is unearned or that Lewis is unworthy of it, but that it sits uneasily. "By bringing such quintessential dishes as shrimp and grits and roast chicken to the plates of trendy restaurants, *Edna Lewis* (1916–2006) showed her fellow Americans the vitality of Southern cooking," offers the Postal Service.[2] In *On Racial Icons: Blackness and the Public Imagination*, Nicole Fleetwood argues: "The racial icon is widely consumed in the midst of persistent, quotidian, and extreme racial inequality and suffering. And thus, the racial icon presents a challenge. . . . *To stand apart* and *to stand for* are the jobs of the racial icon." So, too, in the case of remembering Miss Lewis. Her knowing smile circulates from San Diego to Portland, Maine, but her cookbooks were printed in limited editions. The last restaurant she helmed as chef, Brooklyn's Gage & Tollner, closed and turned into a TGI Friday's. "People's tastes change," shrugged Brooklyn Borough president Marty Markowitz after the Brooklyn institution closed in 2004. In the end, the stamp circulates within political economies of inequality that are not, indeed, *cannot* be recognized through the visual icon of Lewis's portrait. The stamp, instead, presents a flat Lewis, ignoring the complexity of her life and legacy.

To be memorialized on a stamp is itself to become a minor celebrity; the postal stamp is a form of public, historical icon making. The Celebrity Chef stamp series was intended to celebrate "early—and ardent—champions of trends that many foodies now take for granted." But Lewis isn't taken for granted: the image of Lewis reproduced on the stamp is an artist's rendering of one of very few photographs of her that has continued to circulate after her death. And so the image on the stamp does a lot of signifying—Lewis's elegance, her blackness, her black elegance. In her book *Troubling Vision: Performance, Visuality, and Blackness*, Fleetwood calls for non-iconicity, "an aesthetic and theoretical position that lessens the weight placed on the black visual to do so much . . . a movement away from the singularity and significance placed on instantiations of blackness to resolve that which cannot be resolved." Non-iconicity suggests that for an African American chef and writer, a one-inch-wide memorial may be a double-edged sword.

INTO THE ARCHIVES

I suppose it's worth saying that my relationship with Edna Lewis isn't completely random. Her name started cropping up with what felt like uncanny frequency while I was working on a dissertation on living southern chefs' uses of the past. Eventually, I thought I might write a chapter on Miss Lewis, and I went to the archive. I went to the Fales Archive at New York University, to be specific, to learn more about Edna Lewis's presence at Café Nicholson. As associated as Lewis is associated with the seasons, foods, and celebrations of African American life in Freetown, I had been surprised to learn that she spent most of her life and career in New York City. Flamboyant restaurateur Johnny Nicholson filled a rented apartment with European antiques and bric-a-brac and opened a restaurant with Lewis in 1949. Other fine dining establishments in the late 1940s and early 1950s had restrained dark wood paneling or intimate banquettes; Café Nicholson had a resident parrot. Downtown bohemians and the Upper East Side intelligentsia alike were delighted by Lewis's direct, French-accented cooking. But for displaced southerners, Lewis was a tie to home. Craig Claiborne was an early champion of Lewis's work before setting standards for American taste in the coming decades. Truman Capote kept asking for off-the-menu biscuits. Faulkner thought Lewis had trained in France. The juxtaposition between biscuits and béarnaise speaks volumes about the vast cultural and geographic distances between the Upper East Side and Freetown—especially in the late 1940s—and Lewis's unique ability to bridge both.[3] Lewis left after a few years, and in a *New York Times* write-up in 1982, Johnny Nicholson got the credit for the recipes Lewis prepared there.

The incongruous relationship between Lewis's career, albeit a short one, at a non-southern restaurant in New York and her mythic image as the queen of southern cooking continued to nag at me. Is it because the presence of the black Lewis in the kitchen tells an uncomfortable truth about culinary labor—that it is underpaid and often performed by women and/or people of color?[4] Is it because Lewis's career in New York troubles the stable and familiar cliché that to be from the South marks one as eternally southern? Or is it that Lewis herself felt a certain ambivalence about her career on the Upper East Side and preferred to be remembered by celebrating Freetown? I don't know, but I couldn't help digging to find out.

I pored through the Café Nicholson archives for a trace of her unmediated by Nicholson's carefully curated photo albums. A glimpse of her beyond her own cookbooks—heavily filtered as they were through a white, northern editor, a white northern publishing industry, and the white co-authors with whom several of her books were written. I was hoping there would be something of her: her handwriting, perhaps. But I found neither letters in her own hand nor a single candid photograph. Johnny Nicholson saved every review of the restaurant, though. Most mention the décor, Nicholson's personality, the star clientele. Some mention the food, noting its simplicity, the prix-fixe menu. Only one or two note the name of the chef and full partner in the restaurant, Edna Lewis. Torn out of a magazine is a photo of Lewis in which she is upstaged by the elbow of some marble statuary. It seems a fitting image, in fact, since the reviews that laud the simple goodness of the food usually do so only in contrast and relation to the flamboyance of the décor. Reviews claim that patrons can see into the kitchen when they enter—yet the meticulous photographs through which Nicholson details the interior do not show this view. For the "back of the house," there is a staff photograph and a ledger pad noting the waiters' hours. No Lewis. *New York Herald Tribune* reviewer Clementine Paddleford writes, "We saw Edna peering in from the kitchen just to see [the food's] effect on the guests and hear echoes of praise." Paddleford, herself a notable champion of American regional cooking, may have caught a glimpse of Lewis, but these stolen glances never entered the visual archive.

The Lewis of Café Nicholson is not an icon in full detail but a quick sketch in profile. For Lewis, Truman Capote ranks as high as shrimp and grits, as noted in her essay "What Is Southern?" But to the written record, Lewis is a cipher, a witness to the intrigues of high bohemia: never described by the reviewers as a participant but always cast as an outsider, "peering in." Even Lewis's obituary in the *Atlanta Journal Constitution* highlights how she "turned a tiny New York cafe into an artists' mecca where Garbo and Faulkner went to dine on oysters and chocolate soufflé." Lewis's importance to the restaurant is celebrated, not as central, but rather by virtue of the proximity it gave her to the long list of celebrity regulars, the likes of Howard Hughes, Salvador Dalí, Marlene Dietrich, Tennessee Williams, and Eleanor Roosevelt.

The invisibility of the black women who ran the show at Nicholson is only underscored by the visibility of a server named Jean Matlega. Nicholson remembers, in *Vanity Fair*, "The waitress, Jean Matlega, I hired because she was so white, a wonderful contrast to Edna, who was so black. You see, I was already choreographing the place." In this statement, Nicholson explicitly acknowledges the importance of the visual dramaturgy of Café Nicholson and Lewis's role in it as an iconic or even exotic object, rather than as a creatively invested partner in the business—indeed, on whose food the reputation of the restaurant ultimately rested. I keep stumbling across statements like this one, from the *Charleston Post and Courier* in 2016: "It astounded me that her recipe [for suckling pig] would be so extravagant, given her upbringing"—so racist I do a double-take.

Nicholson became a favorite of John Loring, the design director of Tiffany & Co. at the time, not because of the high society usually trotted out as evidence of the restaurant's excellence but in the way that "High Society met High Bohemia" (that's Gore Vidal writing in *Vanity Fair*). Loring wrote, "Food was not good in the 50s. Food was not discovered until the 1960s. But at Johnny's . . . oh, that chicken!" (again from *Vanity Fair*). One wonders just *who* did not discover good food until the 1960s; others, it seems, were eating "oh!"-worthy chicken all along. It is this impulse—the use of black culture, in this case, black cooking, to add value to white cultural capital—that requires reevaluation. Both the good food and much of the high bohemian flair for which Café Nicholson was noted was the unsung work of Edna Lewis. Rhetorics of discovery like Loring's foreground a white subject who gains cultural capital through the embodied knowledge of African Americans like Lewis, even if that fact isn't overtly stated. Of course, this phenomenon (some call it "Columbus-ing") isn't limited to Lewis or the 1960s. Nonetheless, it is her underrepresented labor that facilitated the transfer of good food between Freetown and its discovery in New York.

Lewis may be nearly invisible in the written record of the restaurant, but a turn toward the food itself offers a way to recoup Lewis's contributions to Café Nicholson and beyond. Even ten years after Lewis left the restaurant, Craig Claiborne praised her chocolate soufflé, served with small containers of whipped cream and chocolate sauce on the side for balance, as a "true triumph in the best culinary tradition"; Clementine Paddleford called it "light as a dandelion seed in the wind." Lewis cooked at Middleton Place outside Charleston for only a few years; the soufflé remained on the menu until 2013. These dishes and the feelings they stir up may in fact form a more lasting legacy than a box in a library. The secret to the soufflé, as it turns out, is in the timing—Lewis learned that it needed to be pulled from the oven early in order to survive the walk through Café Nicholson's dining room to the garden terrace. The secret, then, isn't something that can be found in an archive or even taught in a book—it's sensory and embodied. "I can't give you precise timing advice," Lewis cautions in *In Pursuit of Flavor*, "You'll have to figure it out on your own."

TOWARD A HISTORY OF PRESENCE:
ON THE SENSES

A move toward a history of presence—based on less stable, more performative modes of celebrating Miss Lewis—might also help more generally value and account for the lives of women and people of color outside dominant textual or visual frameworks of understanding. In reading and living with Lewis's books, I try not to read against the grain, per se, according to the old deconstructive credo. Instead, I follow intensities in the texts, hoping that they might lead toward a model of knowledge that resides in the body and sensory experience, toward a form of slowing down, of rehoning the lesser senses, moving away from the ease and speed of looking and reading toward a deeper engagement with Lewis's life and legacy. In her foreword to the book *Black Performance Theory*, D. Soyini Madison invites us to pay attention to the specific importance of African American cultural frameworks within broader concepts of performativity, writing, "As much as black performance theory is about politics, entangled within history and power, it is also an enterprise and labor of the senses. *The gift of performance theory is its distinct attention and indebtedness to the sensory* as the senses actualize temporality, enliven desire, and embrace beauty across the poetics of bodies and the aesthetics of their creations" (italics mine). Perhaps Lewis's cookbooks themselves hold the key to an ephemeral, sensory paradigm that might demonstrate the knowledge and cultural value of Lewis's work outside a dominant paradigm.

It's not just knowing when to pull a soufflé from the oven: Lewis's writing is full of evocative sensual description. In *In Pursuit of Flavor*, Lewis shares that the secret to her cakes lies not in the written recipe but knowing how to listen to sense when the cake is done. "You have to know the moment the cake is ready to be taken from the oven," she writes. "I use a cake tester but I also listen to the sounds of the cake after it has cooked for 25 minutes. When it is still baking and not yet ready, the liquids make bubbling noises. Just as the cake is done, the sounds become faint and weak, but they should disappear. Sometimes when I take a cake from the oven, I'll think the sounds are not quiet enough, and so I put the cake back for just a minute. And then all the sounds will be gone after that minute!"

Here, Lewis outlines a theory of embodied knowledge in which one can test the doneness of a cake by listening. The very ethos of southern food is characterized by ways of knowing bolstered by experience, as Sheila Ferguson's introduction to the late 1980s classic *Soul Food* makes explicit: "You cook by instinct. . . . These skills are hard to teach quickly. They must be felt, loving, and come straight from the heart and soul." If Lewis is a celebrity, let her be the celebrity of the inarticulable, or perhaps of the attempting-to-articulate-the-inarticulable and nearly succeeding. Reading through her cookbooks toward embodied, sensory experiences might help recapture the handwork, the embodied labor, and the communal, experiential knowledge that are at the heart of Lewis's legacy.

It is the singularity of these culinary experiences that renders their admission into language both precious and difficult. In *The Taste of Country Cooking*, Lewis describes the Christmases of her childhood evocatively, stressing both the rarity and the sensory and fleeting nature that makes these impressions remarkable: "The bowl of oranges, nuts, and raisin clusters was Christmas. There was no other time of year that house had that particular aroma. It seemed as if the warmth of the hearth fire extracted the oils from the aromatic Valencia oranges filling the house, mingling with the fragrance of pine needles, juniper berries, and holiday baking. . . . There was nothing like the plump, chewy dried raisins, with a sweet flavor mingling with the nuts—flavors we only experienced at Christmas. It is hard to describe the taste of those oranges."

Academics, this one among them, have spent a lot of time thinking through what it means that Lewis cannot describe the taste of those oranges. I've used the phrase "sensory and fleeting" above to describe this scene of smells and tastes, but another way to put it might be "affective," which points to the fact that these senses are not precisely definable or transferrable into feeling or emotion. It's hard to say whether this is a happy scene or a bittersweet one. It is, though, clearly special. In this way, Lewis's writing produces intensities, which "linguistic matter-of-factness" (that's theorist Brian Massumi) dampens. For Massumi, it's not language versus affect—language can work to heighten these vibratory, preconscious sensations (like the sensation of the mingling smells of Christmas and anticipation) or to mute them. For the former, Lewis's books are a master class. The Christmas example is one of many. Descriptions of sounds, tastes, and smells feature large in most of Lewis's writing. Lewis's sense of cooking as an experiential sensory act is clear from her recipes. On canning: "You can tell whether your jar is vacuum-sealed if the top is sucked down tight and makes a hollow sound when tapped; if it is not sealed, the top will bulge out slightly and it has a full, dull sound when tapped." No digital-read thermometers here. Tablespoons and teaspoons are replaced by coins' worth of baking powder or soda. Flour is measured by the palm. This is what Conquergood would call "old wives' tales" in contrasted to the "hard facts" of photographs or the written archive.[5] But looking through the script toward the sensation is the key to understanding the depths of Lewis's contribution to American food. These sensations are hard to quantify, yes. These sensations are also hard to represent: they're non-iconic (that these books lack photographs in favor of line drawings is no coincidence). These experience-based ways of cooking are also common, communal—making the iconic, scripted reception of Lewis as celebrity chef among New York celebrities all the more poignant . . . and all the odder. Something very different is going on here.

EDNA LEWIS REQUESTS THE
PLEASURE OF YOUR COMPANY

I write about food cultures from the vantage of performance studies because performance—with its emphasis on bodies, experience, memory, and other ephemeral intangibles—provides a mode of resistance to the stable legacy of text and the primacy of the visual over other senses. And so I find it quite interesting that there is an *actual* performance about Edna Lewis. As part of their annual symposium, the Southern Foodways Alliance commissions an original performance or art event on that year's theme for its Sunday morning program. In 2013, with the symposium's theme of "Women at Work," the show centered on Miss Lewis. Texas-based writer Shay Youngblood composed a solo performance about Miss Lewis on the topic titled "Edna Lewis Requests the Pleasure of Your Company." I admit that I would have loved to have kept Miss Lewis's company—I imagine many in the audience would have—to have found myself in the presence of the late woman herself.

The play begins with a monologue from Lewis's posthumously published essay "What Is Southern?" It then continues to trace her biography, combining reminiscences from *The Taste of Country Cooking* with the same interview snippets I dug up in my own archival research ("Truman Capote always came looking for biscuits" and "William Faulkner asked if I had trained in France"). The theatrical Miss Lewis holds up each of her books as she describes them, flipping through. The effect is primarily that of autobiographical lecture-performance—the way a John Adams or Thomas Jefferson impersonator might tour a school. The character explains his or her biography in an entertaining, palatable way but does not challenge this very mode of history (of remembrance) itself.

I had hoped for a glimpse of a more living Lewis, to look askance, through her texts and those *about* her, toward something more vital. But of course, Youngblood had to rely on the same slim texts and outsized myths as I did, as most of us who love her do. And in the end, the choice of a one-woman show reduced potential drama, conflict, multisidedness, or polyphony to monologue—the very form at which live theater approaches written text. In "Edna Lewis Requests the Pleasure of Your Company," the language of *The Taste of Country Cooking*—language that I find so enchanting and seductive in its affective dynamism—becomes itself rote, archival.

When introducing the play in Oxford, Mississippi, Youngblood referred to *The Taste of Country Cooking* as "her Bible for getting to know Lewis. I read everything I could find about her." Sound familiar? Although I returned from the Café Nicholson archive with a sheaf of photocopied articles about Johnny Nicholson, I felt empty-handed. As for Youngblood, it was *The Taste of Country Cooking* that I couldn't shake. It was Lewis's books, with their torn dust jackets and sweet potato stains, that I would sit and read in the kitchen while waiting for water to boil and roasts to roast,

that encouraged me to continue writing about Lewis as a way of searching for her. And just like the Edna Lewis depicted in Youngblood's play,
I riffled through these books for comfort—even held them—as though
being close to the material object might somehow bring me closer to the
smells and tastes of Freetown. I cooked from her books, brought pies to
new mothers and biscuits to potlucks. They became a part not only of my
life but of my community.

So *The Taste of Country Cooking*, and its transformation into the performance of "Edna Lewis Requests the Pleasure of Your Company," presents
a double bind. Live performance is used to re-create and celebrate existing
scripts, written texts that, themselves, assert the importance of the non-
verbal, non-iconic, the sensory and embodied. "My education was more
than reading and writing, it was how to set the table for every day," Youngblood's Lewis explains. "It was how to listen to the cake to know when
it is done." Yet this emphasis on the sensory and embodied is lacking in
the form of the biographical monologue and the relatively conservative
staging. The play concludes with Lewis affirming that she would like to be
remembered for her food, family, and friends. What she will be remembered for by most of us, of course, are her books. But at the heart of the
books is something that language can't capture, and the dominance of the
written word threatens, even, to erase.

THE MELANCHOLIA OF COUNTRY COOKING

Listen: it feels awkward telling you about my imaginary relationship with
Edna Lewis. I'd like to be able to create a space where Lewis's true self—
whatever that might be like—can be seen and felt, but the icon flattens
and the archive remains silent; in the end, it remains a one-sided affair. It's
more awkward still because there are people who had *real* relationships
with Lewis. Like Scott Peacock, Edna Lewis's cooking and writing partner
and, in the end, her companion. His description of his own relationship
with Edna Lewis after her death is surprisingly familiar to me in my own,
much smaller, and fainter grief. Laura Shapiro profiled Peacock in *Gourmet*
in 2008 about his life after Lewis. Describing the scene, she wrote, "More
food comes out: Pimento cheese, grits with shrimp paste, fried okra, plum
buckle—everything bursting with personality and clear, rich flavors. He
had eaten these things all his life, but not until he met Miss Lewis did he
start to take them seriously. 'She is part of everything,' he says. 'It is mar-
velous in a weird way, the dynamic relationship you have with someone

who is dead. It continues to grow. I have a breathing, living relationship with her at this point.' He gazes affectionately at the food on the table, seeing beyond it. 'I miss her incredibly. What helps is making biscuits.'"

So what do we want from Lewis? What do *I* want from Lewis? In mourning, we move past grief, but in melancholia, we become attached to grieving, caught in a feedback loop. Critical race theorist Anne Anlin Cheng sees this melancholic process as a good metaphor for the way that race works in America. She writes, "White American identity and its authority is secured through the melancholic introjection of racial others that it can *neither fully relinquish nor accommodate* and whose ghostly presence nonetheless guarantees its centrality" (italics mine). That is, white America understands itself by attaching itself to racial others who are never really inside, never really outside. These racial others are central but ghostly.

In the margins of Cheng's book, *The Melancholy of Race*, I have scribbled, countless times, *Lewis. Lewis. Lewis.* But this concept of melancholia has helped me see what Shay Youngblood and the chefs I interviewed might have been talking about this whole time: Lewis is not a haunting ghost but a living one. Her recipes demand not that we mourn but that we listen.

Often, racial justice is conceptualized in terms of grievances—rightly so, in a political context in which heartbreaking injustices are commonplace, even daily occurrences. But Cheng offers an alternate model, putting griev*ing*, not griev*ances*, at the heart of racial identity. Which is to say, it's not so much concrete acts of political redress as it is thinking of race as a kind of melancholy that America can't fully know and certainly can't shake. Not melancholy in the sense of sadness but rather, in Cheng's words, "as a *sign* of rejection and as a psychic *strategy* in response to that rejection" (italics hers). A deep irony, a paradox: Edna Lewis, having left New York to become the executive chef of the former plantation Middleton Place, living in a converted rice mill where slaves once toiled. What that must have meant to her. The archive at Café Nicholson marks the myriad ways in which Lewis has been rejected from the official record. Freetown, too, lies outside of textbook American history, the rhythms and rituals of African American farm life a mere footnote. At the same time, Lewis traffics as iconic celebrity; we have apotheosized Lewis, given her titles that feel surprisingly out of place in my contemporary mouth: she is a doyenne, grande dame, African queen. Melancholia has two faces. Lewis is dead, but she is decidedly not gone.

Most of the time, I cook by feel. Some recipes, I've memorized—the granola I make every few weeks, the proportions for quiche. Other things I make so often, I've taped recipes to the walls of my kitchen, cribbed in shorthand onto fading Post-It notes. It's interesting, then, that my relationship with Miss Lewis is so different. I always, *always* check the recipe, and I leave the book on the counter as I cook. Maybe it's because I usually end up slowing down, rereading the whole chapter, carried away by the sensory richness of scenes Lewis so tenderly describes. Or maybe it's simpler: because I want her beside me. It doesn't work. But still — almost.

NOTES

1. Which, to reiterate, is why it is so important to put women and people of color into the archive, which might seem an old-fashioned, revisionist activity, because for better or worse, the written record is now online and editable. One might — as Stephen Colbert did on his TV show *The Colbert Report* to prove this very point — delete all references to George Washington owning slaves from Wikipedia, the most often-consulted, public, and free historical record. "Here only what is written is understood."

2. The description of what I presume are meant to be Café Nicholson and Gage & Tollner as "trendy restaurants" shows a conflation of Lewis's own food and cooking with the contemporary language of freshness and hipness, as I expand on below.

3. Faulkner's compliment takes on new meaning now that many award-winning haute-Southern chefs indeed *have* trained in France or Italy but was virtually unthinkable in the 1950s.

4. A line of argument I am delighted to see repeated in John T. Edge's "Debts of Pleasure," reproduced in this volume.

5. Of course, I don't mean to uncritically celebrate this folksy outside to literacy without first considering the lived stakes of illiteracy for countless African Americans long after the end of slavery. As Lewis notes directly after describing the sensory experience of knowing whether a seal has correctly set, "I could sense a great feeling of satisfaction on my mother's face when she had reached the point of placing the labels on the jars after the completion of each batch of preserves and jellies."

Looking for Edna

PATRICIA E. CLARK

—⁃⊱⊰⁃—

My introduction to Edna Lewis came by way of the cookbook she wrote with Scott Peacock, *The Gift of Southern Cooking: Recipes and Revelations from Two Great Southern Cooks*, one day while browsing in a bookstore in 2003, when their book was published. My time with the book was short and my assessment was, perhaps, too harsh. The photo of Peacock, with his arms wrapped around Lewis, stopped me before I could get into the book properly. There was something about the image that struck me as odd, as most staged photographs often do. I pressed on, turning the pages, and there, in the epigraph, were the infamous words uttered by none other than Scarlett O'Hara in Margaret Mitchell's novel, *Gone with the Wind*: "As God is my witness, I'll never be hungry again."

The reference to *Gone with the Wind* unfortunately colored my initial reading of *The Gift of Country Cooking*, especially Peacock's role in its writing. Though coauthored, the voice is Peacock's, which suggests that his and Lewis's relationship was one not of parity but rather one of patronage. (Lewis was ailing at the time of the writing and publication of this book. Peacock became her caregiver.) The voice of the "we, Southerners," in *The Gift of Country Cooking* seemed to me a bit disingenuous, a bitter pill to swallow in that this "we" elides a past and a present that are still, very much, racially divided between black and white. Despite my uneasiness about this particular book, I imagined that Lewis—the person and the subject—was somehow caught in this curious tangle of associations attached to the South and its foodways.

What drew me back into reading Lewis was *The Taste of Country Cooking*, a book that continues to fascinate and to raise many questions for me. I confess to finding it difficult to fully apprehend Lewis in it; this book more so than her first, *The Edna Lewis Cookbook*, foregrounds Lewis's southern past, her early life in Freetown, in what can be considered a food memoir. In reading it, I am reminded of what Maya Angelou felt after reading Zora Neale Hurston's 1942 autobiography, *Dust Tracks on a Road*. In the foreword to the 1996 HarperCollins edition of that book, Angelou praises the fact that Hurston is the author of her own autobiography rather than what had typically been the case through much of the nineteenth and early twentieth centuries — nonblack authors writing for and about black people. However, despite the success of *Dust Tracks*, Angelou finds it "puzzling" that, given the racial climate of the first half of the twentieth century, Hurston "does not mention one unpleasant racial incident" in her account of life in the all-black incorporated town of Eatonville, Florida.

Indeed, everyday life for black people, then and now, did not necessarily consist of a relentless barrage of racial incidents — chores were done, children nurtured and reared, hearth and home happily maintained. And life in all-black towns and communities, like Eatonville — that sprung up throughout the Midwest and South after the Civil War — offered newly freed blacks opportunities to become self-sufficient. In addition, these towns were sanctuaries of sorts, offering some respite from the racial segregation enforced in white-governed towns and cities.

However, blacks were not entirely protected from racial discrimination and violence in these majority and all-black communities. Any misstep of the Jim Crow–style social etiquette that occurred brought to the fore the ugly divide between black and white. Some communities, like Rosewood, Florida — not far from Hurston's Eatonville — were burned to the ground by white terrorists determined to prevent black people from acquiring too much economic and political power and to ensure, in effect, that they stayed in their "place."

Though not daily occurrences, these flashpoints of racial discrimination and violence that punctuated the day-to-day existence of black folks disturbed the peace, safety, and sanctity of family and community life. It is these incidents that Angelou questions in reading Hurston and causes her to wonder just who is Hurston's audience? "There is . . . a strange distance in the book. Certainly the language is true and the dialogue authentic, but the author stands between the content and the reader."

In reading Lewis's *Taste of Country Cooking*, I share a similar view to Angelou's reading of Hurston's autobiography. Lewis as subject and author of her own work is rendered with an intimate familiarity and a peculiar anonymity all at once; her book comforts while it unsettles. The parallels between Hurston's and Lewis's early childhoods are striking, but not surprising. Like Hurston in Eatonville, Lewis lived a happy life in Freetown, according to what she records in her cookbook. Despite what is described as idyllic, it is clear that life was hard in Freetown. The labor of cultivating, harvesting, and preparing food, season after season, was not easy work. Add to this the anecdotes that Lewis provides about her ancestors—detailing what it means to be black, living in this place at this time—from her grandmother's backbreaking labor as a brick mason to the relative who was exceptionally privileged to attend a boarding school. Even more revealing in Lewis's account is what is *not* explicitly stated. One has to read and construct the nuanced black historical narrative that Lewis offers between the lines—that is, if one chooses to go there.

However, one can conveniently choose to bypass the race-specific historical and cultural contexts and to luxuriate in a romance of a South that is benign and devoid of the controversies of slavery, that peculiar institution, and of Jim Crow segregation. Indeed, the ways in which *The Taste of Country Cooking* allows some readers a pass at some of the unsavory elements of America's racial legacy might be one of its ironic achievements. Even as the cookbook allows entry into a bucolic and a wholesome American past, through the many specificities of the food, the land, the region, and the people, *The Taste of Country Cooking* invites a dash of speculation along with the nostalgia it generously serves up. I do not necessarily consider this "strange distance" to be a bad thing, but rather, I think, it serves to complicate the universality of the nostalgia for the past of which Lewis presumably writes.

How to account for this distance? What is called into question here, for one, is the very act of writing as not a singular activity but rather a collective one. Although Lewis is clearly the author of her own work, her voice is interrupted, mediated in ways that render her part of the collective imagination of an American past of which she is often at odds. To put it another way, *The Taste of Country Cooking* represents a multiplicity of voices that feed dominant and prevailing archetypes of African Americans that compete against Lewis's signature and particular voice as an African American female cook. Hence, the Edna Lewis represented in *The Taste of Country Cooking* is scripted by a chorus of others and by Lewis "herself." Lewis, as subject and as author of this book, is understood, simultaneously, in the general (historiographical) sense and in the particular (autobiographical) sense.

In the general sense, Lewis, as an African American female cook, is cast as both exceptional and anonymous. Lewis's reputation as exceptional encases *The Taste of Country Cooking* since its publication: she carries the title of "chef" and is often referred to as "doyenne of southern cuisine." The jacket cover of the thirtieth anniversary edition boasts that the book has become, over the years, "a Great Southern Classic." These labels highlight the distance between the everyday black female cook in the kitchen and the chef. Add to this her association with the famous clientele that dined at Café Nicholson, including Truman Capote, who pined after her biscuits; the many awards and accolades she received in her lifetime; her cofounding of the Society for the Revival and Preservation of Southern Food with Peacock; and the essays, articles, and documentaries about her, and Lewis's legacy has been permanently etched for generations of cooks, most especially black women and men who have not been recognized for their singular contributions to U.S. cuisines.

Lewis's exceptional status plays against and within the legions of anonymous black women who labor in the kitchens and are unknown, in the particular, but are known, ironically, en masse. The reputations of these anonymous women precede them and are crystallized as icons and mascots—they are named as Aunt_____ (fill-in-the-blank), as members of the legion of black women whose labor marks them. These icons and mascots help fuel and perpetuate feelings of nostalgia for the life and customs of the old, antebellum South. Rememorializing Mammy and Aunt_____ in perpetuity provides an anodyne for many in all regions of the United States, especially the progeny of the Old South who continue to embrace the ideas of the so-called Lost Cause. The iconography of the black female cook grants these women an identity, albeit a collective one that robs them of their individual and singular contributions to the American food landscape. The pervasive images of black aunties and mammies that dot the food landscape (on food products, on postcards, on kitchen utensils and other objects and ephemera) mark both their presence and their absence. She does not have a name of her own.

That Lewis is named and is called chef is a departure. Although she has become a figurehead for countless, anonymous black women in the kitchen, Lewis's designation as chef places her in a different category—singular and set apart from the others by fate and talent. From the late 1980s to the present day, historians, scholars, chefs, and writers such as Doris Witt, Jessica Harris, Psyche Williams-Forson, Michael W. Twitty, Toni Tipton-Martin, Scott Alves Barton, and a growing list of others have worked toward making visible black people's imprint on U.S. culinary histories. Although this lack of recognition and inclusion is being redressed in their scholarship and food writing, the projects of identifying erstwhile anonymous cooks and establishing a list of black "firsts" call attention to just how many remain in the background, unnamed and unspecified.

The gap created between those black women cooks who are known versus those who are not known is determined by fate (or luck—as some might have it) to a degree, but largely by cultural and ideological forces that allow singular and exceptional black subjects to emerge at particular junctures in history. We know Edna Lewis, but also we now know Abby Fisher and her book, *What Mrs. Fisher Knows about Southern Cooking*, published in 1881, and Malinda Russell and her book, *A Domestic Cook Book: Containing a Careful Selection of Useful Receipts for the Kitchen*, published in 1866, and more. But are the full force, impact, and complexities of African and African American peoples' culinary contributions felt and accepted in mainstream circles? Even today, the answer is, not often enough. What is clear is that the ennobling and necessary enterprise of identifying and naming our black culinary forebears is not fully divorced from its troubling past.

This play between Lewis's exceptionalism and the iconic anonymity of the black female cook is brilliantly exemplified in John T. Edge's essay "Debts of Pleasure" (reprinted in this volume), in which he questions the identity of the black woman in Karl Bissinger's famous photo "Salad Days" (1949). The image, whose composition is reminiscent of Édouard Manet's 1863 painting *Le Dejeuner sur l'herbe* (The Luncheon on the Grass), shows a black woman wearing an apron and carrying a tray with a teapot atop. Obviously, she is serving the people, sitting around a table, who have just finished lunch in a garden courtyard behind a restaurant. The place—Café Nicholson on New York City's Upper East Side—and the people—movers and shakers of that current artistic and cultural scene: Tanaquil Le Clercq, Donald Windham, Buffie Johnson, Tennessee Williams, and Gore Vidal. All are identified except the black woman with the tray and the teapot.

What is interesting about this omission is that the composition of the photo begs for the black woman's identification. In fact, Edward Weintraut, then of Macon, Georgia, wrote a letter to the editor responding to Gore Vidal's 2007 article in *Smithsonian* magazine, titled "Salad Days." Vidal wrote of one of Bissinger's photos of Café Nicholson's garden, nostalgic for the restaurant's heyday as a meeting place for the bohemian elite; Weintraut wondered why the black woman in the photo was neither identified nor acknowledged by Vidal. The composition of the photo is triangular, with the members of the lunch party on each side of the shape, receding in the frame to the apex, where the black woman is positioned.

Patricia E. Clark

The viewer is forced to reckon with this figure. Who is she? All facts point to the possibility of Lewis being the person in the photo. At the time, she was the chef at Café Nicholson in New York City; Lewis was "known" by many of the notable and famous patrons who ate at the restaurant, the likes of Truman Capote, Katherine Anne Porter, Tennessee Williams, and other transplants with a yen for southern-by-way-of-Virginia-style home cooking. (Though Lewis's and Johnny Nicholson's idea about the type of food at the restaurant when it opened was "truck driver," not southern.) But it certainly is conceivable that she was not the sole black woman in the kitchen at the restaurant.

Edge discovers that the black woman, who was "not-Edna," had a name and a reputation. Her name was Virginia Reed, a waitress who, according to Peacock's secondhand account, was a "character." Lewis writes about Reed with greater affinity in *The Edna Lewis Cookbook*, mentioning her uncanny sense of time in determining when "to set the soufflés in the oven for each table." It seems that Reed was more than a waitress, given how indispensable she was to Lewis, who, at the time, "was unaware of all the supposed pitfalls of soufflé making." With Virginia Reed identified as the black woman in Bissinger's photo, what else do we know about her? Where and how did she develop her knack for timing soufflés? Did she cook on that one stove and oven at Café Nicholson? The questions persist and are relentless.

Along with this general sense — the historical and cultural narratives and contexts that determine who Lewis is — there is she, as author, writing about herself in the particular. Lewis writing her autobiographical text is not a singular act but is, once again, part of a collective — an editor, a recipe developer, a photographer, an illustrator, and countless others who are involved in the production of the book. This collective frames how Lewis's particular account of her life and her cooking are subsequently read and recirculated through other media by diverse audiences for ostensibly different purposes. The production of the book and the attendant editorial and other decisions might be yet other reasons for the "strange distance" I read in *The Taste of Country Cooking*.

A closer look at the writing and production of Lewis's first two cookbooks — *The Edna Lewis Cookbook* and *The Taste of Country Cooking* — alongside an earlier cookbook I mentioned, Fisher's *What Mrs. Fisher Knows about Old Southern Cooking*, might help to illustrate the point I make here.

Abby Fisher, author of one of the nineteenth-century cookbooks discovered in the twentieth century, was encouraged by a group of women in San Francisco to put down, in writing, her prize-winning condiment recipes. Fisher, who could not read or write, had to dictate the recipes to the women who then transcribed the manuscript for the book. With this transcription came the introduction of errors; the women heard one thing and transcribed what they thought they heard. One such mistake is in the recipe for Jumberlie, which, in reading the ingredients in the recipe, is clearly one for jambalaya. The woman transcribing the recipe did not understand Fisher's words. This error and others in print make apparent the disconnection between what Fisher *knew* and what the women, recording her in good faith, *thought* they heard and knew *about* her.

Lewis, unlike Fisher, could read and write eloquently enough to write, with Evangeline Peterson, her first cookbook, *The Edna Lewis Cookbook*. The book was born out of years of conversations between Lewis and Peterson, who urged Lewis to write it. Lewis, bored from convalescing at home with a broken leg, having recently been forced to close Café Nicholson, "suddenly recalled our forgotten conversations about a cookbook. As soon as I could maneuver about on crutches, I called Evangeline and we met to talk about the possibility of our writing together."

Lewis's imprimatur in her first cookbook is apparent; she writes in a style that speaks to her love of cooking and her friendship with Peterson. She divulges information about herself, her background from the beginning to her life to New York City. Though sparse in autobiographical details, in the book, Lewis gives readers a taste of who she is and what her passions are. We learn about a bit of her life with her husband, Steven Kingston—they raised quail on a farm in New Jersey. Living in Harlem, she writes that she is upset and disturbed by what she sees around her. However abbreviated, one gets the sense of how her entire life moves forward organically, with a glibness that is as facile as it is friendly with the facts and, certainly, not stuck in one particular place and time. The "we" she evokes in her recipes points to the warm camaraderie she enjoyed with Peterson and others, cooking in a kitchen together—be it at home or at Café Nicholson. The genesis and the writing of the manuscript for *The Edna Lewis Cookbook* seems to reflect the ebb and flow of her life then.

The Edna Lewis Cookbook was on its way to the printer when Judith Jones urged Lewis to write another cookbook. In the preface to the thirtieth edition of *The Taste of Country Cooking*, Jones recalls the conception of the manuscript with Lewis. Peterson bowed out of this project, leaving the task solely to Lewis. Jones wanted Lewis to write a book that focused on her childhood in Freetown. When Lewis presented Jones with a draft of the book, Jones was dismayed and thought the voice "inauthentic," "not-Edna." Jones began the process again by talking, face-to-face, with Lewis, "asking questions and prodding for more detail," with the hope of pulling out a more authentic rendering of her voice and her childhood in rural Virginia. Jones heard what she wanted to hear during this session, and she sent Lewis away to write it all down "while we were still giddy with her total recall." Lewis returned with pages, handwritten on yellow, legal-sized notepads, which met Jones's approval. The result of Jones's prodding and Lewis's writing is the book *The Taste of Country Cooking*, her first publication with Knopf.

Jones's shepherding of Lewis's writing process raises several questions regarding what happened to the handwritten pages that were edited, published, and mechanically reproduced as a book. What did her pen strokes reveal? What landed on the pages of her legal pads that did not make it into print? No doubt, Lewis's recipes were aided by the work of a recipe developer. Lewis, reputedly, cooked by instinct, trial and error—or at least her method was hands-on, as evidenced by the recipes and instructions in *The Edna Lewis Cookbook*. Interestingly, Lewis's manuscript for *The Taste of Country Cooking* was produced in a similar fashion to Abby Fisher's; both Fisher's and Lewis's texts and words were subject to the ideals of the women capturing their respective voices. What the women in San Francisco heard, in Fisher's case, and what Jones read (and heard), in Lewis's case, was printed, mechanically reproduced, effectively hewing their particular identities to fit collective archetypal (and stereotypical) ideas of black women cooks. Fisher's book bears some witness to the errors in transcription and poetic license taken by the writers. However, with Lewis's *Taste of Country Cooking*, one wonders what ended up on the cutting room floor, excised out of those yellow legal notepads, for reasons that may or may not be discovered or known.

In an October 28, 2015, *New York Times Magazine* article (reprinted in this volume), Francis Lam writes of *The Taste of Country Cooking*: "It stands as an exemplar of American food writing, a complex, multilayered, artistic, and even subtly subversive document. And it stands on the other side of a cruel tradition in cookbooks from the first half of the 20th century, one in which black domestic cooks often had their recipes recorded and written by their white employers, who tended not to flatter the help in the process." I agree with the "complex, multilayered, artistic, and even subtly subversive" assignation to Lewis's book; however, I would add that the "cruel tradition" of mammy books and Lewis's account share the same sense of nostalgia that either casts blacks eating and cooking food pejoratively or overcorrects the stereotype by positively lionizing the black cook in the kitchen. That is, Lewis's book is not entirely "on the other side," as the sense of nostalgia it evokes makes room for both the black female chef and the mammy.

That *The Taste of Country Cooking* harks back to early cookbooks written by black women *and* to pamphlets and books written by white authors in blackface and drag is significant and reflected by what contemporary readers might read or see in *The Taste of Country Cooking* and how the multiple interpretations of it fall along cross-sections of race, gender, socioeconomic status, among other positions. The common ground for all readers of *The Taste of Country Cooking*, though, is its evocation of a time past that is as romantic as Marcel Proust's madeleine cake reverie. However, the realities of the past bring to bear a more complex and divided embrace of it. These divided and elective affinities are evinced in the final cut of Lewis's account of her life in *The Taste of Country Cooking*.

Lewis's autobiographical account of her life is situated within historical and cultural contexts that are both affective and factual. By this I mean that *The Taste of Country Cooking* compels readers to feel a particular way about the past while at the same time basing these feelings in real places, people, and events. What is indeed interesting about the book is the way in which the affective pasts, for Jones and Lewis, don't exactly marry up. What is heard or remembered (or known) by each is rhetorically at odds in this book, hence the "strange distance" between the book and the reader, with Lewis standing squarely in the middle.

Consider the place, Freetown, yet again, as an example. In the book's thirtieth anniversary edition, whatever historical traumas and hardships Lewis's people experienced as founding members of Freetown is glossed over, first by Judith Jones in her preface and then again by Alice Waters in her foreword. Waters praises Lewis's work and her depiction of her "idyllic" childhood, her bringing "her lost paradise of Freetown back to life." In *The Taste of Country Cooking*, one is comforted by Lewis's snapshots of Freetown framed by Jones — the recipes and the dishes, the painstakingly loving ways in which hogs are butchered and smoked, chickens are killed, and small fowl are hunted, murdered and dressed for dinner. This image is a far cry from the killing scene in the kitchen that Alice B. Toklas records in her cookbook where she is forced to murder a carp "in the first, second, and third degree." Instead, readers imagine the willing sacrifice these animals

Patricia E. Clark

have made for the sustenance of the entire community of Freetown. That there is no blood spilled carelessly in Lewis's account of the South during a period of hostility and violence against black people.

Simply calling Freetown a "farming community" misses the point of the larger significance of the community's name and its place in history. How Lewis describes Freetown in *The Edna Lewis Cookbook* compared to in *The Taste of Country Cooking* is instructive here. In her first cookbook, Lewis writes: "I was born in Freetown in Orange County, Virginia. This small community was named by the freed slaves who had settled there after the Civil War. My grandfather, who had been one of the founders of Freetown, lived in the center of the village, and my parents, brothers, sisters, and I lived there with him." In contrast, Lewis writes in *The Taste of Country Cooking*: "I grew up in Freetown, Virginia, a community of farming people. *It wasn't really a town. The name was adopted* because the first residents had all been freed from chattel slavery and they wanted to be known as a town of Free People" (italics mine).

The Freetown in Lewis's first book is its own, distinct "village," intentionally named in an active and deliberate way *after* the Civil War. This declaration of the emancipation of her people in this place and time attests to the pride Lewis feels and knows about her forebears. There is a direct connection to the history of black towns established throughout the South and West — such as Nicodemus, Kansas; Boley, Oklahoma; and Mound Bayou, Mississippi. Promoters of these towns, like Benjamin "Pap" Singleton, who escaped from slavery in Tennessee in the 1840s, traveled and distributed pamphlets and posters in black communities to convince prospective settlers that emigration and segregation were the only viable solutions to America's race problem. Many of the towns established became incorporated; and for virtually all, the principal source of revenue came from farming, the one skill that was in abundance among freed blacks.

Freetown, which shares its aspirational name with other Freetowns across the globe — namely Freetown, Sierra Leone, and Freetown, Jamaica — connects to a broader history and community of people across the African diaspora, stirring in the same pot, adding their own ingredients to this global freedom gumbo. And this history was likely known to Lewis's forebears post–Civil War. Why, then, is Freetown's status as "village" denied in *The Taste of Country Cooking*? Why does Lewis redact her statement from *The Edna Lewis Cookbook* and, instead, declare that Freetown "wasn't really a town"?

Indeed, editorial decisions play a hand in this framing of Freetown in

The Taste of Country Cooking. In addition to Jones declaring Freetown a farming community in her preface in both editions, the book's marketing materials reinforce this image of the town as a bucolic paradise that "jes' grew" without much intent; from the front cover of the first edition: "She evokes the tantalizing aromas of a farm kitchen. She brings back the fresh, natural tastes of the wonderful cooking she was raised on in Virginia"; on the back cover of the first edition, as well as the jacket flap of the thirtieth anniversary edition: "In recipes and reminiscences equally delicious, Edna Lewis celebrates the uniquely American country cooking she grew up with some fifty years ago in a small Virginia Piedmont farming community that had been settled by freed slaves." While these blurbs are somewhat descriptive, it is difficult to get a sense of Freetown the place and what it means, really *means*, that slaves "settled" there.

It is important that there is a "village"; and Lewis evokes the village of Freetown despite its not being labeled as such in *The Taste of Country Cooking.* Lewis notes pride and cooperation as hallmarks of family and community in Freetown. Family is central to Lewis's memories of food practices there. The labor required to cultivate, harvest, process, and cook food does not seem thankless. Giving thanks for bountiful harvests, good foods, and the land and hands that made all possible is the soul of the food—the true antecedent of the ways black folks have traditionally eaten and lived. She notes how each and every member of the families that made up the entire community of Freetown was valued. "Everyone shared in the work," even the children. The cross-generational respect and honor each person received had a lasting and profound effect on Lewis: "I guess that is why I have always felt that the people of Freetown were very special. They showed such love and affection for us as children, at the same time asking something of us, and they knew how to help each other so that the land would thrive for all." This sense of cooperation and community is not unique to Freetown but was characteristic of many all-black towns and segregated sections of many urban and rural areas scattered throughout the South.

Given her love for the people of the "village" of Freetown, one wonders why there is no moving tribute in recognition of the death of her parents. In *The Taste of Country Cooking,* she does not hint at any trauma she experienced losing her parents, both before she turned eighteen years of age—first, her father at age nine and then her mother at age sixteen. What she recalls, then, covers a short time, barely two decades. One can certainly assume that the adults who "showed such love and affection" toward the children included her parents. Lewis does mention "Mother" in some of her recipes, but we don't get too close to either parent in this regard. Lewis writes movingly about the passing of the founders, her grandparents, her surviving siblings, and herself: "Since we are the last of the original families, with no children to remember and carry on, I decided that I wanted to write down just exactly how we did things when I was growing up in Freetown that seemed to make life so rewarding." This statement is striking in that Lewis suggests that this is end of the "village"—there are "no children to remember and carry on"—despite acknowledging her niece Nina Williams as her faithful transcriber and typist in this book. Lewis not only has the "village," but she also has close family members in addition to the book itself. Why, then, is Lewis cast as orphaned in this way, abandoned not only by parents, whose loss is not fully captured, but also by others—generations past and future? Wasn't Lewis prodded by Jones to give greater detail on her particular relationship with her parents? Or was she encouraged to avoid the painful details of their loss altogether? What of the family matters that tie Lewis's past to her current legacy?

That Lewis's parents are not as important to the story of Freetown as the founders is interesting, in that this piece of her affective reality as a child is not regarded. In light of editorial decisions made in *The Taste of Country Cooking*, there is something to be said about the ways in which the "founding" narrative takes precedent over the "foundling" narrative. Or, perhaps more accurately in the case of Lewis, the foundling story is reconstructed in ways that repress what she might have *really* felt. Instead, her life is portrayed as one of almost complete joy and bliss.

Hers was a simple life, according to *The Taste of Country Cooking*. But simple is not what it seems. The recipes and the autobiographical anecdotes that make up the entire book, in concert, contribute to a familiarity and a sense of not-knowingness about Lewis. Consider the language that surrounds the book: the countless readers who identify with the work wherever they are located who assign a universality of experience to Lewis's account that unintentionally—even innocently, I would say—elides the specific historical time and place of the book. The word "simple" and its derivations predominate the several descriptions of *The Taste of Country Cooking*.

In her blurb on the back cover, M. F. K. Fisher writes that Lewis's "book is fresh and pure, the way clean air can be, and water from a deep spring. It is in the best sense *American*, with an innate dignity, and freedom from prejudice and hatred, and it is reassuring to be told again that although we may have lost some of this *simplicity*, it still exists here . . . and may be attainable again" (second italics mine). In his blurb, James Beard writes with a similar sense of longing. He states how her book "makes me want to go right into the kitchen and start cooking. . . . It's a delicately drawn picture of an interesting period when American cooking was a series of family events, and I found such honest satisfaction in the *simple* delights of Miss Lewis's descriptions and recipes" (italics mine). Waters writes in the foreword to the thirtieth edition of *The Taste of Country Cooking*: "Thanks to this book, the glories of an American tradition worthy of comparison to the most evolved cuisines on earth, a tradition of *simplicity* and purity and sheer deliciousness that is only possible when food tastes like what it is, from a particular place, at a particular point in time" (italics mine).

The "simple delights" and "simplicity" of life and foods that Fisher and others read in Lewis's account present a particular view of America that belies the full body of experiences Lewis and her family encountered in a community of newly freed blacks in an all-black town in the South. Also, I wonder what "best sense" of the American and of America that Fisher reads in Lewis's book; if this is the best sense of the nation and its citizenry, this position is hardly one of simplicity, but rather of a complexity that one dare not utter, especially in the context of readings that insist on a pure, unadulterated simplicity in Lewis's book. Echoes of Langston Hughes's "I, Too" are heard here, his "best sense" of the America/n that was not fully realized during Lewis's childhood:

> I, too, sing America.
>
> I am the darker brother.
> They send me to eat in the kitchen
> When company comes,
> But I laugh,
> And eat well,
> And grow strong.
>
> Tomorrow,
> I'll be at the table
> When company comes.
> Nobody'll dare
> Say to me,
> "Eat in the kitchen,"
> Then.

Patricia E. Clark

"The dignity and freedom from hatred" that Fisher reads in *The Taste of Country Cooking* gives one the ironic sense, again, that she, Fisher, is keenly aware of the place blacks have occupied both historically and in her and Lewis's time, a place that is mutually understood. No racial strife or radicalism is mentioned in explicit detail in Lewis's book, though the historical record tells us that the time and region in which she lived were turbulent.

Questions punctuate this past by what we learn about Lewis post-Freetown—in the snippets of information offered in the preface and foreword to *The Taste of Country Cooking*. After the death of her parents, Lewis moved to Washington, D.C., and then to New York City, as she references in the preface and foreword to the book. In New York, Lewis met and marries Steven Kingston. Curiously, we learn nothing about her marriage to Kingston, a radical member of the Communist Party, or of Lewis's own ties to the party, especially her work on the *Daily Worker*—in which she is variously referred to as a typesetter or a writer for the paper in other sources. In their first meeting in 1972, Jones describes Lewis "as a regal presence" in her African-style dress. The African dress was Lewis's signature style beginning in the 1970s (or thereabouts) and was likely a deliberate choice, a visible, sartorial nod to her African ancestry and connection to all the Freetowns, everywhere, current and past.

To be considered, too, is the period in which *The Taste of Country Cooking* was written: the 1970s. Did she identify with the movements of this turbulent decade in the United States—if not the politics and tactics per se, then their resonances with the self-sufficiency and pride touted by black nationalists? Her stories—her personal tale, memories interwoven throughout the book—belie more than they reveal. Although she has come to symbolize all things that are "authentically" southern, the other legacy that belongs to her and her people is a history of reticence and reluctance not to tell all their business to white folks.

Edna Lewis, indeed, stands between the content and her readers. I think this is okay, because what she has left us with is a conversation and many questions. We don't have her to ask these questions of, but what she has written down (or not) in her books, what she has said to a body of witnesses, and what she has given her people—her kin and everyone—continues to stand the test of time. Vidal advised all to study Bissinger's famous photo. I agree. Study it, and study it hard. And read Lewis's cookbooks. Cook her recipes. For in these, you might find out what Edna Lewis *really* knew.

PART THREE

At Table with Miss Lewis Today

I Had, of Course,
Heard about Her

An Interview with Nathalie Dupree, April 14, 2016

SARA B. FRANKLIN

Sara: Can you start by telling me how and when in your trajectory you started focusing on southern food?

Nathalie: Oh my. Well, that's pretty easy for me. I mean, I started focusing on it, really, when I was in England in '69–'70 because I started missing the food. And I would eat an English scone and realize I missed a biscuit with butter. There's such a similarity. I missed the greens and the southern peas. I really missed the peas that we had, among other things. So I can put my finger on it as being in the late 1960s when I was away from it, when it was not accessible to me.

S: And had you studied cooking at that point?

N: No. That's when I started my cooking classes at the London Cordon Bleu.

S: Okay.

N: And some of them, you know, like frying chicken, some of that resonated with what I knew, and others not.

S: And then the other question for you, for context, is, where did you grow up?

N: Well, I grew up in Virginia. I was born in New Jersey during the war when my father was stationed up there, then Ohio for kindergarten. We moved to Virginia when I was in the first grade. I lived there through high school. My freshman year I went to Texas Western with my father, who was stationed in El Paso, and then my sophomore year I went to George Washington.

S: I see. And where in Virginia did you live for most of your childhood?

N: I lived in Alexandria and then in Fairfax, close to Mount Vernon. It was very different then. I crossed Shirley Highway on foot to go to school. Washington, D.C., was the city, and far away, even though it was close in mileage.

S: And were both of your parents also from Virginia?

N: No, neither one of them were. My mother was of Danish extraction. My grandmother married a half cousin and moved to Minnesota, where they had a farm. Her husband, my mother's father, was killed, so they moved to Chicago. My father was from New York. So I was not of southern heritage per se, but easily influenced and surrounded by it. I ate at my neighbors' houses as a child. There was southern food there, too. I've lived in the South sixty-two years.

S: So, you absorbed it quite early in your life.

N: Yes.

S: So, let's shift over to Edna.

N: She was Virginian, too.

S: Do you remember the first time you encountered Edna Lewis?

N: I had, of course, heard about her, and knew of her. But when she was at Middleton Place, I made it a point to go down to meet her. I might have met her casually sooner, but I remember making that trip shortly after she got there. Before that she was in North Carolina at the Fearrington House. Jenny Fitch had called me and said that Edna was there and that she needed some help, that she really couldn't do the cooking by herself there, asking if I knew anyone to help her. I suggested Walter Royal, who is now the head chef of a big steakhouse in Raleigh. Walter Royal was an African American full-time student of mine for the three-month professional class who had been a psychologist and wanted to change careers. When Jenny's call came in, I said, "Look, you'll learn more from Edna than you will from me. You have to go help Edna!" So I made him quit my school and move to go work with Edna.

S: And that would have been, what, in the early to mid- or late 1980s? And what do you remember about that first meeting with her?

N: Oh, we had a wonderful time! I had lunch at the restaurant, and then we went for a long walk around the lake. She showed me where she lived. We talked about the ghosts of the past slaves that were there and how they spoke to her, and that she was very aware of them when she walked down to her home on the lake at night, in particular. We saw a special tree of hers. She spoke of how close she felt to the past of slavery, because her grandfather had been a slave and Freetown was a town of former slaves. And she felt very close to the ghosts of the people who had never been freed, or the people who had lived and died before emancipation.

S: And what do you remember of her personality or of her presence?

N: Well, you know Edna always had a presence, but when I met her, it wasn't in a crowd, it was just in a nice one-on-one, and so everyone talks about being struck by her elegance and her beauty. And that's certainly true. I'm suspicious of it being the first thing that people say about Edna—her beauty and her statuesqueness—because she had been a model, she did know how to comport herself. And in some ways I kind of felt like, I *feel* like, it diminishes the real Edna. She was a beautiful woman, very elegant, and everyone speaks to that, as Judith Jones does. But there's something about it that makes it sound like it's not to be expected, you know? As if an African American woman couldn't be expected to be elegant or beautiful. When you stress someone's elegance and beauty, it's sometimes as if, "Well, I didn't expect her to be that way." And I had already heard about that, so it wasn't something necessarily that I was looking for. I had read about her, and read her books, I already knew what she looked like. I was more interested in the person and in the conversation about food and about her life, and just very glad to meet her. I felt a kinship. We talked about Walter. And I was aware then, all of that time, that she was not necessarily able to be a full-time chef in the sense of being a chef. I mean, any more than I could be right now, my goodness! The time of hauling pots and pans comes long before your sixties. She wasn't a young chick—she was born in 1916—so she must have been close to seventy. I was admiring of her for even being able to do it all. But that's when I became very aware of the fact that she really didn't have any independent income, that she really hadn't made any real money from her books, and that there wasn't any fallback for her. She had to work. In some ways, it was the same role as an executive chef—one of those men who supervise the line cooks and set the menu, et cetera, but she was also cooking.

S: Speaking of her books, I'm assuming you first encountered her in print.

N: It might've been books, it might've been a story about her. And there was also a time, and I don't remember when it was, when I was asked to come up and give her an award from the New York culinary group or New York Cooking Teachers, headed by Norman Weinstein. It was held at Raoul's, where we had a suckling pig. But I knew *The Taste of Country Cooking* before I met her. When I first met her she talked passionately about foods needing flavor, and attributed it, of course, to fresh food.

S: Do you remember impressions of her or her food through her book early on? I mean, you were also writing and talking a lot about southern food.

N: Edna had a lovely voice, and she had a different perspective, because she was from a different part of Virginia than I knew, a more rural area than where I had been living in Atlanta. People tend to think that southern cooking is all the same. And that just because they have ramps in her part of Virginia, there are ramps in the middle of Georgia. We didn't know from ramps! So, it's that whole thing of people thinking that all southerners are alike, and not recognizing that there are climate zones and that there might've been ramps in north Georgia but not in mid- to southern Georgia, and not away from the hills. So I was entranced by *her* South—a loving community of relatives and friends, all helping each other, foods fresh from the earth, the familiarity she had with food.

The same thing was true in reverse in Middleton. We spoke about that, that the Lowcountry was, in fact, a very different place for her than where she had been before, even in North Carolina. And that these were all parts of the South that were not the same South to her. And that's kind of where she felt she was instructed by the history of the slaves there. Here she was plunked down in the middle of the Lowcountry, learning about rice and sesame, when she had been living in Virginia and North Carolina. Very different! Very different climates, different heat, all of that! People act like rice was everywhere. Well, rice wasn't everywhere! In Atlanta, you'd see much more of potatoes and other starches. And Edna and I talked about the difference in Middleton and what she was cooking with there. It was different than it was in Virginia and in North Carolina even. It was always irritating to me, it *still* is irritating to me, that southerners are all lumped together. Fearrington had a little store there, and was nipping at the heels of growing fresh vegetables and serving fresh vegetables and so forth. And Edna was part of that transition. But what was available seasonally was not easily available to her, and particularly at Middleton in those days, its early days as a foundation,

Sara B. Franklin

too. She knew we grew much of the produce on the property for my restaurant in Georgia in the 1970s and that I searched out farmers for things I didn't grow and shopped for the rest locally. I never used a commercial vendor. We had that in common.

She, too, searched out local farmers. She was always so interested in meeting them, as was I, so that was something we had in common wherever we went. We would try to find the farmers together. And she had mentioned that she was trying to find farmers there. But Edna didn't drive, so she was handicapped by that. She didn't drive, so she couldn't have a free-ranging kind of a spirit. She did get special local farmers and dairy to deliver to her at Middleton after searching them out.

Edna spent a lot longer in New York City than I did. I never lasted more than six months or a year, but she spent a lot of her lifetime in New York. Over fifty years. And a lot of her cooking training came from New York. Her mother did cook and did teach her to cook, of course. But a lot of her training come from the French, even if secondhand, as did mine! It took us learning another cuisine to really recognize our own. It's only when you get away that you recognize what you have. You see Edna's nostalgia in her books and her description of Freetown and its food.

S: You had mentioned to me that you wanted to speak about Edna and farmers' markets.

N: She just loved them. And I remember when she came to Atlanta, we went to the Atlanta State Farmers Market, which was, at the time, the only one. There was one that started in Virginia-Highland [a neighborhood in Atlanta] that my former food stylist started, but I don't think it had begun yet at that time. So we went to the Atlanta Farmers Market, which was so brutally depicted on the cover of *White Trash Cooking*. Edna didn't feel that it was a true farmers' market. It was the only time I saw her terribly disappointed. She saw the huge trucks and, you know, the conglomerate trucks coming in as well as smaller farmers. But you had to go by every stall to figure out which ones were the smaller ones and the real farmers. And she wanted to talk to the farmers, not the salespeople, not the truckers or their assistants. She wanted to talk to the people who dug in the ground. She wanted to find out more about the earth, you know? In every area that she was in, in every area where she was—what grew there? How did it grow? You know, she loved the earth. She loved it and planted wherever she was. She planted a garden at Middleton, she planted a garden at the restaurant in Atlanta where she first worked, and where she met Scott Peacock.

S: I think of that as an important part of the message that comes through in her writing. But how else might you characterize her sense of mission, to the extent that she had one. I mean, you and many other people have spoken about the ethnic garb that she sewed herself and always wore. . . .

N: I can't remember what she had on at Middleton. Every other time I saw her in ethnic garb. I do not remember any time that I did not. But I could not tell you on the jury stand that she had on ethnic garb at Middleton. But it seems to me that she would have, because she made her own clothes so frequently, and those were very easy to run up on a sewing machine. I don't remember seeing her in anything but ethnic garb and chef's whites. But she might possibly have had a chef's white jacket over it, as she wore one several times when we cooked together for functions.

S: Last we spoke, you also mentioned that she was always engaging people in political discussions. What was the character of those conversations?

N: Well, Edna was a liberal, and at one time — when it was fashionable among the intellectuals and bohemians — a communist. And so we had that in common. My grandfather was a socialist. I think we talked about Eleanor Roosevelt and different people that she had known that my father's father had known and that overlapped. She was always an admirer of Eleanor Roosevelt and all that she had accomplished. We just loved talking about politics and racism and equality together! Edna's flirtation with communism was very typical of that generation, and it was one of the few places where integration occurred.

S: Was that rare in the food community, such an explicit political bent?

N: You know, there wasn't a food community there like you're talking about. There was a New York mafia — Craig Claiborne and Jim Beard, who both loved Edna — and certainly there was a New York southern mafia, Craig, Jim Villas, Jean Anderson, Jeanne Voltz, and all those people at the *New York Times*, Johnny Popham, Howell Raines, et cetera. And they were by and large liberals.

We started IACP [the International Association of Culinary Professionals] in 1975–76 because there wasn't that kind of food community then the same way that there is now. When we started it, it was because we wanted to build a food community across the United States that was talking to each other. We didn't know who was out there. People [Bill Rice, from the *Washington Post* and then the *Chicago Tribune*, for instance] would tell me that they were teaching at a cooking school in Texas, and I didn't know who that teacher was. So whether or not there was politics, I tend to mostly talk to liberals anyway! I seek them out. I don't think it is rare. I think food people are very fundamental and they understand the hardscrabble of life. There are the gourmands, I suppose, that are Republicans. And the owners. But the real food people, I think, are egalitarian and understand the necessity of being good to the dishwasher, and that we all have to eat. All classes of people have to work together and are interdependent in the restaurant kitchen.

S: Right. That's really important. I think that in the cooking community there is that understanding.

N: And I sense that about the writing community, too. I don't know that I've ever met any archconservatives in the food writing community. Have you?

S: No, I haven't. But that's not to say they don't exist!

N: Edna and I were both feminists, too.

S: Yeah, I can imagine! I would expect that.

N: I mean, we just both knew that women did not have a very good place in the world. And we knew it well.

S: Let me try to rephrase my last question. To the extent that Edna was wearing ethnic garb and presenting a real Afrocentric pride and often talked about the legacy of slavery, do you have any sense of how the public responded to her race politics? Were people accepting of that, admiring of that? Was there a sort of disregard for that?

N: (long pause) You know, I think the same thing is true. You wouldn't have been with Edna, you wouldn't have stuck around to find out what she had to say, if you weren't liberal in some way. You know? If you weren't accepting, at least superficially. Her asset was this elegance, and the fact that she affected the African garb. I suspect that was a very nice shield for her. Once you wear ethnic garb, people treat you differently, as if you are special. I think she figured that out long before, and the bohemians of the era certainly made it possible. [Café] Nicolson prided itself on being bohemian. I think she knew that when she was in New York, if she wore ethnic garb, she would be treated well and as an exotic, and stand out. I don't want to say that she manipulated it, because I don't know that she did, but she was not unaware of the fact that you weren't just treated like any "Negro" cook in a diner if you wore ethnic garb. There is a kind of a courtesy extended to foreigners, no matter their color, so her clothes helped pave the way for better treatment. Then, once you spoke to her and heard that lovely voice and accent, people would treat her with respect. And she knew how she wanted to be treated. She was an egalitarian and she saw herself as good as anybody else. So I don't know if I would ever think of anybody not being respectful to Edna in the exterior world. But obviously, obviously, as we know, racism is alive and well everywhere. She was always respectful to others as well. But using the back door would have made her very unhappy, and did when she was young.

S: You made a comment about Julia Child back when we spoke last June, and you said to me, "I don't think she had gotten beyond a certain point in the civil rights era." How did that affect Lewis's place in that fledgling circle, with Judith Jones, with Julia Child?

N: Well, they were liberals. Julia, you know, was from the West and she worked for USIA [United States Information Agency]. She had traveled extensively. But I never think that people *not* from the South are the same toward African Americans one way or the other as people from the South. Jack Bass, my husband, who has written on race and politics for a long time now, has a phrase where he says, "In the South you can get close as a black person"—you know, people grew up together on the farms and so forth—so you can get close, "but not high. In the North you could get high, but never close." And I find that's true. Northerners are willing to accept an elegant African American who appears cultured to them and promote them but not necessarily be close to them. When I go to the North and I expect a kind of closeness with a northern African American, I don't get it. Whatever I say elsewhere can be misunderstood by someone black, where in the South it's not so liable to be misunderstood, because there's a closeness. But at the same time, it's a lot harder for African Americans to get in a higher position in the South, but we "do for each other."

S: I think there's a lot of truth to that, which is why I'm so interested in Edna's reception in New York circles. You had spoken last time about a feeling that Judith Jones had tokenized Edna.

N: I don't think there's any doubt that Judith and the ilk—I don't think they had any experience in *not* tokenizing. It's not a vicious charge, it's just the fact that she was exotic. You can even see it in the way that Judith wrote and spoke—speaks—about Edna, as if she was a rarity. And she was a rarity, but she also wasn't. How do you say it? When you're from the South, there is an understanding that's almost implicit about food and the farm and growing up within a certain sense of that. African Americans always had their own little gardens, even if they didn't come from a place where they had more access to farmland, like Edna did. But remember, she left when she was sixteen. So she didn't stick around for that, either. But there's no way that Judith ever understood that. I don't know how often Judith ever came south, or if she ever did. To this day, I don't know that she's been south, you know? So how could they do anything other than tokenize Edna? And there is still a lot of tokenization of Edna. What did her being a model, a fashion designer, or a seamstress have to do with her passion for food? Was she making a living at it? If so, why did she start working at Café Nicholson? Sounds exotic, sure enough, but only as a token.

S: Oh, sure.

N: I mean, it's in part because she was physically stunning when she walked into Judith's office, and in part because she was in ethnic clothes. Edna didn't come in there wearing a black suit, like I probably did. Edna came in there not complying with anything Judith knew. And Edna came in there having been associated with liberal elite intellectuals and models, knowing writers, having worked in these kitchens. So she was high in the North. But she never got close, except perhaps to the southern writers who understood the closeness who were her friends at Café Nicholson. But Faulkner, Paul Robeson, Tennessee Williams, Truman Capote, Craig Claiborne, Jim Villas—they were easy with her. They understood the closeness.

S: Would you say that you and she got close?

N: (long pause) I would say that we had a real understanding, an easiness and candor, and a certain kind of closeness. Would've been more so if we had more time. But I saw her every time I went to New York. We always went out to eat or drink together at least once, so I think we had a kind of understanding and a closeness. Certainly for twenty years or more. Yeah. And she confided in me about her family, her income, her status.

S: What were those times in New York like? Did people know Edna in the restaurants?

N: Oh, yeah. Well, let's see, when I wrote *New Southern Cooking*, which was in the mid-1980s, and my publisher was Judith Jones, that was when I realized that Edna was also published by Judith. Toula [Polygalaktos], Judith's assistant, put us in touch, and Toula, Edna, and I would all go out together to these restaurants. I always wanted to take Edna to places she hadn't been and places I hadn't been. So we would go to places that were very fashionable at the time. When we went to the Four Seasons, when I was at the bar, nobody paid any attention to me. Edna came in, and we went and sat in some chairs adjacent to the bar area. Sergio [Vacca] saw Edna when he was walking by, did a U-turn, and stopped and invited us to all come upstairs to a special room where he just fêted us with food. He was very happy to see her. I don't think he'd ever met her before. Same was true when we went to "21." Jerry [Berns] saw us in the lounge—saw *her*—and made a beeline and treated us very well.

S: So she had quite a reputation locally?

N: She had quite a reputation. She had certainly been written about, and that was where her visual—once again, if she was in the black suit that I was in, nobody would have noticed her except as a stunning black woman, but not as a cook. So, she utilized that garb, whether it was influential to her, whether she meant it as a respect of Africans or meant it as her persona, and it certainly was easier for her to do that than keep up with the black suit, financially as every other way. Her clothes weren't expensive, and that fit her budget as well as her outlook.

Let me be clear. Edna Lewis was the first woman in the twentieth century, way before Julia, to jump the line between being a cook and a chef. She was the leader of the way for women in general to achieve a status on their own in the kitchen. That she was black was integral to her persona, but not to the achievement she made on her own in the kitchen. She led the way for black *and* white women. Remember, Julia Child was never, ever in the professional kitchen. Edna Lewis was the first woman in a professional kitchen who was not an owner or front of the house, but the most important back-of-the-house woman in the twentieth century as she broke all the barriers. Certainly, Mama Dip and others, for instance, ran their own restaurants and became famous, but that was an organic evolution in their lives and the recognition of their status. Edna achieved it, and achieved it in New York City, where restaurant culture as we know it now was really emerging. She got there through her own persona, through her dress, through her self-education. Edna was well spoken, well read, and very knowledgeable about current affairs. She was able to converse with the top writers who frequented the restaurant. She bridged that separation I was talking about earlier—the North letting you get high in status, which she did—and the ability to be close to these important southern novelists because they understood closeness between races. It was her ability to brook these differences that made her stand out. If she hadn't understood that she was equal—something learned through her marriage, through her attraction to the intellectual components and freedoms promised through communism, her bohemian phase—could she have operated so well in the public arena? I doubt it.

S: So that's a way in which she distinguished herself knowingly. Was there any extent to which you saw her embracing a persona of celebrity? Was she aware of her recognition?

N: She surely was aware of her recognition, and she had wonderful publicity and fame in magazines and newspaper stories. The list of places that wrote about her is impressive, and we're seeing a resurgence of that today. The flip side, though, is it didn't get her much of anywhere in terms of . . . she got some jobs that she wouldn't have gotten if she hadn't had had it, like Middleton, and Gage & Tollner, the big one, because she had cachet. Gosh, no, she had cachet, and people like Alice Waters, James Beard, and Craig Claiborne were delighted to meet her. But she never had any money. I suppose as a communist when she was young it wasn't her goal. And then they lost whatever they had with the pheasant farm that went bust. So, she had some celebrity-dom but never had a permanent place to live or any mobility. She had a rent-controlled apartment, but her sister and brother-in-law sublet it from her, and she and her husband never gave it back to Edna. I suppose they thought it was theirs as they had paid the rent all those years, but she complained bitterly to me about it. That's why she moved to Atlanta. She didn't have a place of her own. She didn't have a place to root. So what good is having a reputation and being a celebrity and being fêted if people don't make sure that you also have an income and throw jobs your way? But she did get the ones like Middleton Place and the Fearrington House because of her cachet. They didn't always last long because she was older and not able to necessarily keep up, and they were both isolating in their own way, being rural and out of the city atmosphere she loved.

Because she couldn't do it all by herself anymore. No matter how much you respected and loved her, if you were hiring her as an executive chef, you had to get her an assistant. She couldn't turn out food at that time, any more than I could now! But she could communicate her love of food and how to do things, how to add the touch of grace to the food.

S: Was she unique among your peers—I mean, you talk about the food community being very small—but was her financial situation unusual? Were people making more than Edna?

N: Dammit, she never made any money from her books, is what she told me. One time I said something about it being nice to get the royalty check, and she said she had never really gotten any royalty checks. I mean, Judith was stingy and didn't promote or anything. And Judith could have helped Edna more, she just didn't. Judith was very important in that she recognized Edna's abilities, her status, and her cachet. Without her help, perhaps Edna would not have found a way to have a national publisher or have her books kept in print for so long. On the other hand, I fault Judith for not giving her more of an advance, for not promoting her books, and for patronizing her writing. You had to do your own promoting—they didn't do any for you, if you were Edna or, for that matter, me, at Knopf. I was fortunate in that I had a television show and a publicist. But Edna didn't have that. And Judith didn't particularly help her in that way. I mean, Judith made no bones about the fact that she sat and helped Edna write her second book at her desk, and that she would then give things to Edna to take home and work on, and vice versa. She said Edna would bring in yellow lined pads full of her writing. Which was fine, you know, that was the editorial role that maybe people had then. But then Judith said to me, for the next book, "Well, I can't do that for Edna for the next book. I really did it for the first book, but I can't do it this time. I need to get her a coauthor," which is when she got Mary Goodbody. But you know, that just meant that Edna really didn't earn that much from that book either! And Mary probably didn't make enough, either.

I mean, it's bittersweet, as without Judith, Edna would not have had a vehicle so well suited to publicize her, and obviously her first [*The Edna Lewis Cookbook*] book didn't sell well, so this was an important step for her, to have a book like that. And to have Judith help her so was flattering and encouraging. Certainly, Judith brought a great deal of good out in Edna. The bitter part is that Edna didn't earn according to the station that the book, the press, and her relationship with Judith conferred on her. Judith couldn't help her New England nature, and Edna couldn't make herself bargain for more; she was a product of her times in that regard. It was hard for women to negotiate for themselves until very recently—it still is, even now. We weren't taught how to assert ourselves, and southern women even less so. And although Edna had that quality of assurance and quiet strength, negotiations for money were so hard for all of us. I don't think she had an agent, and I did not when I published with Judith either.

S: Did Edna seem bothered or insulted by her financial situation?

N: Maybe not insulted, but it got to her, when I once said that I had received another royalty check in the mail just before I went to New York. That probably hurt her, as then she knew Judith didn't do right by her. I wouldn't have said it if I had realized the situation. I assumed that Edna was making a nice living from those books, from *The Taste of Country Cooking* especially, because it was so recognized there. But not, according to her. And, gee, I mean it lanced her, I think, when she realized that people actually made royalties, that there was a little sinecure I was getting every year at the time that she wasn't getting one. And what a difference it would have made to her life! And, you know, who knows how many of those jobs that she had in between Café Nicholson and Middleton Place, how many of them paid her Social Security? Where was she cooking at that time, what was she doing? What did she do in those years? When she catered, did she pay into Social Security? So many freelancers don't or can't. And I don't know what her role at Gage & Tollner paid there at the end, but I do think they paid her Social Security.

S: It's quite veiled in the record. At some point, it just starts to become, "Scott took care of her." That's the popular narrative.

N: Right! And I don't mind it, but when Francis Lam did that article for the *New York Times*, for which he got his award, and he gives all the credit to the African Americans and cooks of the world, and so forth, it's the same kind of patronization. I wish someone from the South had written it. Certainly, an article in the *New York Times* about Edna was going to create a flurry of attention, so that is wonderful for her legacy and makes me happy. But how sad it is that someone didn't write it who had known and loved her writing and maybe even her, and who understood race relations during her time and her place in them. Edna was a very special person. It was more that the audience for whom she wrote was not the black home cook of the era when she wrote. But in my experience, young black women know who Edna is and are very aware of her imprint on the cuisine. I just think he missed the nuances, by and large. He had a viewpoint that didn't enable him to see her as she was, or how people regarded her, certainly in black-and-white terms. In all fairness, he interviewed a number of knowledgeable people about Edna, but as always, an author picks and chooses the quotes. Still, I'm happier it was there than not and have made my peace with it.

Judith's goal for Edna's book was much different. Her target audience was not black cooks or the black middle class, as they, as a demographic, were not known for supporting book-buying in those days. Judith certainly helped Edna reach the level of a top cookbook writer. She was a peer, if you will, of all the best. And that was Judith's goal for the book. God bless her for that, as it positioned Edna again as a peer to anyone. But it was a very different book than the average cookbook. It was a memoir of sorts, and thank goodness it captured the era of Edna's youth, which was gone.

But, anyway, where Edna was in those interim years is something that I do not know. Judith must know!

S: Judith does not know. They really fell out of touch toward the end.

N: That is probably because of the money. Edna was pretty available. I mean, whenever I called we would get together. She didn't say anything about not being able to as she had a job.

S: The sense I've gotten is that she gigged. She really was essentially a freelancer for most of her life.

N: That's what she was! Did a little catering here and there, and so forth. So, she probably had a minimum of Social Security that she was living on when she was living with her sister and brother-in-law in the rent-controlled apartment, in New York, but things weren't going well with the brother-in-law. So, that was just a few years, and then she was out of there, and came down to Atlanta. And once again, I didn't get to see her too much. There was this movement to help

Sara B. Franklin

Edna, which she certainly needed financially, but they took her out
to the suburbs, and all she saw was white people. She commented
about it. She was lonely for black friends. I did pick her up and once
brought her in so that she could see one of the girls that she brought
up who she called her foster daughter, who was from, I don't know,
Haiti maybe? The Dominican Republic? Someone that she had semi-
adopted, had taken into her life somehow. She had an address, so I
drove her over there. She didn't have any other way to contact the
girl, no phone number. But she complained about not having trans-
portation and being stuck out in this white area with no African
Americans. I don't think she drove. So many years in New York.

S: That's really interesting. Really interesting.

N: And see, it's the same kind of thing that's happening to Vertamae
[Smart-Grosvenor].[1] She gets in situations where white people have
the financial resources and do for her, but she tires of living in an all-
white environment, and they don't really understand her, even in a
nursing home, you know? Or assisted living.

S: Yeah.

N: Julie Dash, the movie producer, is trying to get her [Vertamae] into
an African American . . . finding an African American place that's af-
fordable, for women that have some intellectual and individuality is
very hard! Very hard. It seems to me Vertamae and Edna didn't really
know or like one another very much.

S: Do you know why that was?

N: Well, they were totally opposite. Vertamae was very flamboyant, and
Edna was not. Edna was a quiet-spoken person. Edna was not flam-
boyant, she just didn't have the inclination. Like, for instance, when
I mentioned to Judith that I wanted to have Edna on my Christ-
mas show, Judith said, "Oh no, she just couldn't do that." And I said,
"Why couldn't she do that? I think she'd be good on television." "Oh
no, oh no, she's just too shy." All part of Judith's patronizing of Edna.
Well, I had her on anyway, and she did wonderfully.

S: Had you worked with Edna at all leading up to putting her on television, and why did you feel it was so important to put her on TV?

N: Well, she was then, to me, the premier southern woman in the way
that Craig Claiborne was the best known of the southern men. And
then I had Paul Prudhomme as a guest as well. So those were people
that were very much representative of the cuisines. Craig was Mississippi, very different again from Cajun. And it was Edna in the

Upper South way. So, I wanted to have them on that show. Her being African American was important, but it was her southern voice and outlook we wanted on that Christmas show. Edna was the most important southern restaurant cook—male or female, black or white—from the late 1940s to perhaps the 1980s. Who else was there, man or woman, black or white?

S: Did you let Edna have control of what she cooked on that show?

N: Absolutely. Told her to cook whatever she wanted to. And she wanted to cook greens. It was so funny—I wrote about it later—we carefully measured how much fatback she put in there, but we had to write the recipe for the book. And she really didn't write the recipe. And so we wrote the recipe, we measured everything carefully, and then when I put it in my next book, which was *Matters of Taste* with Judith, Judith was furious because there was so much fatback in there. So she changed the recipe in my book.

S: Really?

N: Yes. We had measured every sliver that went in there, because we wanted to have Edna's recipe exactly. But Judith—and I don't know how much that influenced any of the recipes in Edna's books, you see—because Judith had her own opinions. Judith is a skinny, ascetic New England woman. And I'm sure she imposed her own opinions, just like the first editor I had who kept wanting me to take the pork out of the southern cooking, which is why I left her. We will never know exactly what influence Judith Jones had on Edna's cooking. What made her appealing to the target market was not necessarily the use of fatback and streak o' lean.

S: Really!

N: Yeah! These New York women did not want southern cooking to be southern cooking. They did not understand the role of the broth or of meat as a seasoning, but that's all people ate! You know, maybe with turnip greens and cornbread. They didn't get that. And so, I wouldn't doubt that she fiddled with Edna's recipes. *In Pursuit of Flavor* had a good amount of fat in its greens—but Judith didn't do those recipes with Edna, Mary Goodbody did.

S: I've never really thought about that, but all those recipes were definitely worked through a filter.

N: Oh yeah, they went through a filter. And then, by the time she got to cook with Scott, she was what, seventy-five, eighty?

Sara B. Franklin

S: Yeah, it was quite late. *The Gift of Southern Cooking*, she was quite old when that book was published.

N: Oh yeah. So he interpreted what she did, too. Boy, that food was good, though! When Edna was working with him and he was working there all the time, it was good! When he got disinterested in the restaurant, it really slumped. This was the one in Virginia-Highland, where he was working when the book came out. You know, we had that wonderful time, the American Institute of Wine and Food really embraced Edna. I brought her down for an event there, and once again she got very upset because there weren't any farmers there. I don't know what she expected! At the international convention of Les Dames d'Escoffier, we awarded her — our first grande dame. I guess it was twenty years ago, something like that.

S: How did she seem to feel about receiving that honor?

N: She was always happy when she was acknowledged, but modest. It was just a shame that there was no financial benefit to her from any of this. You know? But that was true of M. F. K. Fisher. That is one of the things that happened to these women, and I guess it happens to men, too. They get this stature, they get touted, but they're not catapulted into anything financially. Part of it is not being in a population center that is welcoming when they're of a certain age, and it comes late. You know, God bless Scott. I know there's a lot of whoop-de-do about that, but at least he found a place for her to live and make sure she had enough to eat. And he battled some of his own demons so he could keep her company and take care of her.

S: Yeah, I was always struck when Judith told me that late in her life, M. F. K. Fisher was still commuting down to San Francisco to teach at a community college because she just had no money. She had no cash!

N: She had no money! And part of that was because Judith didn't help them. You know, she didn't give them advances. It was all royalty stuff. Well, why shouldn't they have gotten these big advances? Judith would discover and solicit writers, but she wouldn't pay you. Why didn't Judith want to part with money for those women? All her parsimoniousness. I think that was the way she cooked, too. Anyway, you know that letter Edna handwrote to Eugene Walter that they published in *Gourmet*?[2] They printed that verbatim, and I have wondered if that is her only piece of public writing. Her true voice. Unless Judith took down verbatim what she said for *The Taste of Country Cooking.* I mean, Edna really did resent that Mary Goodbody came on for that next book, because every little bit of money would have helped. I think Mary did a good job capturing a lot of Edna's voice. I told her that recently. But do you notice a difference between those two books?

S: Yes. I think there's a sort of purity, maybe a puritanism, and more reference to race in *The Taste of Country Cooking* than there is in *In Pursuit of Flavor.*

N: Yes, the puritanism was Judith's, because Judith picked a northern person to write the second book. Why didn't she find a southerner? She could've found a southern person to do that. She just didn't even think of it! But there is a fair mention of race in *In Pursuit of Flavor,* too. In *Taste* it is more subtle.

S: I mean, really, everything Edna wrote was filtered through a northern voice — every book Judith edited was filtered through her particular northern lens, whether it was about the South or Italy or the Middle East or China. Okay, the last question I have for you today is a big one. I was going to ask you anyway, but when you spoke about Lam's piece, I wanted to ask you even more. So now that I've primed you . . . What do you see as Edna's legacy? What matters about her memory?

N: Well, what matters is that finally the food world decided that there was someone who they could put on a pedestal that was African American and a cook, who had in her own self a persona and a love of the land that could be communicated. I mean, I guess in each case, whoever comes to the fore is a personality. But Edna wasn't necessarily charismatic that way — it was her looks as much as anything that did that. And good for her! I mean, it was great that she was commanding. And she was a survivor. But she didn't have a charisma the way Paul Prudhomme has it, or Bill Clinton. Edna didn't have a forceful personality, she was soft-spoken. She was lovely. But that was the first thing people would say about her, that she was statuesque and all that, and that gave her an entrée that other African American women didn't have. I mean, the question always comes, "How many other African American women were there that were just ignored?" Because they didn't wear African garb and weren't beautiful? And I don't mean that to distract from Edna in any sense, I just mean that it sure has taken a long time. The young black women I mentor complain to me that for so long the culinary world has acted like there was only room for one black woman in any position of power or focus. Now, happily, there can be a number of women.

S: So is there anything in her cooking that is a powerful or worthy legacy, the way you see it?

N: Her love of the cooking is certainly there, and that increases, of course, as you get older. The love of your native cuisine. Because that's what's familiar and those are the tastes that you remember, that imprinted themselves on you. So the imprint of southern cooking and growing up in that rural area was really important. And she did mix the French with the southern, and that was of that era, and that's an important thing to show! I mean, Continental cooking was seeping in all over, and there's nothing wrong with that! It's combination cooking, and there's someone recently — maybe it was Lam in his piece — that talked about Edna cooking a soufflé. I don't care what anybody tells me, Edna Lewis's mother did not cook a soufflé at home in Virginia when Edna was growing up. She did not! Edna did not learn French cooking until she went to New York. Now, she may have come back to visit and cooked it. But she didn't do it during her childhood, and her mother didn't do it before Edna was sixteen. You just trust me that that was true! They weren't there beating egg whites in a copper bowl making soufflés. But let us not forget that Edna was a groundbreaker. She left the most important legacy — being the first American woman professional in the kitchen who was treated as a peer in the New York culinary world, which was mostly men, European men at that. And she was the first African American woman who broke race barriers in the kitchen and was not the cook — the hired help — in the southern way, or the back-kitchen help in the northern way. She was a partner at Café Nicholson.

One thing about her cooking — her recipes were part of her. She didn't refer to any recipe when she cooked turtle soup for an event we were cooking for. And she supervised or did it herself every step of the way. She wanted to touch the food, by snapping or shelling the peas herself, and she would invite you to join her so that you could have a social visit as you shelled peas, just as generations of southern women have done. That's that "southerners get close not high," regardless of race, thing. You are going to be close to someone you shell peas with. She would invite the lowly and the high to shell peas with her. From the dishwasher to the owner of the restaurant. She knew no divisions.

S: Well, and *The Taste of Country Cooking* was written well after Edna moved to New York, so of course her time there had influenced her.

N: I mean, this is not a pure book any more than anybody else's book is pure, in terms of southern cooking. It's an amalgamation. She had lived in New York and cooked. She did bring some of her southern cooking to New York, and was a good cook and caterer of southern food for that reason. But she learned things that pleased the people she cooked for, and those were the foods of the era. Fortunately for that last book, Scott was southern. She also had the influence of those men southern writers at Knickerbockers who adored her. That fed her soul, I'm sure of it. They also taught her how to knock back a drink or two, and hold it. She loved a good drink.

I never heard her ooh and aah because she served a famous person or brag about it. She served Eleanor Roosevelt, all those famous authors, the southern ones, Gore Vidal, all the famous bohemians, the ballet dancers, the artists. But she didn't let class into her soul. And that does shine through, no matter who her editor was. It's not a sin to be from the North, as Judith was, or to expect someone to write for the audience one wants for a book, it's just that it changes the lens with which Edna is seen. I don't want to diminish Edna by saying she was filtered through New Englanders. And yet, who else is ever going to say it? Was there more she wanted to say? She was integral to women being accepted in New York kitchens, as well as African American women as being skilled and up-to-the minute with soufflés, not just someone who could only cook home-style cooking. She brought home-style cooking to New York with style and grace, and it spread to the places she worked and the people she touched. God bless her.

NOTES

1. Vertamae Smart-Grosvenor died September 3, 2016, not long after this interview took place.

2. Dupree is referring to "What Is Southern?" published in the January 2008 issue of *Gourmet*, as referenced in Jane Lear's essay in this volume.

It's Not All Fried Chicken and Greasy Greens

MASHAMA BAILEY

Around the age of ten, I started cooking breakfast for my parents. I enjoyed the feeling of control I got from being in the kitchen. Breakfast, at the time, was the only meal I knew I could prepare independently. I liked standing at the stove stirring eggs in the pan or whisking grits into boiling water. We lived in Queens, New York, our kitchen was small, and there was not a lot space for many appliances. I would spread butter on sliced bread then carefully place it in the broiler. Sometimes we would eat our eggs with bacon and sometimes with leftover slices of ham.

Despite the sense of satisfaction preparing food for others brought me, as it turned out, I wasn't a very good cook back then. The grits would clump. The eggs would brown. The toast would always burn. My proud ten-year-old self would scrape the burned edges from the toast, then cut the slices diagonally so they would be easy to eat. I would put a slice of American cheese over the grits so that the lumps did not matter. As for the eggs, they tasted pretty good.

My parents never told me that my breakfasts weren't perfect. They always accepted my Saturday morning offerings with big smiles and great pride, and ate everything—even the charred toast. For years, I actually thought they preferred burned toast. I found out some years later that I had been mistaken.

Despite the joy I found in the kitchen, I was never the cook of the family. Both of my grandmothers cooked very well, and my older cousin Alan would experiment at the stove to impress the family with all types of hotpot concoctions that he could think up. I was shy and stayed in the background, but somehow I always seemed to end up in the kitchen asking questions.

I came from a working family. My parents were young, and both went to college after their children were born. I was the little mama, the oldest of three, and the support for my parents. I picked up my brother and sister from school and daycare. I made them snacks and helped them with their homework while we waited for our parents to come home. During the week my mother cooked quick meals like pasta with a salad or canned soup with sandwiches.

But Sundays were different. On Sundays, she cooked all day.

My mom was born and raised in Waynesboro, Georgia, a small town just south of Augusta. It was on Sundays that she reminded her young family where she came from. She would roast chicken and serve it with rice and gravy and greens. We ate glazed ham with sweet potatoes and cabbage. She didn't bake, but there was always cornbread or biscuits on the table. And the real treat, fried chicken! She made the best fried chicken. She used a cast-iron pan and grease she had saved, to be used only for chicken. It was a meal that took hours, and we only had it sometimes. She would always make pan gravy, mashed potatoes, and sweet peas to go alongside the crispy meat. Really good fried chicken is still one of my favorite foods.

Mom's Sunday cooking—now that was food to me. Living up North, soul food and southern food were commonly considered to be one and the same. People think of soul food as BBQ ribs, macaroni and cheese, buttermilk biscuits, and sweet tea. Our Sunday dinners taught me about my family and what we ate, and helped me distinguish *real* southern from soul food. But I had no idea that there was so much more.

In 2000, I decided to change my career path from social work to becoming a chef. My decision was prompted by a few work dinners where coworkers complimented me on my sweet potatoes and roasted chicken. With a half-cocked aspiration, I left my job in Brooklyn and decided to attend culinary school.

The school I attended was French based, like all culinary schools at the time and the majority, still, today. I had chosen it because it was geared toward career changers and had an excellent work-study program. I also liked that the school took the view that French food was the mother of all professional cuisines, so my education's foundation of principles, I thought, would be priceless.

During the first phase of classes our chef instructor asked us to write an essay about someone who inspired us to cook. My mother, of course; so easy, I thought. I would interview her when I got home that evening. But our teacher insisted that it be someone professional, like Escoffier or James Beard. My dilemma was that the only chefs I'd heard of were the ones on TV: Julia Child, the Frugal Gourmet, and the Cajun chef Justin Wilson.

I wanted to write about someone who looked like me, and like my mother and grandmothers. I began my search for a chef that I could admire. I started trolling around on the Internet without finding much on the subject of notable black women cooks. I searched at the public library, and after some digging, I found an article about a woman called Edna Lewis.

Edna Lewis's search for taste, as well as her story, stuck with me. A black woman from the South, Miss Lewis moved to New York to start a whole new life, first as a laundress, later as a seamstress and restaurant chef. She was never formally trained, but she had grown up cooking in rural Virginia, was hardworking, and loved wholesome food made with fresh ingredients. This sounded like many of the women in my family before me. As the opening chef at Café Nicholson in New York in the 1950s, she showcased simple food and was heaped with praise for it. Through Miss Lewis I realized that there was a history of black women, like me, in professional kitchens, and that I wasn't alone.

My cooking school was diverse. We had students from all types of backgrounds, but in class, African Americans were poorly represented. So I decided to use tell my classmates about my discovery of Miss Lewis. Many of them haven't heard of her. My culinary instructor had, though, and told me about her cookbooks. *In Pursuit of Flavor* was the first cookbook of Miss Lewis's that I read. I prepared her boiled Virginia ham recipe with mustard and rosemary for our final exam. I got an A−.

Armed with my new base of French gastronomic knowledge and ready to pursue a career in fine dining, I spent the next few years bouncing around from restaurants to catering to personal chef work, trying to find out where I fit in in the culinary world and what was I going to do. Like most young cooks, I did not have a plan. And, like many of my planless peers, I decided to travel. I signed up for a stage at a cooking school at a château in France.

Château du Fey was located ninety-five miles south of Paris in Burgundy. It had a garden that we could explore and pick from for both our guest and staff dinners. I learned about farming, different herbs, slow cooking, and preserving. I loved how people in the French countryside lived. It was a slower pace of life from that of New York City. Working people in

France had afternoon breaks that allowed them to go home and care for their families. I realized that the only place in the States that seemed to have anything in common with the French lifestyle was the South.

I was born in the Bronx, but the South has always intrigued and had a pull on me. As a kid, I would do almost anything to associate myself with the region. Growing up, I liked to say, "I'm one generation removed 'southern.'" During my time in France, I started to reminisce about visiting my relatives in Waynesboro during summers growing up. We would sit out on the porch and watch the cars go by. A few times a week, someone would pull up in front of the house with bushels of all kinds of vegetables. They would bring my grandmother fresh butter beans, green beans, corn, and summer squash. She picked up samples of every fruit or vegetable to smell them before buying anything. My uncle could tell when a watermelon was ripe by balancing the straw from a corn broom straight across the fruit.

I also started noticing similarities between French and southern food. At the château we made coq au vin, a braised bird cooked down in wine, onions, and bacon. The dish instantly brought me back to chicken and dumplings, just replacing the wine with a bit of broth and adding dollops of bready dough before cooking. In France we prepared a gratin of summer vegetables; at Grandmamma's house, she made squash casserole. French cooking, I found, made sense to me because of the memories of southern food and culture it evoked. It was the sort of food I was not only interested in cooking but wanted to eat, too.

I began to think of Edna Lewis again, and how she was always cooking in such a way as to get better flavor. Simple, pure food. The château had a ton of cookbooks, and I was surprised to find that they had all of Miss Lewis's. I read *The Taste of Country Cooking* and was amazed to find how close the dishes were to the foods of my mother's past. Blackberry cobbler, baked ham, green beans and pork, and sausage patties! These were the foods that my mother grew up eating!

By the time I returned home to New York, I'd decided that I wanted to become a restaurant chef. I worked as a line cook for three years in some of New York City's busiest restaurants, attempting to reinstate myself into the community. When I thought that I was ready, I applied to Prune in the East Village. I had heard that the chef there, Gabrielle Hamilton, was a legend in her own right. She had the reputation of being a badass with a serious perspective on food. Lots of people knew of Prune for its fantastic brunch menu, but I wanted to work there because I knew it was time to move my career to the next level. I was finally ready to become a sous-chef, and I wanted to work with a chef who had a point of view, a voice, and something to say.

I arrived at Prune right after Gabrielle completed her first book, *Blood, Bones, and Butter*. The restaurant was a hotbed for creativity. We all found ourselves buzzing around the tiny space, excited just to be there and ready to work.

Working with Gabrielle and her staff, I noticed that there was an underlying theme threaded through every meal, from brunch down to our staff meals. It was "Cook what you want to eat!" I like to call that grandma cooking, this idea of providing people with a sense of time and place through food, reminding them of why they like a particular dish in the first place. Is it because strawberries are in season or because you can smell the sugar being stirred into the iced tea that took hours to make? Again, I found myself thinking of Miss Lewis.

At that point, I began to understand why she had become such a recurring fixture in my life. It wasn't because she looked like my elders; it was because she cooked like them. Miss Lewis cooked from her heart and with the support of all those childhood memories of taste. Her food had a sense of time and place. But above all, she cooked how she liked to eat. This is what I love about cooking and, I realized, why I wanted to become a chef: I want to preserve history and celebrate it one meal at a time.

A few years later, I decided it was time for me to move South. With the help of Gabrielle's recommendations and advice, I headed to Savannah, Georgia, and I opened my own restaurant, The Grey. At The Grey, we cook the kind of food I like to eat, the very sort of food Lewis, my mom, Hamilton, and all my women culinary influences have given me the confidence to cook professionally.

Every so often, I open *In Pursuit of Flavor*. I boil some Virginia ham the way Miss Lewis says to, just so I can eat it with soft scrambled eggs, creamy grits, and toast that is the shade of brown the makes you remember why you love toast anyway. This breakfast is a far cry from the ones I made as a child, but it brings back memories nonetheless.

Boiled Virginia Ham

Virginia ham is uncooked and cured for six to eight months. Miss Lewis, like many southern women, ate these hams boiled and then baked. The following recipe is inspirited by both Miss Edna and my grandmother, whose addition of ginger ale gives this rendition a distinct flavor. For a breakfast like the one I sometimes treat myself to, serve grits hot with a spoonful of eggs and as much sliced or diced ham as you like.

{MAKES 16–20 SERVINGS}

13–15-pound uncooked Virginia ham
2-liter bottle ginger ale
24-quart pot

Scrub the ham with a stiff brush under cold running water. When the moldy outer covering has come off, rinse the ham well and put it in a pot. Cover with cold water and soak overnight in a cool spot.

In the morning, pour off the soaking water and add the ginger ale and clean cold water to cover the ham. Cover and bring to a boil, then lower the heat to a simmer. Cook for about 5 hours. After 4½ hours, lift the ham out of the water to see if the skin is bubbled and soft. If not, let the ham cook until it is, another ½ hour or so.

Remove the ham from the cooking water and let it rest in a shallow pan. When it is cool enough to handle, cut the skin off with a sharp knife. As you remove the skin, trim a bit of the fat, leaving enough to help retain the moisture.

Soft Scrambled Eggs

{MAKES 2 SERVINGS}

4 large eggs
½ teaspoon kosher salt
2 ounces heavy cream
1 tablespoon butter

Crack the eggs into a medium bowl. Add the salt and heavy cream. With a whisk, whip the eggs until completely homogenous and pale yellow, about 30 seconds.

Heat the butter in an 8-inch nonstick skillet over medium-low heat. When the butter has melted, add the eggs and cook, undisturbed, until a thin layer of cooked egg appears around the edge of the skillet. Using a rubber spatula, push the eggs all the way around the entire skillet, then across the bottom, making a figure eight with the tip of the spatula. Continue to push the eggs around and across the skillet until fluffy and barely set, about 2 minutes; they should still look runny on top.

Creamy Grits with Cheese

{MAKES 4–6 SERVINGS}

3 cups water
1 tablespoon kosher salt
1 cup stone-ground grits (good quality like
    Jimmy Red or Anson Mills)
3 tablespoons unsalted butter
3 ounces shredded cheddar or Swiss cheese
Kosher salt and freshly ground black pepper, to taste

Bring the water and salt to a boil over high heat in a heavy-bottomed pot. Rain in the grits while stirring constantly. Continue stirring until the mixture returns to a boil, at which point it will become creamy and begin to thicken. Reduce the heat to low and simmer slowly for 45 minutes to 1 hour, stirring often, until grits are tender and very creamy. Stir in the butter and cheese. When the cheese is completely melted, add salt and pepper to taste.

Building an Appetite

Seasonal Reflections on the Farm

ANNEMARIE AHEARN

I wasn't born in the countryside or raised on a farm. I was born in a hospital in Milwaukee, Wisconsin, and spent my childhood and teenage years in the suburbs. But one of my closest friends lived in a grand, old, sprawling farmhouse, farther out of the city. We spent afternoons barefoot in the creek, snatching up crawfish and then frying their tails or riding an old horse named Sugar, two at a time, bareback, through the woods. Out in the barn were two dozen mixed-breed chickens and a rooster, making so much noise, you could hear him from just about anywhere on the property. My friend's mother was always finding ways to use up the eggs, making beautiful cakes with an older French woman who would come by. A vegetable, herb, and flower garden was just out behind the kitchen, and I relished walking along the pea stone dividing paths and inhaling the scents of fennel, chamomile, lavender, and rosemary. In my memory, my friend's home is a wild kingdom of life and activity; there was work to be done, every day and all the time, in order to maintain the farm. I held onto this bucolic vision all my life.

Twenty years later, it was the view from an Adirondack chair, high on the hill, looking out over the ocean that ultimately called me to Maine. My father's family had owned a blueberry farm in the small town of Dresden for generations. Each July, we'd drive a 1981 Volvo station wagon from Wisconsin to Maine to spend a week picking blueberries with my cousins. My father's lifelong dream was to buy a piece of land on the coast. One dreary afternoon, my family drove east and parked the wagon in a ditch off Route 1, across the street from a rundown, abandoned motel. After bushwhacking through about a hundred yards of brush, there in the distance, through the spitting rain, were the ocean waves breaking on the shore. With a beaming smile, my father said, "Girls, this is where we are going to spend the rest of our lives." My sister and I looked at each other dismayed, my mother forcing a smile in support of her husband.

I was eighteen when my folks bought the twenty-five-acre property on the Atlantic Ocean. The piece of land was an old sheep farm, with hordes of dead trees, lots of standing water, and a fairly dramatic slope down to the coast. But the land faced south, which in a northern climate is hugely beneficial in terms of encouraging plant growth. My father and I had visions of one day building a farm. We constructed a cottage in which we'd spend summers, with four Adirondack chairs perched up on the hill, overlooking Penobscot Bay. I had just begun studying for my undergraduate degree in Colorado but spent summers in Maine, working as a waitress at the local lobster pound and as a prep cook at a little bistro that had received national acclaim. Maine was growing on me quickly. Before leaving at the end of each summer to go back to school, I'd sit in one of the Adirondack chairs to say a final and unwanted good-bye.

After college, I spent seven years in New York City's food industry, working the rounds. I worked at a food magazine as a fact checker, then enrolled in the culinary arts program at the Institute of Culinary Education. It was at ICE that I conceived of a cooking school of my own in Maine, aimed at home cooks. I spent six months writing the business plan that would bring it to life, but I still needed experience.

I spent a summer cooking at a renowned Manhattan restaurant, making raviolis and working the sous-vide machine, crouched under a staircase for ten hours at a time. Realizing that prep work wasn't satisfying me, I got myself hired as a personal assistant for a famous chef (as it turns out, I'm not very good at playing the role of a travel agent). I tried my hand at personal cheffing for families who lived in lavish homes along Central Park, spent weekend mornings doing cooking demonstrations at Greenmarket, and wrote a column about cooking and dating for a Brooklyn-based magazine. Although New York City felt like the center of the culinary universe, it never quite fit right.

My parents were building a barn on our land in Maine, and I proposed that we design a summer kitchen — a large space set away from the house overlooking the garden — and that I teach classes there. I wanted nothing more than to farm to the point of exhaustion in the spring, cook endlessly all summer long, and preserve every last gift from the garden in the fall.

My parents agreed.

I began my first season with a head full of book knowledge on crop rotation and laying hens but no practical experience. There were endless tasks and projects and never enough hours in the day. I quickly found that nothing gave me greater satisfaction than a finished task: a cleaned-out chicken coop, a turned-over and well-shaped soil bed, a bowl full of shelled peas, or a dozen jars of packed tomatoes, put up for the long winter ahead. Working for food was a novelty, one that satisfied my obsession with daily progress. And working all day made me hungry, which made me want to cook all the time. In leaving the city and starting life on a farm, I had found the engine that to this day, eight years later, keeps me running.

It was during this first summer that I came across a book written by Edna Lewis, titled *The Taste of Country Cooking*. Edna Regina Lewis grew up in Freetown, Virginia, knowing the land and the work of the farm and kitchen as her world. But unlike me, she didn't choose it.

She speaks fondly of running around the farm with her cousins, tackling the day's chores and standing around the stove, watching carefully as her mother made supper for the family. I didn't realize it at the time, but I needed guidance. My mind was flush with ideas about sustainable living and objectives for the school, but it wasn't clear how everything would take shape. And really, though I knew how to cook, I didn't know yet how to teach.

As I was beginning to plan my cooking classes, I was also immersing myself in a new way of life. As I read through the seasons' introductions and recipes in Lewis's book, I noticed a style of instruction that was revelatory in its simplicity. Her words were careful observations of her surroundings on a farm in Virginia and a culinary response to those observations. She wasn't delivering highly technical tips and techniques but rather a sort of commonsense cookery that resisted making a fuss of things.

She breathed life into her cookbook through descriptions that illustrate why a dish is made at a precise moment in time: "Blackberries were always a favorite for us and fortunately the small berries ripened just about the time the wheat was harvested so that we could have a cobbler for the dinner." Or, in reference to why fresh skimmed sweet cream was used to make gravy, "We used cream a lot in summer because that was the time when calves were weaned and it was plentiful, just as was the green grass for them to graze on."

It struck me as profound.

Lewis led me into a world in which days are spent providing nourishment to a community of family and friends, and told how this work can bring tremendous pleasure. Pleasure of the senses, all of them: the sweet taste of a sun-ripened peach, the feel of kneading a soft dough on the palm on your hand, the earthy smell of an autumn mushroom just after the rain, the sight of a young lamb springing about in the paddock, or the sound of chickens cooing while taking a dust bath on a warm summer afternoon.

In Maine, I felt humbled by the elements: the thick fog that passed over and through the hills, the northern winds that forced the vast sea to thrash about, and the stillness of the deep woods in the morning, save the sounds of the woodpecker. Though Lewis's Virginia was hundreds of miles, many degrees warmer, and culturally a world apart from my place in coastal Maine, I found much that resonated with me both then and today.

Although Lewis writes often of the work that is associated with eating well, she also reminds us that preparing food can be a rather methodical act, a wonderful way simply to pass the time. It is a means of calming the nerves, satisfying the soul, and finding a sensory tranquillity in the familiarity of the kitchen. "Stews and thick soups cooked leisurely in the side of the hearth and were enjoyed before a lively fire that sent up loud reports of snaps and crackles as if it knew we were enjoying our meal after a day of ploughing through the snow to feed the stock and gather in the evening wood." Lewis helped me to learn and to notice, and she continually reminds me of why we cook.

The following text is a call and response of sorts — excerpts from Lewis's observations living on a farm in Freetown, followed by my own seasonal journal entries from Salt Water Farm. It is the daily work of tending the farm to bring food to the table, shaped by the inevitable progression of the seasons, that informed Lewis's teachings through her writing. It is the same rhythm that shapes my teaching today. Despite the dramatic differences in our time, place, and cultural contexts, I am struck by the similarities in our daily routines and emotional responses. It is this that leads me to feel that Lewis's work and legacy are truly transcendent.

Spring

This was truly a time of birth and rebirth in the barnyard, field and forest. Early morning visits to the barnyard extended into the woods as well, which was just across the stream from the barn. The quiet beauty in rebirth there was so enchanting it cause us to stand still in silence and absorb all we heard and saw.

Soaring high above the stream, swollen with water, are the cormorants, waiting for the alewives to run. Some stand stoically on river rocks drying out their wings from the last dive. Spring is a time when the waters fill with new life, as do the fields. A small fox family lives in a burrow alongside the ocean cliffs of the farm; in the early morning, the mother trots through the meadow in search of a small meal. We are careful to mark the chicken coop with our own scents to deter the fox from snatching up a bird for breakfast.

Naturally, there is much work to be done in the spring. Garden beds need shaping and amending, the greenhouse must be cleaned out and re-organized for planting, and raised beds need to be mended from winter's frost. Perennials begin to reveal themselves—lovage, sorrel, and chives emerge in the herb garden, asparagus spears push the cold soil, and the rhubarb plant begins to form its leaves.

Spring begins in our glass greenhouse. Once the evening lows start hovering closer to the freezing point than dipping far below, we plant seedlings. I always pick sunny days to start this process; it's magical to feel the warmth generated by the sun in a greenhouse when the ground is still covered in snow. A burst of vitamin D goes a long way this time of year. The dogs walk the pea stones of the greenhouse floor while I lay out plastic seedling trays across potting tables and sprinkle them with compacted soil.

There is an order in which we plant. Some crops prefer direct seeding when the threat of frost has past. Others benefit from getting a head start in the greenhouse and then being transplanted into the ground, once conditions permit. Cold-weather crops, such as peas, radishes, arugula, spinach, beets, carrots, and kale, can withstand chilly nights, and their seeds can go into the ground as soon early as April. Hot-weather crops, such as tomatoes, eggplants, cucumbers, and peppers, must wait until the weather has warmed significantly. The timing of transplants is critical to their success: too soon and the cold will stunt their growth, too late and they won't mature until late summer. Planting this early in the season gives me a head start, so that come August, I will have big, fat, and juicy tomatoes, ripe for the picking, and peppers that are swollen and glistening, ready for the grill. On a rainy spring day, standing in the greenhouse makes me feel warm and sheltered, and with a little music playing, there's nowhere else I'd rather be.

By early May, the seedlings have established little roots and are ready to be repotted into larger vessels or transplanted out of doors. It is common practice to harden the plants by setting them outside during the day to adapt to the elements of wind, direct sun, rain, and fluctuating temperatures and then bringing them in for protection at night. After a few days of exposure, I'll leave them out through a night or two, and then they are ready to move into their home in the garden. If the plants are hot crops such as tomatoes, cucumbers, squash or peppers, they are not quite ready for these cool spring nights. Until the heat of summer arrives, they need to be moved to bigger pots, with generous handfuls of compost to feed them, and kept inside.

Summer

Another late afternoon feast would be the melons my father had gathered in the early morning from the melon patch while the dew still lingered on them. He would put them in a tub of water or underneath the shrubbery until we were ready to eat them. Before he ever sliced open a melon, he would always plug it — by cutting out a small piece which he would taste to see if it had the proper flavor.

Early in the morning and when the tide is high, my father slips out of the house in his fishing gear and heads down to the shore. He tips his kayak into the sea, and in the still water and bright light, he hangs a mackerel lure off the boat: three little shiny rigs twittering through the briny water. Mackerel swim in schools, like many fish, and when you catch them, you are likely to catch two or three at a time. They are the most beautiful small fish, silvery blue and sparkling. Mackerel are an oily fish and are best eaten either raw with a bit of preserved lemon or grilled whole and stuffed with lemon and herbs. In early July, they are still young and the bones are small, but by August, the fish have swollen in size and the fillets become quite meaty. Some days, they are running like crazy, and my dad will bring up a long wooden stick with eight or ten of them strung up in a glorious display. If he times it just right, I'll be in the midst of teaching eight students about local fish varieties, and my dad will perform a fish-filleting demonstration with his boning knife, which hangs from his neck in a sheath and is always kept sharp. Watching my father fillet a fish is a rather nostalgic image; I have watched him, with his patience and precision, fillet fish since I was a kid. I always thought it was a special skill. If he doesn't get around to cooking the fish up the day that he catches them, he always pickles them in a little white wine, Pernod, fennel, and aromatics to be eaten for breakfast all week.

The busy season of harvesting vegetables and canning brought many delights at mealtime: deep-dish blackberry pie, rolypoly, summer apple dumplings, peach cobblers, and always pound cake to accompany the fruits or berries that would be left from canning.

Berries are the much-awaited gift of July, nature's way of apologizing for a hard and cold winter. The soil in Maine is acidic, which berries love. Berry bushes of all kinds creep and crawl along fences and old rock walls, across fields and even the seashore. I first discovered wild blueberries on the backside of a mountain range called Maiden's Cliff. The dogs and I were taking an afternoon hike when, all of the sudden, the path opened up to a big, blue sky and acres of wild Maine blueberries, stretching as far as the eye could see. I bent down and began picking them and popping them my mouth. The dogs followed suit. There is no comparison between the taste of a wild Maine blueberry and a commercially grown berry. The wild berries are not too sweet, not too tart, and not too tannic. They have a gentle flavor and taste mostly of summertime. Standing in a sea of blueberries, the mountain and its fruit all to myself, I was reminded of why I left New York City.

Each year, our berry bushes put off more and more fruit, calling for culinary application. Usually, I'll start by eating as many berries as my stomach will allow. Then, I'll make a handful of pies and tarts, trifles and sauces. When I've satisfied my need for all fresh dishes, I'll cook down pounds of berries with sugar and pectin and fill Mason jars with the hot, bubbling preserves so that all winter long, I can spread summer's jewels on homemade bread. Jam must be made at the height of the fruit's freshness so that you are bottling the sweet, fresh tastes of summertime. The joy of making a strawberry tart in June lies mainly in the fact that we have waited nearly a year to taste the first summer strawberry, watching it fruit out in the patch, ripening little by little until it's ready to be picked.

The main crop of the garden vegetables would be coming in at this time: new cabbage, potatoes, cymling (a white squash nearly flat and round with scalloped edges), butter beans, string beans, tomatoes, eggplant, and roasting ears.

Annemarie Ahearn

Come July, we celebrate our first true harvest of sizable vegetables. If planted at just the right time, fruiting plants such as cucumbers, zucchini, summer squash, and even cherry tomatoes will begin offering their first fruit in mid-July. There is tremendous satisfaction in knowing that there has been enough heat, enough rain, and enough sun in our northern climate to grow warm-weather crops. This is the time when I begin introducing panzanella and gazpacho to our menus at the cooking school and supper club, dishes that highlight and celebrate the garden's offerings with little more than olive oil, salt, lemon, and crusty bread.

By mid-September, you can be sure that an excess of perfectly edible vegetables exists in the wilds of your garden (or at the farmers' market), and it is your duty as a cook to put up the extras for winter. Not to mention the pleasures that come from biting into a crisp cucumber in the late fall, spooning onion relish on your cheesy toast at a holiday meal, or laying a few dilly beans across a steak sandwich well into the winter.

The first hams of the season would be cooked about July and August in case an unexpected summer guest dropped in.

August is the height of the summer season in Maine. Traffic lines up for miles, both north and south of our tiny town, and tourists with Massachusetts and New York plates drive slowly, scanning the storefronts for shopping opportunities. As a community, we depend on this business, as it represents a shocking percentage of our annual gross sales, but truthfully, we'd prefer to be tucked away on a secret path in the woods or lying across a warm rock on the lake's edge. But, alas, there is money to be made, and so we work day and night to capture a living.

There is no time for meals in the month of August. We are simply too busy food-shopping, cleaning, preparing recipes, doing laundry, setting the table, harvesting from the garden, pickling and preserving . . . the list goes on and on. And because our job involves food and usually tasting, nibbling, or sitting down to a meal with a table full of paying guests, there is really no need for cooking outside of work. Dinner consists of leftovers from the business, which my husband has never complained about. Clients always ask me how I stay so thin, and the answer is simple. In the summertime, I never stop moving or sit down for more than a of couple minutes.

The availability of mushrooms depends largely on the rains and moisture in the earth's surface. In August, at the farmers' market, there are piles of fragrant, foraged mushrooms, such as chanterelle, black trumpet, and oyster mushrooms. But the ultimate treat is to find them yourself in the wild. On hot August days, we take a little inflatable boat out into Penobscot Bay on island adventures. Off the back, we drag fishing lines. Once we are close to shore, we pull up a half-dozen mackerel. We often gut and fillet the fish right there on the boat, their flesh still warm with life, squeeze a bit of lemon on the meat, and pop it into our mouths. After the boat is anchored, we swim in the cold water to the shore to explore the island. A trail of chanterelles, all perfectly ripe for picking, gets our attention. We gather them in our T-shirts to sell them to local restaurants. On the rocky shore, we drink beers kept cold in a pool of saltwater and relish the day's work.

Fall

Unlike other seasons of the year, the coming of fall was looked upon with mixed feelings. When the leaves began to fall, all the visitors were gone, and the whistle from the train passing through Orange gave a long, lonesome, shrill sound as it rolled through without stopping to let off any passengers.

Fall brings with it a bitter sweetness, now that the hot days of summer have passed. The cool breeze that blows between the hills reminds us that we've earned our keep, and it's finally time to slow down and relax. The tourists have headed south, leaving us to make do for the long winter ahead. Autumn is the time of year to turn our attention to the home, which will again become a sanctuary. It is also time to order cords of firewood, a hot commodity in Maine in the fall. Firewood does more than keep you warm as the weather cools; its gathering and carrying provides a daily routine that gets your blood flowing each morning and offers comfort throughout the day.

Pickles, relishes, spiced fruit, jellies, and jams played an important role in the make-up of each meal, especially the meals of fall and winter.
    Pickling, as was other canning and preserving, was woven into her everyday work.

I quickly came to understand the importance of food storage in Maine as the long stretch of winter provided little nourishment. My father and I began to explore food preservation through methods of salting and smoking. In the fall, I packed beans and cucumbers into vinegar and cooked down berries with heaping cups of sugar. I put away as much food as I could, imagining how people in Maine learned these skills as a means of survival hundreds of years ago. Food preservation became as important as food growing, a bookend to the season.

Hunting season was as much a part of harvesting as hog butchering, turkey picking, gathering of nuts, berries, persimmons, and apples. Rabbit, quail, squirrel, plover, snipe, woodcock, and wild turkey lived in the woods and surrounding fields feeding upon hickory nuts, hazelnuts, persimmons, corn, and other cereal grains and frequently feeding with backyard flocks. Hunting was not a sport of killing but a way of adding variety to the food supply, making our meals more interesting and delicious.

There are plenty of culinary projects worth pursuit in the fall. In October each year, my father and I head up to Blue Hill, Maine, where George, a dear friend, takes us through the brush, shotguns in tow, and we listen carefully for the flutter of grouse or the peeping of Maine's most prized hunting bird, the woodcock, which you can track by what it leaves behind. Just before woodcocks take off in flight, they defecate on the ground below, marking the leaves with a white trail. While I have held and shot both my father's and George's guns, I prefer to act as the dog, rustling the underbrush to send the birds into the sky. Of course, there is the slight risk from the bullets flying overhead, but the two of them are pretty good shots, so I figure that my odds aren't bad. After a long day of bushwhacking and walks along the blueberry barrens—now red in their late-season dress—we head back to George's mother's house (built two centuries ago), deep in the Maine woods, and sit by the fire sipping Scotch out of small shot glasses painted with tiny woodcocks. We hang the day's hunt and pull from George's reserve of birds that have been hanging in the garage for days, flavoring the meat. We defeather and gut the birds in the sink and then prepare them whole in the oven, brushed with a little butter. The entrails are made into a paté and spread on toast as an appetizer. A sauce, made of huckleberries or currants, accompanies them. The meal is a fine reward for the day's hunt.

An apple orchard was a basic part of every homestead. It supplied all of the fruit used. The orchard was also a kind of nursery for baby calves when weaned from the mother cow, and a haven for birds, especially bluebirds and robins. The little bluebird always made its nest in the hollow of an apple tree.

On fair-weather days, we gather apples and pears from the orchards and press them into cider to be consumed fresh or fermented and distilled into a harder beverage. My father and I spend the better part of the morning grinding the fruit, then loading it into the barrels to age for a day or two, then pressing it on my great-grandfather's hundred-year-old press, which is hard and time-consuming work. The juice runs down the sides of the press into the wooden spout and then fills the glass stills that allow for its distillation. We often celebrate the day's work with a sip of last year's cider, to remind us of why we continue the tradition, despite our sore backs.

Winter

The main meal was served in the evening because the short daylight hours of winter and the early feeding of the stock. This was the time to draw upon the canned vegetables and fruits that had been prepared during those unbearable hot days of the past summer. In addition, there was sausage, liver pudding, spareribs, wild game from the hunting parties, and wild watercress.

I love to watch the leaves from my kitchen window gather on the ground, the wind whipping them around in circles and then rescattering them. As a result of daylight savings time ending, the chickens take a break from laying in November, and we take great care to put them in before dusk, after which the fox and other predators are scouring the neighborhood, looking for their own food to put away for winter. In daylight hours, the chickens enjoy their last days of roaming the still-green grass, foraging for any living remains and shaking out their feathers in the sunshine. Often in early winter, the chickens molt and lose much of their plumage, leaving them looking as though they've weathered some sort of storm. Their tails become thin, and they develop big bald spots under their wing sockets.

Annemarie Ahearn

Meat features prominently on our menus throughout the winter, both game and farmed animals slaughtered in the fall. Many folks keep a deep freezer in the barn full of pork, venison, or beef so that they can eat local meats year-round. The quality of meat depends entirely on its origin. Take a pig, for example. A well-raised, well-fed, and well-butchered pig results in naturally delicious meat. Smothering a good pork chop in flavorful sauce or a dry rub, in my opinion, devalues the work that went into its production. When you think about food in terms of the quality of the ingredients themselves, cooking becomes a far less daunting proposition. Success lies in simplicity. I try to impart this lesson throughout my cooking classes at Salt Water Farm. It is wonderful to watch my students achieve this realization. For years, they have been overthinking dinner, which takes the joy out of cooking. Oddly enough, going back to the basics is a mental hurdle for some.

Many folks used to have a cellar; a cool, dark place to store root vegetables for winter. (In many corners of Maine, the tradition still exists; many use their unfinished basements for such a purpose, or a dugout hole in a hillside with a cover for protection.) For most people, though, the most convenient dark and cold place for roots is in the refrigerator, where they will last many months, if properly stored.

In the woods, the start of winter is hunting season, and it's absolutely mandatory that blaze orange be incorporated into your wardrobe. You cannot go for a walk or a hike without hearing a gun go off. Mid-November is when the season opens for deer hunting, a strong tradition in Maine's northern woods. A quick trip to the grocery store or the post office, and you're likely to see a truck bed with a deer carcass or just a pair of hooves hanging off the back, a blaze orange hat resting above the dash. It's a defining part of northern culture, a tradition that is cherished by most of the state of Maine.

It was in between these daily chores that the people of Freetown found more time for visiting each other.

The best part of winter is the luxury of time. We host and attend dinner parties all through the week and into the weekend, catching up with friends and telling stories about our frenzied summers. We pore through cookbooks and make recipes that we have never made before; we bake breads and make cakes in celebration of the holidays. During the short daylight hours, we skate on the ponds, cross-country ski through the woods, and take the dogs on long walks down snow-covered paths. A fire always warms us at sunset, along with the company of good friends and family.

In the summer of 2016, I began teaching a class called "Honoring Edna Lewis: American Southern Cuisine." It was quick to sell out, because Lewis's legacy resonates with so many people. In this class, we discuss the significant value of growing food as a chef, the relevance of time and place in the conception of a dish, and the richness of food traditions. We also study the importance of regional fare in the American culinary landscape and why it's considered the only true form of American cuisine. Last, we craft a meal inspired by Edna Lewis and Freetown but made with ingredients that are native to Maine, with a nod to our own regional cuisine, that of New England. The menu is simple and straightforward, a reflection of the life and breath of summer in Maine. Despite differences in time, place, and historical context, the lessons in regional home cooking are much the same on Salt Water Farm in Maine or in a well-stocked kitchen in Freetown, Virginia.

A Summertime Sunday Supper

Sweet Tea with Anise Hyssop

Green Bean Salad with Summer Tomatoes

Slow-Cooked Skillet Onions

Spoon Bread

Pan-Fried Chicken with Creamy Gravy

Blackberry Cobbler with Sweet Cream

Sweet Tea with Anise Hyssop

On our group tours through the garden, I always insist that my students sample a small piece of anise hyssop. It's an unassuming little green leaf with magnitudes of floral and licorice flavor. It makes a wonderful addition to sweet creams and salads, but its most refreshing application is in summer sweet tea. We always use honey rather than sugar to sweeten teas since honey is less harsh.

{MAKES 1 PITCHER}

5 black tea bags (PG Tips or English Breakfast)
½ cup honey
30 anise hyssop leaves
1 lemon, cut into quarter rounds
A few handfuls of ice

Fill a large glass pitcher three-quarters of the way with water and pour into a large pot. Bring to a boil, then turn off the heat. Add the black tea bags, honey, and anise hyssop. Let the tea bags steep for 10 minutes, then remove. Let the anise hyssop steep for another 10 minutes, then give the pot a stir. Strain back into the glass pitcher and let cool. When ready to serve, add the lemon rounds and ice. Give the pitcher another stir and pour into iced tea glasses.

Green Bean Salad with Summer Tomatoes

This dish is a declaration that summer has arrived. Cherry tomatoes ripen on the vine, tender green filet beans hang by the dozens, and herbs grow in abundance throughout the garden. You can garnish this dish with an assortment of colorful edible flowers, such as nasturtiums, calendulas, or daylilies.

{MAKES 4 SERVINGS}

For the salad

1½ pounds green beans, cleaned and stems removed
1 pint cherry tomatoes, cleaned
1 bunch chervil, leaves picked from stems
Edible flowers for garnish
Sea salt to taste

For the vinaigrette

1 shallot, skins removed and roughly chopped
Pinch of kosher salt
Juice and zest of 1 lemon
⅓ cup sherry vinegar
¼ cup packed parsley
¼ cup packed basil leaves
6 tarragon sprigs, leaves picked from stems
½ cup olive oil
Kosher salt and freshly ground pepper

Bring a large pot of well-salted water to a boil. Prepare an ice bath and outfit yourself with a set of tongs or a slotted spoon. When the water is at a rolling boil, add the green beans and cook for 3–4 minutes or until just tender. Then plunge them into the ice bath, so that they retain their color, and let them cool fully. Lift them out of the ice bath with a slotted spoon and dry them on a clean kitchen towel or in a colander.

To make the vinaigrette, in a blender or food processor, pulse the shallots with a pinch of salt. Add the lemon juice and zest, sherry vinegar, parsley, basil, and tarragon, and blend on low until smooth. Add the olive oil and pulse again. Taste for seasoning, adding salt and pepper as needed.

Cut the cherry tomatoes in half. Toss the beans and cherry tomatoes with half of the dressing. Garnish with chervil, edible flowers, and sea salt. Serve with additional dressing in a little bowl on the table.

Annemarie Ahearn

Slow-Cooked Skillet Onions

Nothing is more satisfying to me than a well-cooked onion. Onions are the foun-dation of so many dishes, the base for building a flavor profile. They are won-derful cooked in a myriad of ways: grilled, sautéed, buried in ash, slowed baked, and braised. But every so often, it's important to honor the onion, a member of the allium family, all on its own.

{MAKES 6 SERVINGS}

4 tablespoons butter
2 tablespoons honey
4 small garden onions (such as Tropea, Redwing, Cippoline, or
    sweet), peeled and cut in half lengthwise (roots still attached)
Kosher salt
2 cups water
2 tablespoons apple cider vinegar

Heat a large cast-iron pan over medium-low heat. Add the butter and honey. When the butter begins to foam, add the onions, cut side down, along with a big pinch of salt. Cook slowly for 25–30 minutes. Each time the pan dries up, add a couple tablespoons of water and move the onions around a bit. When the onions are golden brown on the bottom side and nearly cooked through, flip them over. Add the cider vinegar to the pan. Continue cooking for 10–15 minutes or until cooked through.

Spoon Bread and Fresh Butter

The act of making spoon bread should comfort any cook because it is simple and soft and delicious. It's important to whisk the eggs with vigor so that they incor-porate enough air to give the bread a bit of lift. And spoon bread must be served with generous amounts of fresh butter and a sprinkling of sea salt.

{SERVES 6}

For the homemade butter

2 cups heavy cream
1 quart-sized Mason jar with a wide mouth
Sea salt

5 tablespoons butter
1 cup all-purpose flour
½ cup white or yellow medium-ground cornmeal
2 tablespoons sugar
1 teaspoon baking soda
2 teaspoons baking powder
½ teaspoon kosher salt
4 eggs
1 cup buttermilk

For the butter, take the cream out of the fridge and pour it into the Mason jar. Let it come to room temperature, about 30–45 minutes. Place the lid on the jar and seal tightly. Shake, shake, shake, and then shake some more. After about 10 minutes of shaking, the butter will thicken into a cream. You can remove the top to check it. Then keep shaking, and like magic, the butter liquids will separate from the butter solids, offering up butter and buttermilk. Pour off the buttermilk and reserve it (you can use the buttermilk to make the spoon bread). Then move the butter into your hands and squeeze off any additional buttermilk. Give the butter a rinse with very cold water and place in a crock. Sprinkle a little sea salt on top and chill slightly.

For the spoon bread, preheat the oven to 400°. Place the butter in an 8-inch cast-iron frying pan, and let it melt in the oven. In a mixing bowl, whisk together the flour, cornmeal, sugar, baking soda, baking powder, and salt. Make a well in the center. In a small bowl, whisk the eggs with gusto for 2–3 minutes. Slowly add the eggs and buttermilk to the well. Remove the pan from the oven, swirl the butter around to cover the bottom and sides of the pan, and pour the excess into the well. Stir the batter with a spoon until well incorporated, then pour it into the pan. Place the pan in the oven and bake for 40–45 minutes. Remove when the bread is golden brown and set in the center.

Pan-Fried Chicken with Creamy Gravy

Edna Lewis offers poetic instruction on the subject of fried chicken in The Taste of Country Cooking. Her mother took great care to give the cooking pan her full attention, turning each piece of poultry several times to brown the surfaces properly in a medley of fresh butter, home-rendered lard, and a slice or two of smoked pork. After browning the breasts, she lay them atop the legs and thighs and allowed the residual heat of the pan to complete their cooking. The gravy was then built in the pan with a few tablespoons of flour and skimmed sweet cream, which was plentiful when the calves were being weaned. Even in the North, we wouldn't dare stray too far from her recipe.

{SERVES 6}

For the fried chicken

1 whole chicken, cut into legs, thighs, breasts (cut then
    again in half), and wings (tips removed)
1½ cups all-purpose flour
½ cup whole wheat flour
2 teaspoons kosher salt
½ teaspoon freshly ground black pepper
8 tablespoons (1 stick) unsalted butter
½ cup canola oil or lard

For the stock and gravy

Chicken carcass and wing tips
1 yellow onion, diced
2 carrots, roughly chopped
3 celery stalks with leaves, roughly chopped
12 peppercorns
1 bay leaf
1 herb bundle (2 parsley sprigs, 2 thyme sprigs, 2 rosemary sprigs)
4 tablespoons fat (unsalted butter, oil, or lard)
3 tablespoons all-purpose flour

Rinse each chicken piece and blot it dry with paper towels or a chicken cloth. Combine the flours, salt, and pepper in a shallow medium bowl. Mix until evenly seasoned. Dredge each piece of chicken in the flour mixture on all sides and set aside on a platter. Let the chicken rest for 1 hour, allowing the meat to absorb the flour so that it sticks when fried.

To make chicken stock for the gravy, place the chicken carcass, onions, carrots, celery, peppercorns, bay leaf, and herb bundle in a large pot. Add water just to cover. Bring to a boil, reduce to a simmer, and skim off any foam that rises to the top. Cook for 45 minutes. Using a colander, strain into a medium saucepan. Reserve 3 cups of stock for the gravy.

To fry the chicken, place the butter and oil (or lard) in a large cast-iron pan on the stove and heat the oil to 375°. Add the chicken pieces one at a time, fitting them all snugly in the pan. They should sizzle when they go in, and the oil should come halfway up the chicken pieces. Cover and cook about 12 minutes, lifting the lid occasionally to keep an eye on the chicken and moving pieces around to brown all the parts. Flip each piece and cook for 12 minutes more, again making sure to brown all parts while leaving the cover on as much as possible.

Remove each piece to a sheet pan to rest. If additional cooking is desired, put the chicken pieces in an oven preheated to 400° for 5 minutes.

To make the gravy, pour off all but 4 tablespoons of the fat from the frying pan. Whisk the flour into the fat, slowly toasting until the roux turns medium brown, about 3 minutes. Slowly whisk the chicken stock into the roux and cook for 15 minutes. Taste for salt and pepper and season accordingly.

To serve, pile the chicken on a platter. Dress with gravy. Serve hot with spoon bread.

Blackberry Cobbler

Come late August, the blackberry brambles that stretch over the rock walls of our seaside farm are bursting with berries. Each morning, I go out to collect a handful for breakfast, and later in the afternoon, with a basket in hand, I collect larger amounts for jams, pies, cobblers, and muffins. As much as I love the bitter, sweet, and tart nature of blackberries, they are a reminder that berry season is coming to a close and autumn is around the corner.

{SERVES 6}

For the pastry

2¼ cups flour
1½ teaspoon baking powder
¾ teaspoon baking soda
¼ teaspoon kosher salt

6 tablespoons sugar

6 tablespoons cold unsalted butter, cut into pieces

1 egg yolk

½ cup heavy cream

For the filling

3 pints fresh blackberries

1 cup sugar, plus 2 tablespoons for topping

2 tablespoons cornstarch

4 tablespoons unsalted butter, cut into small pieces

¼ cup sliced almonds

For the pastry, sift together the flour, baking powder, baking soda, salt, and all but 2 tablespoons of the sugar into a mixing bowl. Use two knives or your fingers to work the butter into the flour mixture until it resembles coarse meal. Whisk the egg yolk and heavy cream together in a small bowl and stir into the flour mixture with a fork until the dough just begins to hold together. Wrap the dough in plastic and let it rest for 20 minutes in the refrigerator.

For the filling, preheat the oven to 425°. Pour the blackberries into an 8 × 8 × 2-inch baking dish, sprinkle with the sugar and cornstarch, and gently mix to incorporate. Distribute the butter pieces throughout the berries.

Pinch off walnut-size bits of dough and arrange them evenly over the berries, then scatter with the almonds and sprinkle with the remaining sugar. Bake until the berries are bubbling, the pastry is golden, and a toothpick inserted in the center comes out clean, 40–45 minutes. Set aside to cool for 20–30 minutes before serving.

The Wisdom in the Pages

VIVIAN HOWARD

🙖 🙖

I wonder: Is it appropriate to call someone you've never met and know only through books your mentor?

I worked briefly in other chefs' kitchens in New York. Scott Barton inspired me to start cooking at Voyage in the West Village. The kitchen culture and command of technique at Wylie Dufresne's WD-50 impressed and humbled me. I gained confidence and speed in the early days of Jean-Georges Vongerichten's Spice Market. But in my years of apprenticeship and training, I never worked for, alongside, or under anyone who helped me develop my voice more than Edna Lewis has.

My husband, Ben, laid the *Taste of Country Cooking* on top of a stack of cookbooks next to my bed during what I'll call my tomato petal period. The restaurant we run together in eastern North Carolina had been open about a year, and we were moderately busy, a miracle in a downtown where more buildings were condemned than occupied. The way we saw it, Chef and the Farmer was committed to three things: helping tobacco farmers become food farmers, educating our salad bar–loving clientele on the finer points of dining out, and staying open.

I made seasonal, tasty food, but it was all over the map. On any given night our menu offered a mishmash of things like chicken samosas with cilantro yogurt, duck confit pappardelle, smoked goat cheese raviolis with tomato petals, and chocolate molten cake with roasted banana ice cream. I studied Thomas Keller's *French Laundry Cookbook*, rolling and poaching foie gras torchons, whisking beurre monté, and steeping lobsters in their shells exactly the way Chef Keller told me to. I read *Not Afraid of Flavor*, by Durham, North Carolina, restaurateur pioneers Ben and Karen Barker, front to back and cooked nearly every recipe in between. I went to bed with Alice Waters's *Art of Simple Food* and woke up primed to shower her austere plates in a torrent of tomato petals. But after all that, I failed to do anything other than cook versions of Keller's, the Barkers', and Waters's food in my own kitchen. I was an earnest, hardworking cook who wanted desperately for my food to do more than just fill bellies, but I didn't know what "more" was.

It must have been frustrating for Ben to guide hopeful diners through a menu muddled by multiple genres with a "global" focus, because after watching me flounder for a year, he went to Amazon.com for help. His goal was to find cookbooks that better represented our place in the world. He used the words "country" and "southern" to guide the search. Miss Lewis's book rose to the top, like cream in a pail of fresh milk.

I dismissed *The Taste of Country Cooking* initially and left it for lost in the always growing stack of books next to my bed. I had never heard of Edna Lewis and was particularly quick to snub all of my husband's suggestions at the time. Furthermore, I had spent the better part of my adolescent and adult life trying not to appear or sound "country." While living in New York, I altered my accent so dramatically that people often asked me if I was from England or New Zealand. By the time Lewis's book arrived in my life, I had come to terms with living in the country again, but I had worked hard to shed signs of my backwoods upbringing. If I was going to read about southern food, it was going to be southern city food. I already knew about, and was frankly embarrassed by, the country kind.

But one Sunday morning a few months later, I woke up early, rolled over, and found *The Taste of Country Cooking* on top of that stack again. Miss Lewis — regal, wise, and warm — stared back at me from the cover of her modest-looking book.

I generally read cookbooks from beginning to end like novels, interested as much in the author's story as I am in their recipes. I approached Miss Lewis's book the same way.

"I grew up in Freetown, Virginia, a community of farming people. It wasn't really a town." These, her first two sentences, whispered me in, made me think we shared a history. I grew up in Deep Run, after all, a similar-sounding place, not founded by freed slaves, but a community of farmers organized around a general store and a school — definitely not a town, definitely country. I instantly felt as if I knew Miss Lewis, as if she was in the room telling me her story.

I spent that day and many that followed lost in the Morning-After-Hog-Butchering breakfasts, the Hearty Midday dinners, and the Cool Evening suppers of Miss Lewis's youth. I had been drawn to the new techniques, flavor combinations, pictures, and lengthy recipes in other cookbooks, but

Miss Lewis's story itself—her memories of life in Freetown, her deceptively simple recipes, and her familiar, matter-of-fact voice—resonated with me and forced me to look at the food of my place in a new light. *The Taste of Country Cooking* wasn't just organized around the seasons; its menus took shape around the work that came with a given time of year, and I related to that narrative.

Our summers in Deep Run revolved around topping, suckering, and barning tobacco. We started work before 7:00 a.m. because of the heat and ate big, hearty breakfasts, fortifying midmorning snacks, light dinners (which we called lunches), and early suppers. My grandfather carried a roasted sweet potato in his pocket to fight off afternoon hunger in the field, and my dad drove a pickup carrying sleeves of salt-roasted peanuts and coolers of Pepsi to offer end-of-day energy. I grew up hearing about hog killings, celebrating with pig pickings, putting up corn, and shelling butter beans. My grandmother made fruit preserves and picked medium cucumbers and dropped them in salt brine for pickles just like Miss Lewis's mother did. And we celebrated the harvest and hunkered down for the winter much as Lewis described that she and her community did. By writing about it, Miss Lewis celebrated the rural way of life I had been so ashamed of. She made country living seem magical, and her stories began to reshape my own memories. *The Taste of Country Cooking* wasn't a cookbook like the others in the stack next to my bed; it was a love letter about family, survival, and community told through the lens of food. In the pages of Miss Lewis's book, I learned what my food at Chef and the Farmer had been missing. It lacked a connection to my place and my people. It was void of emotion. My food didn't have heart.

Although I've only cooked about a third of the recipes from Miss Lewis's classic book, I found my voice amid hours spent in its pages. Miss Lewis taught me to exalt the mundane; in the everyday, the commonplace, lies the love. So I started to look at the ubiquitous dishes of my region, the foods that were a part of my DNA, as a starting point.

To celebrate my mother's chicken and rice, I sought balance with lemon juice. I added bright notes with fresh herbs, and I created texture with crispy chicken skin. I preserved figs, peaches, and blackberries in syrup just as the farmers' wives of eastern Carolina would have. Then I rounded those preserves out with aromatics and vinegar to make complex sauces for meats. I took eastern Carolina's sharp vinegar-based barbecue sauce and tamed it with the deep sweet of blueberries. I fried teeny tiny hushpuppies, my region's companion for fish and barbecue, and called them croutons. I stewed collards with ham hocks, pickled their stems, and stuffed it all in a potato as a companion for steak. I swapped field peas in for cannellini beans, sage in for oregano, cornbread in for ciabatta, added some salt pork, and made a country ribollita. I did all of this with both my roots and my customers in mind. I wanted to honor the food of my people, but I also wanted my food to appeal to a modern audience. At the restaurant, I don't make my mother's food, my grandmother's food, or the food found on buffets and covered-dish suppers around eastern Carolina, but I'm inspired by all of it.

Miss Lewis taught me to lead with the story—the whys and whens— because stories make an impression and provide context. So with nearly every dish I introduced to my diners, I provided a story about the concept for the dish itself, about the person who grew the ingredient, or about something I learned while making it. And because I could see bits of myself in her, Miss Lewis showed me that food and cooking can be a means to connect with people, a universal way for us to see the things we have in common rather than the ways we're different. These lessons are the foundation for my work. They define, nurture, and tune my voice.

Years after first finding Miss Lewis, I wrote my own book. In it I tell the story of eastern North Carolina through its food. I argue that our country cooking is as worthy as any cuisine in the world, and I organize the whole thing according to the trajectory of my personal and professional journey. Before I started writing, I put away all of my cookbooks, including Miss Lewis's. I worried that I might accidentally emulate someone's style, plagiarize their work, or generally psych myself out with too many role models hanging around. Throughout the entire two-year process, I cracked nary a food tome. Honestly I'm still queasy and unsure of myself when I open one up today. So imagine what it was like to revisit *The Taste of Country Cooking*'s timeless, streamlined bucolic sensibilities for this tribute. Humbling—that's what it was.

Country Ribollita

Like Lewis was, I've been permanently etched by the classic techniques and dishes of European cuisines, once—not so long ago—judged the world's only sophisticated cuisines. Part of my reckoning of identity was a realization that the American South has culinary traditions no less worthy of the term cuisine than the gastronomic traditions of the Continent. It took me a long time to learn this truth; Lewis, on the other hand, seemed to know it in her bones.

Ribollita is a classic Tuscan soup based on vegetables, beans, and stale bread. In this eastern Carolina adaptation, I've got all that going on, but with field peas, lima beans, cornbread, and salt pork, the foods of my home region.

Yes, it's a big pot of soup. I can't make a small one. I usually make this on winter weekends to eat throughout the week. Ben poaches a couple of eggs in it and eats a huge bowl for breakfast. Basil or arugula pesto makes a nice, bright condiment.

{MAKES 4 QUARTS; SERVES 10}

1 cup dried lima beans
½ cup dried field peas or black-eyed peas
10–11 ounces cured pork seasoning meat
2 medium yellow onions, diced
⅓ cup olive oil, divided
½ teaspoon salt
6 garlic cloves, sliced
2 celery stalks, diced
2 medium carrots or 1 large carrot, diced
1 cup red wine
4 cups canned diced tomatoes
1 teaspoon dried sage
½ teaspoon dried thyme
2 bay leaves
½ head green cabbage, cut into 1-inch dice
6 cups cubed day-old cornbread
1 cup grated Parmigiano-Reggiano

Soak the lima beans and peas in water separately overnight. The next day, combine the pork with 10 cups water in a 4-quart saucepan or Dutch oven with a tight-fitting lid. Cover and bring to a boil. Cook for 30 minutes over medium heat.

Add the field peas and simmer for 10 minutes. Then stir in the limas. Cover and cook an additional 30–40 minutes. The field peas should be tender and the limas cooked through. Some of the limas will be falling apart. You want this to happen because it will make the finished soup a bit creamy. If this is not the case, continue to simmer the beans until it is. Once the beans are as they should be, take them off the heat, pluck out the pork, and set it aside. You may want to put little bits of it in the final dish.

In a separate 4-quart Dutch oven, sweat the onions with 2 tablespoons olive oil and the salt over medium heat for 5 minutes. Add the garlic, celery, and carrots and cook for another 3–4 minutes. Don't let anything brown.

Add the red wine and cook for 3–4 minutes. Stir in the tomatoes, sage, thyme, bay leaves, and all the beans, as well as their cooking liquid. Bring to a boil, cover, and cook for 15 minutes. Stir in the cabbage, cover again, and cook for another 10 minutes.

In a perfect kitchen, you'd make this in an actual 4-quart Dutch oven, chill it down overnight to let the flavors marry, and then bring it out the next day about an hour before you wanted to serve it. You'd preheat your oven to 375° and heat the stew gently on your stove just to take the chill off. Then you'd toss the cornbread with the rest of the olive oil and Parmigiano, sprinkle it on top of the stew, and slide the whole pot onto the middle rack of the oven. You'd bake it for 30 minutes. During that time you'd see the cornbread toast and the stew bubble up some around the sides. Then you'd serve it to people who were really excited.

If you don't cook in a perfect kitchen—like me and everyone else I know—you can still serve this to people who are really excited by tossing and toasting the cornbread with the remaining ¼ cup olive oil and the Parmigiano and serving it over the hot stew.

Their Ideas Do Live on for Us

Edna Lewis, My Grandmother, and the Continuities
of a Southern Preserving Tradition

KEVIN WEST

On June 8, 1861, the citizens of Blount County in east Tennessee—567 square miles of fertile valleys and wooded foothills that climb toward the Smoky Mountain crest—paused from their work in fields and towns to cast ballots in a referendum on the state's Ordinance of Secession, which had been shepherded through the General Assembly by Governor Isham Harris. Blount County voted against, by a count of 1,766 to 414. Strong secessionist majorities in middle Tennessee swung the other way, and Tennessee became the last state to join the Confederacy.

None of my living family members knows with certainty how our Anglo–Scotch-Irish ancestors voted, but the Wests have lived in Blount County long enough that our family lore stretches back almost to that day. My father heard his great-grandfather tell that, as a young boy, he saw Union soldiers pass his window at the end of the cataclysm. That ancestor was Payton West, born on my birthday, May 22, in 1860, so his memory of boyhood must have been either unusually acute or, more likely, informed by stories he later heard and adopted as his own. Payton went on to study law and to keep a farm, although without much success on the latter count. He had a bookish and moody nature—I suspect today he'd be diagnosed as depressive—and his land produced poorly. The family lacked. Payton's son, Burgess, had a clearer mind and a stronger back. With poverty as his goad, Burgess acquired land at a steady clip and died with 500 acres. One of his ten children was my grandfather, John Riley West, born in 1912. Pappaw married my grandmother, Mary Eloise McGill, in 1930, and five years later they settled on 126 acres near the town of Greenback. Gran had been born in Blount County in 1916, and she died there in 1981, when I was eleven, an age at which I was old enough to feel the pain of loss but too young to have a sane measure of its proportion, and so her death became the traumatic center of my childhood.

Many years later, in April 2008, I was at a farmers' market in Santa Monica, California, at the peak of strawberry season. It's a story I've told often, because often people want to know how a person's life changes course. The sight of so many strawberries made me impulsive, and I bought a whole flat, then realized I couldn't eat them all before they went bad. I thought of Gran's strawberry jam and decided to make some. With no one to explain preserving to me, my first attempts were a bust. The formula to describe what happened next would look something like this: desire + frustration = obsession.

Five years later I emerged from my rabbit hole of research, cooking, and writing with *Saving the Season: A Cook's Guide to Home Canning, Pickling, and Preserving*. It's a collection of 220 recipes inspired by my family, southern ingredients, southern traditions, and historic English and American cookbooks. I explored or adapted preserving recipes from, among others, Edna Lewis, Rufus Estes, and Abigail Fisher, not because I went looking for African American contributions to southern preserving, but because their recipes connected me vividly to childhood memories of Blount County in the 1970s, on the eve of land-use changes that saw farming replaced by tract housing.

A little more about Gran's death, and a ghost story: that summer I turned eleven, Gran went into the hospital for her heart and didn't come back. I last saw her in a little sitting room off the kitchen, where she kept a covered crock of fourteen-day sweet pickles. Miss Lewis gives a similar recipe in *In Pursuit of Flavor*, although she mentions in the headnote that "changing times have produced hybrid cucumber varieties, which have affected the way we make pickles." Still, the general outline holds. You ferment the cucumbers (fewer than fourteen days are needed for "improved" hybrid varieties), stabilize them with vinegar and sugar, and season the pickle with the traditional blend of mustard, allspice, pepper, cloves, ginger, and such. Gran made them every summer. When Pappaw died in 1999, the year I turned twenty-nine, the farm on Maple Lane sold to a developer. The last time I went to see the place, bulldozers had already scraped away the farmhouse. I sat stupefied and red-eyed on the red clay ground and looked in vain for shards of Gran's pickling crocks. Some years later, after I moved to Los Angeles, I booked a session with a psychic energy healer as research for a magazine piece on alternative medicine. She laid me on a table and performed her hocus-pocus. My mind drifted back to Gran and Pappaw's farm. "This is strange," said the healer as she kneaded the air around my body. "I'm getting a smell of pickles."

I was mired in a depressive and alienated phase then, wounded by my buried grief about Gran's early death and homesick for Blount County. I went to a therapist, sometimes twice a week, in hopes of a talking cure. Then, for whatever reason offered by a mind in psychic turmoil, in the spring of 2008 I seized on strawberry jam as synecdoche for Gran and Pappaw's farm, for the childhood idyll, for the lost *locus amoenus*. After my first failed attempt to conjure Gran's jam, I riffled cookbooks for knowledge that could help me, and among the books I found were Miss Lewis's.

Like my grandmother, Edna Lewis was born in 1916 in the upland South. This is most of what the two women shared, other than that they both grew up in communities of farming people in former Confederate states and they both made strawberry preserves.

In *The Taste of Country Cooking*, published by Knopf in the bicentennial year, Miss Lewis proposes a menu for a late spring lunch that includes a ring mold of chicken sauced with wild mushrooms in cream, a salad of loose-leaf lettuce and scallions, and biscuits with strawberry preserves. Note that adverb, *late* spring. Someone who has lived close to a garden or cooked from one knows that the seasons have their seasons. Early spring brings cress, polk, and asparagus—the first shoots and leaves. Crops of mushrooms and strawberries—two types of fruiting bodies—need longer to mature. In her next book, 1988's *In Pursuit of Flavor*, Miss Lewis wrote that she always tried to get home to Virginia in late April or early May for wild strawberry picking. Strawberries were a cause for celebration in Freetown, as they were in Blount County when I was young, because they came in once a year, a seasonal occurrence that marked both natural cycles—orbs spinning in the solar system and all that—and cultural traditions. Strawberries were an *event*. Miss Lewis made strawberry preserves for the same reason one made the effort to preserve any food: to extend the shelf life of a desirable and fleetingly abundant crop. At its most basic, preserving is the way to storehouse seasonal calories, nutrition, and flavor for later use. "Having preserves on the pantry shelf," wrote Miss Lewis, "is like having a little taste of summer in the middle of winter." Preserving is how abundance prepares for want. It's saving the season.

Miss Lewis's recipe for strawberry preserves in *The Taste of Country Cooking* is standard: three cups of crushed fruit cooked down with 2½

Kevin West

cups of sugar. (Her use of crushed fruit suggests to me that the final product will be more of a "jam" than "preserves," but the distinction between the two categories always blurs.)

Miss Lewis's experience, the source of her authority, shows in her written instructions. For example, she'll have you crush the berries with "a clean, odorless, wooden pestle"—not, in other words, the same one used for spices or garlic—"or a strong coffee mug." When the fruit and sugar meet in the preserving pan, "it is much better to skim while it's rapidly boiling, because that seems to cause the scum to remain in a mass, and it's easy to dip it out without getting too much of the syrup." Her prose shows an intimate knowledge of what actually happens in a kitchen—sometimes you don't have a clean, odorless, wooden pestle handy—and sings with the folksy tune of oral tradition. That is, the instructions have been honed by repetition over time. An older relative might have told the young Edna Lewis that bit about skimming, and in turn Miss Lewis instructs us.

I don't rightly remember how my grandmother made her preserves, but I do know that Gran made biscuits nearly every day of her married life, and they usually went on the table with small jars of strawberry or wild blackberry sweetness. She used jelly jars that looked like juice glasses and sealed them with paraffin; sometimes they would come up from the earthen cellar with a spot of mold where the wax cap met the glass rim. Life on a farm had turned Gran into an able and efficient cook, and her kitchen afforded her no luxuries, certainly not the luxury of being squeamish. She could wring a pullet's neck or ax its head on a stump, and she didn't hesitate to spoon out the clean strawberry preserves beneath the mold. Preserving food was part of her year's work, and she reflexively used traditional techniques that reliably safeguarded against spoilage. The underlying science—not that Gran ever paused to consider it—was sound, and it confirms the speck of mold as a localized blemish, not pervasive decay. In brief: strawberries' natural acidity suppresses pathogenic bacteria, including those that cause botulism, while the addition of granulated sugar and the extraction of moisture through boiling lowers the "water activity," meaning that the finished strawberry preserves lack sufficient "free" water for dangerous microbial proliferation. (Pappaw applied the same principle in curing his country hams: a fresh pork leg will rot on the counter; salted and hung to dry, it cures.)

Edna Lewis, while not a household name, was certainly admired by the professional chefs who influenced me. I remember reading that Alice Waters called her a major voice in American food writing or something along those lines. Then in the wary and militant semidecade between the 9/11 attacks and the Great Recession, home canning underwent a revival, one of various niche specialty skills practiced within a broader food movement — let's call it conscientious eating — that also embraces local agriculture, organic and sustainable farming, farmers' markets, seasonal ingredients, traditional foodways, and home-based food production. A dozen or more substantive contemporary cookbooks on preserving, including my own, have been published since 2008's financial crisis, most of them marketed to affluent urban and suburban kitchen enthusiasts. One explanation is that the new jam movement grew out of the farmers' market movement. A focus on cooking seasonal ingredients led to the wish to preserve them.

During the time I spent on Gran and Pappaw's farm in the 1970s, preserving was not yet in need of revival in the rural South. People just did it. Gran and many other women in rural communities, including my maternal grandmother, put up homegrown summer produce out of necessity. Others did so from habit or custom or to meet a family member's special request or to satisfy their own personal taste. My late Tennessee friend Ada Mae Houston grew up in a remote hollow that didn't get electricity until November 5, 1948, when she was thirteen. Before then, her family ate what they raised, and they made it through winter with supplies of canned, fermented, cured, and root-cellared food. Ada Mae never characterized this reality as a hardship but rather considered it a mode of self-sufficiency, something many rural southerners used to call "living at home," as in providing for their needs at home rather than going out to buy necessities. Pappaw had a slightly different phrase for the same idea. He called it "good living," which I like better inasmuch as it conveys a belief that healthy food, family coherence, neighborliness, and individual self-determination cannot be purchased at large. "Good living" suggests an ideal of country life that is as old as the *Georgics*, as deeply American as Thomas Jefferson's yeoman farmer, as radical as Wendell Berry's critique of industrial agriculture, and as current as Berry's ideological heir Michael Pollan. It hews to the Aristotelian logic that *eudaimonia*, the good life, requires the exercise of virtue, *arete*.

By the time I knew Ada Mae, she could have eaten from the grocery store, but into her seventies she still put up hundreds of quarts of green beans and tomatoes every year. Why? Ada had no children but liked to serve her grand-nieces and grand-nephews the food she grew up on, and she admitted that she always craved home-canned tomatoes "when the snow flies." Preserved food, it seems to me, is particularly adhesive to such nostalgia, placing it among other occasional foods such as Sunday desserts, holiday pies, and Christmas cookies that merit heirloom status as family recipes. The preserving recipes get passed down, preserving ancestral variations on regionally iconic dishes such as chow-chow, fourteen-day sweet crunch pickles, pickled peaches, and strawberry jam.

None of us Wests are sure what happened to Gran's recipes—or, more accurately, the skimpy chicken scratches she relied on to jog her memory from one year to the next. Pappaw remarried after Gran passed, and Gran's kitchen became someone else's. Without Gran's gravitational pull, the West clan spun apart. Things scattered.

In the introduction to *The Taste of Country Cooking*, Miss Lewis announces that her purpose is to safeguard against such scattering. It's an important paragraph, one that reveals the scope and consequence of her writing:

> Over the years since I left home and lived in different cities, I have kept thinking about the people I grew up with and about our way of life. Whenever I go back to visit my sisters and brothers, we relive old times, remembering the past. And when we share again in gathering wild strawberries, canning, rendering lard, finding walnuts, picking persimmons, making fruitcake, I realize how much the bond that held us had to do with food. Since we are the last of the original families, with no children to remember and carry on, I decided that I wanted to write down just exactly how we did things when I was growing up in Freetown that seemed to make life so rewarding.

Miss Lewis doesn't claim the recipes that follow as her inventions, although most of her readers would surely grant her that privilege. Instead, she places her cooking within a larger historical context. "Although the founders of Freetown have long since passed away, I am convinced that their ideas do live on for us to learn from, to enlarge upon, and pass on to the following generations." Implicit in this paragraph, which in effect spans the generations from slavery to the 1970s, is something my West kin might well recognize. When the Wests talk about food, we're talking about more than just food. We're talking about a specific way of life—in a specific place, with a specific understanding of the land and its inhabitants, and a specific commitment to sustaining those relationships across the generations. We're talking about "good living."

Miss Lewis also lets us in on her secondary purpose. To preserve recipes means to preserve culture, or how a body of knowledge exists within a set of social practices. If a single recipe is akin to a story—or, perhaps better said, if a single recipe is a vehicle for a story—then collectively Miss Lewis's recipes align to form a grander narrative. This narrative chronicles one farming community's signal achievements, which included political liberty and economic self-reliance, as well as the exercise of such virtues as personal dignity, cordiality, cooperation, reverence for family, joy in companionship, neighborliness, skill at farming, stewardship for the land, and intimacy with nature and its cycles. It's a narrative about good living.

Admittedly, the story is idealized. It elides negative counterforces such as racist neighbors or abusive family members. But as an agrarian model, Freetown nonetheless prefigured more recent experiments in social reorganization, including back-to-the-land communes of the 1960s, as well as written explorations of traditional craft skills, such as the Foxfire books and post-9/11 neo-homesteading blogs.

Wendell Berry implores us to see eating as an agricultural act. Miss Lewis's books speak to that in readily apparent ways. She also reminds us of another set of connections inherent in the act of eating. A recipe documents what happens when a shared or communal form (an iconic regional dish, for instance) is shaped by local use and played on by individual ingenuity. In other words, home cooking is a folk performance, and a jar of strawberry preserves is like a twelve-bar blues or a mountain reel, two folk musical forms in which a soloist will improvise on a commonplace riff snatched from a community memory bank.

Miss Lewis was a particularly fine soloist in the kitchen; her lasting achievement was that she wrote it all down, both her own experience—her improvs—and the commonplace riffs she borrowed from Freetown's collective memory bank. Miss Lewis's recipes turn the autobiography of her kitchen life into what you might call an autoethnography of her community. Her writing is telescopic in both senses; it unfolds pleasingly, unexpectedly, and it sees far.

If you take a very long view, food preservation is as old as human culture. Drying is a primordial technique that has hardly required further refinement—fish, grapes, stone fruit, and tomatoes are still dehydrated under open skies—and dried foods have long provided staple nourishment around the world. The first Europeans who came to North America stocked their ships with dried cod, and once here they met Native peoples sustained by pemmican, a mixture of dried meat and dried berries bound with fat. Techniques for preserving vegetables are only relatively more recent. On the Korean peninsula, kimchi has been a staple side dish since the beginning of agriculture. I suspect that sauerkraut has similarly ancient roots in Europe, and at the very least, Cato's *De agri cultura* describes cabbages and turnips preserved by salting. Our word *pickle* plausibly derives from an obscure Teutonic root word meaning "to prick"—a reference to the pickle's piquant taste—and modern usage was established by the fifteenth century. (The OED cites *Le Morte d'Arthur*, published in 1485: "with pekille and powdyre of precious spycez," an antecedent of the spice blend Gran and Miss Lewis used for their pickles.)

As for the sweet preserves, they were scarcer in antiquity because sweetness was hard to come by in the wild, and refining sugar from sugarcane required skills and technologies that restricted production until the modern era. One early written recipe comes from Rome, where epicures knew the quince as a peculiar type of apple, astringent when raw, that became succulent when cooked in honey and kept for months. They called it *melimelum*, honey apple, and Roman legions carried honey-cooked quince on their long march to the Iberian Peninsula. The travel-battered word emerged in Spanish as *membrillo*, used today for both the fruit and a dense fruit paste made from it. In Portuguese, a *marmelo* cooked with honey—or, after the fourteenth century, sugar—was *marmelado*, "quinced." Tudor England imported quince sweetmeats from Portugal, and the Anglicized word proved flexible enough to describe both quince paste and a "dry marmelet of peaches," in Thomas Dawson's *Good Housewife's Jewel* of 1596/7. It also eventually applied to an eighteenth-century citrus preserve eaten with breakfast toast, orange marmalade. Incidentally, Dawson gave a recipe, "To Preserve Quinces All Year through Whole and Soft," that would have looked quite familiar in ancient Rome, apart from his use of sugar in the Portuguese manner.

Always desirable, sugar and sugary foods remained precious until after the Columbian voyages. Then New World sugarcane plantations established with enslaved African labor created vast exports from the Caribbean "sugar islands," and at the time of the American Revolution, sugar, once a rarity, had become a mere luxury. (Homegrown sorghum and maple syrup provided the Republic with cheaper everyday sweetness.) By abolition, inexpensive sugar had reached most pantries, and Freetown's founding coincided with the golden age of sweet preserves, thanks to the convergence of a ready sugar supply with another historical anomaly, the nineteenth-century South's immense horticultural diversity, which represented gatherings from Europe, North America, Africa, and South America, as well as extensive tinkering on American soil.

A principal author of that nineteenth-century garden, and by extension the farmer whose experiments would define a distinctly American cuisine, was none other than Thomas Jefferson. His garden at Monticello—the "rich spot of earth" he conjures in his famous letter of 1811 to the painter Charles Willson Peale, in which he also says of himself "but tho' an old man, I am but a young gardener"—is described by Monticello's longtime director of garden and grounds Peter Hatch as a "revolutionary American garden" for the 330 varieties of 99 species of plants and herbs that Jefferson grew. As Hatch wrote in *"A Rich Spot of Earth": Thomas Jefferson's Revolutionary Garden at Monticello* (2012), the array represented a "world of edible immigrants," including such novel crops as asparagus, tomatoes, okra, Brussels sprouts, cayenne pepper, rhubarb, and peanuts. Hatch muses that the Jeffersonian recipe for okra soup, attributed to the president's daughter, Martha Jefferson Randolph, was an apt metaphor for the entire Monticello garden.

> The Jefferson family gumbo is a rich blend of "native" vegetables like lima beans and Cymlings, or Pattypan squash, that were grown by American Indians on the arrival of the first Europeans. It also included new vegetables found by Spanish explorers like potatoes, an Andean discovery adopted by northern Europeans, as well as tomatoes, collected in Central America and embraced by Mediterranean cultures as early as the seventeenth century. Binding the soup was an African plant, okra, grown and "creolized" by both the French and enslaved blacks in the West Indies. The dish was ultimately prepared by African American chefs trained in the fine arts of French cuisine in the kitchen at Monticello.

Jefferson's enthusiasm for horticultural experiment extended equally to his Fruitery, which encompassed 400 trees and multiple berry patches that supplied his favorite fruits in season: Albemarle Pippin and Esopus Spitzenburg apples, Green Gage plums, Moor Park apricots, Seckel pears, peaches, and cherries. The Old Man/Young Gardener also loved strawberries. Wild strawberries had been harvested in the New World since before colonization; the first Europeans delighted in their abundance. The surprise is that in Jefferson's day, garden strawberries—including new strains hybridized in France by crossing New World and Old World stock—were only infrequently cultivated. A letter from Jefferson to his granddaughter Anne Cary Randolph in 1808 demonstrates the attention he paid his strawberry patch, advising that the soil be dressed with sand and manure so that "the waterings would carry both down into the clay and loosen and enrich it."

Strawberry preserves almost certainly found a place in Monticello's larder. Jefferson's kinswoman Mary Randolph, reckoned to be the best in cook in Virginia, included two recipes for preserved strawberries in her 1824 cookbook *The Virginia Housewife; or, Methodical Cook*, which culinary historian Karen Hess called the most influential cookbook of the nineteenth century. Both recipes are brief, but they neatly demonstrate the difference as it is usually drawn between strawberry "jam" and strawberry "preserves." For the former, Randolph has you cook down one pound of ripe strawberries with one pound of loaf sugar, stirring frequently to break down the fruit, until the mixture reduces to a thick spread, or "jelly" in Randolph's terminology. (This recipe parallels *The Taste of Country Cooking*'s Strawberry Preserves made with crushed fruit.) Randolph's "preserves" recipe, on the other hand, refines the normal sugar + fruit + heat technique, applying more skill to keep premium berries whole. You stew the "largest strawberries, before they are too ripe," with an equal weight of sugar, "taking them out to cool frequently, that they may not be mashed," until the fruit is translucent with absorbed sugar. The candied fruit suspended in clear syrup is then transferred into "small glasses or pots," covered with brandy paper seals, and tied under additional layers of paper.

Miss Lewis's recipe for wild strawberry preserves in *In Pursuit of Flavor* differs from Mary Randolph's only in small particulars. Lewis has you boil the precious wild berries—"I have always treasured them"—for a spell, rest them in their syrup overnight to plump with sugar, and carefully boil them a second time before canning. She gets away with less sugar (that is, less preservative) as a consequence of storing her preserves in sterilized Mason jars that are double-sealed with paraffin and fitted lids. Otherwise, Miss Lewis and Mary Randolph might be swapping recipes between neighbors, albeit neighbors separated by 152 years.

This retrospection from Freetown kitchens to Mary Randolph's (which also spans a chasm of race and class) calls for a further look back, because there was nothing new about Mary Randolph's preserves, either. They hardly differed from contemporaneous English preserves, including the definitive recipes given in Eliza Acton's *Modern Cookery for Private Families*, published in 1845 but fragrant of earlier Regency cooking. From there, it is only a short culinary step from *The Virginia Housewife* of 1824 to *The Good Housewife's Jewel* of 1596/7. Randolph and Dawson agree on how to preserve quince, oranges, cherries, lemons, pears, plums, and pumpkins. Their recipes for preserved gooseberries might as well be interchangeable. (He has strawberries, too, but puts them in a pie.) If we can draw a direct line from Edna Lewis to Mary Randolph, we can also confidently extend that line back another 228 years to Tudor England. And why stop there? The line fades across the next thousand years, but Dawson's quinces preserved "whole and soft" point back toward honey apples stored in covered clay pots, so we can at least infer a very distant Roman lineage for Miss Lewis's strawberry preserves.

The point is that a curious exchange occurred in the kitchen at Monticello and in other kitchens staffed by enslaved African women. The exchange was unequal and transacted under the abhorrent circumstances of slavery, but it mirrored the so-called Columbian Exchange in which, for example, apples and sugarcane came to the New World and tomatoes and potatoes went back to the Old. Multiple ecologies and multiple cuisines converged in the early American kitchen, and the influences ricocheted in unpredictable directions. Black cooks preparing food for white owners left their "thumb print," as Karen Hess says, on every recipe they touched; their forced service also required them to learn cooking techniques to satisfy white tastes, and some of those techniques outlasted slavery to inform subsequent African American cooking.

As for our strawberry preserves, English preserving techniques based on sugar—a double legacy of slavery—passed through the hands of Miss Lewis's Freetown ancestors until their thumbprints had marked the recipes as Freetown heirlooms. Miss Lewis wrote them down to memorialize her African American cultural inheritance, "how we did things when I was growing up in Freetown that seemed to make life so rewarding." What we as readers take away, in turn, is not just a sense of one kitchen, Miss Lewis's, but a glimpse into the domestic economy of a whole community of independent, land-owning yeoman farmers. In this light, Freetown comes across as a vigorous proof of the Jeffersonian concept, even as it also sharply rebuked Jefferson's failure to imagine his yeomen citizenry as anything but white. Freetown's gardens, lush and sweet, bloomed in the rubble of American history, always close to the surface in the rural South. Miss Lewis quietly acknowledged as much with *The Taste of Country Cooking*'s Emancipation Day menu.

I eventually learned from reading her obituaries that Miss Lewis had been a political activist, a registered Communist, and a volunteer for FDR's second presidential campaign in 1936. But from my first brush with her story, as told in *The Gift of Southern Cooking* with coauthor Scott Peacock, I had intuited political shadings to her culinary pride. Her African-influenced dress and self-possessed, statuesque personal bearing reminded me of Nina Simone (whose song "To Be Young, Gifted, and Black" featured on the 1970 album *Black Gold*) and of Aretha Franklin at her 1972 performance at the New Temple Missionary Baptist Church in Los Angeles, which was recorded live and released as the best-selling double album *Amazing Grace*. Just as Aretha was known as a queen, Miss Lewis's dignity and talent—she was "gifted"—inevitably called down the honorific *Miss* Lewis for those who knew about her.

During research for my book, I read Miss Lewis's essay "What Is Southern?" published posthumously in 2008, and my understanding of the particular gift of *her* southern cooking finally came into sharp focus. What Miss Lewis left behind—apart from a guide to good eating—was a manifesto about good living, a coherent set of ideas that protested against the diminished farming and cooking practices of today in contrast to the richer agrarian model of Freetown. It bears remembering that Freetown as she knew it had passed by the time of her writing; it existed only in her pages, among the phantoms of memory, a verdant but ghostly place.

Wendell Berry's *Unsettling of America*, a milestone in American agrarianism since Jefferson, came out the year after *The Taste of Country Cooking*. Different in all obvious ways, Berry and Miss Lewis nonetheless inked their pens from a common well. Both trusted their experience of rural life and doubted professional agricultural expertise. They shared a belief that the health of the individual, the community, and the earth were indivisible, and they understood that traditional rural life possessed but fragile defenses against the mighty force of industrial agriculture. Their prescience has earned them iconic stature among conscientious eaters today, when we have all the more reason to distrust agribusiness.

Miss Lewis and Wendell Berry both laid bare for me the urgent need for a cook's aesthetic considerations—how food tastes—to fit honorably within larger ethical and political realities—how food is grown, by whom, and under what social and economic conditions. Miss Lewis's cookbooks are not overtly political, I know, but still I'd categorize them, if such a category existed, as radical pastorals.

There is another overlooked commonality between Miss Lewis and Berry, and it is something I share with them in a modest way. Both left the rural South for the metropolis, where they moved in privileged literary and artistic circles before they began to espouse in print their rural visions. Perhaps I connected so strongly with Miss Lewis because she remembered Freetown from the perspective of her life in New York and I was a southerner living in Los Angeles. We were both exiles. Memory served as the necessary bridge to our subject, which was located in the past—which *was* the past. Miss Lewis's cookbooks had a different tone and shape than the other cookbooks I studied, how-to books like *The Virginia Housewife*, Mrs. S. R. Dull's *Southern Cooking*, *Charleston Receipts*, Rufus Estes's *Good Things to Eat*, and *What Mrs. Fisher Knows about Southern Cooking*. It's not just because she was the more gifted writer. *The Taste of Southern Cooking* was also a why-to book, and it was frankly nostalgic.

I don't mean to say that Miss Lewis was merely wistful. Historian Eric Foner argues that "as a wholesale rejection of the present, nostalgia can serve as a powerful mode of protest." Miss Lewis's nostalgia was of this potent kind. Her essay "What Is Southern?" focused my work in *Saving the Season* because it allowed me to realize that in preserving food I was also preserving my family past and my southern heritage—to say nothing of my sanity. I seized on the additional idea that preserving could be a protest against the greed of the contemporary food system and the banality of contemporary consumer culture. Putting up strawberry jam was a finger in the eye of agribusiness. Preserving my memory of Gran's strawberry jam was, to use Miss Lewis's words, my way "to learn from, to enlarge upon, and pass on to the following generations" the joy I'd felt on Gran and Pappaw's farm. I realized that I could preserve in my jars an inherited belief in good living, which included notions of self-reliance, reverence for family and friends, awareness of agriculture's impact on health and the environment, cordiality, generosity, and other such virtues that would have been equally familiar to Miss Lewis.

The exile, by definition, is writing from the perspective of distance, of separation, of loss. The exile's impulse to write is complex. It takes in a wish to re-create, if in imagination only, the lost homeland, and it encompasses the wish to protect its memory. Miss Lewis's cookbooks issued from this displaced perspective and they took the form, to borrow Eric Hobsbawm's phrase, of "a protest against forgetting." Her books remembered something fine and laid up a store of past knowledge, the necessary seeds for revival on the far side of some future lapse.

Toward the end of my work on *Saving the Season*, I experienced an intense dream. I was riding a train through springtime woods abloom with serviceberry and wild apples. The train delivered me to Gran and Pappaw's farmhouse, and they ran out to the porch to greet me. "Get in here, you old rascal," said Pappaw. My shrink declared it a termination dream, meaning that we could safely end my therapy. I had returned from exile.

My book's publication date the following summer, chosen by my publisher with no input from me, fell on June 25, Gran's birthday. Aware that she would hover over the publication party in Los Angeles—another uncanny apparition—I decided to serve biscuits and preserves. What could be, to answer Miss Lewis's titular question, more southern? At a subtler level, I also wanted to show how a southern-inflected preserving tradition could adapt to other ecologies and subsume other influences. (I sourced berries from a favorite grower in San Bernardino County and flavored them with splashes of Bandol, Alice Waters's favorite wine.) More personal still, biscuits and jam would bring together, if only in my imagination, the two otherwise unlike women who shaped *my* southern cooking and helped me find my way back from the pain of exile. A friend put me in touch with Scott Peacock, and after I explained myself, he agreed to fly from Alabama to Los Angeles to make the biscuits, an extraordinary gift. We met in the kitchen on the day of the party, two gay men who cherished southern cooking and the women who had taught us most about it. We swapped stories, talked about food, and laid out trays of lard biscuits with jars of strawberry and blackberry sweetness. The moment was southern in spite of the obvious ways it was not. We remembered. It was good living.

Afterwords

A Family Remembers

RUTH LEWIS SMITH AND
NINA WILLIAMS-MBENGUE

---

*Ruth Lewis Smith (age ninety-three at the
time of writing), sister of Edna Lewis*

My sister Edna—who was eight years older than me—was an example to me every step of the way, from our childhood in rural Virginia through her later years. Her calm demeanor was as striking as her neatly styled hair and side profile.

Edna began cooking early. Our mother assigned her to cook breakfast for all of us (there were six of us children who survived—Edna, me, Naomi, George, Lue Stanley, and Virginia) so everyone could eat before school. The breakfast was not quick fast food but rather meat, scrambled eggs, fried apples, and stovetop-cooked homemade bread. In addition, she prepared our lunch, which was the envy of our classmates.

Family members shared recipes with our mother, and this enhanced Edna's meal planning ideas. I can see her now, just as she is depicted on the covers of two of her books, selecting a variety of vegetables from the huge garden and gathering some flowers along the way. Edna loved flowers almost as much as she enjoyed food.

Our father passed away when we were young, so Edna did domestic work in our community to help pay bills. Like many from the South, Edna, along with one of our other sisters, Virginia (who went by Jennie-Mae), headed north. Edna left before finishing high school. In New York, Edna found domestic work that included cooking, so she had an opportunity to explore her culinary talents.

Edna was an excellent seamstress and clothes designer. In addition to making clothes for me, she always made whatever she wore. This eye for design landed her a job as a window display designer for department stores in New York. We wrote each other often to share what was going on in our lives.

Our mother became ill with cancer, and Edna went back to Virginia whenever she could to check on our mother.

After some years, Edna was invited by two entrepreneurs she had become friendly with downtown to become the head chef at Café Nicholson in New York. Her signature dishes were fried oysters, fried zucchini squash, and baked Virginia ham. After our mother died, I followed my sisters to New York, and after a stint doing domestic work, I worked at Café Nicholson for a time; in today's world, I would have been known as Edna's sous-chef. I assisted her by preparing the shrimp for frying and made both chocolate and cheese soufflés. The restaurant was very popular with celebrities, and drew the likes of Eleanor Roosevelt and Jackie Robinson.

Edna and her husband, Steve Kingston, bought a small farm in New Jersey, and she began to raise pheasants. I remember visiting her there, but that venture didn't last long. Pretty soon she realized a dream, owning her own restaurant in Harlem on 125th Street and Seventh Avenue (I don't remember a sign on the door, and strangely, none of us can recall the restaurant's name).

My daughter, Mattie, spent the first summer of the restaurant's operation as a waitress. She recalls fond memories of daily restaurant goers coming in to order the special of the day. Everything Aunt Edna cooked was special.

I don't recall when, but at some point Edna broke her leg; after that, she never went back to the restaurant.

During her time in New York, she lived in the Bronx with her sister Naomi and helped raise her niece, Nina, who was instrumental in putting together the manuscript of *The Taste of Country Cooking*. As Edna developed recipes, she loved to return to Virginia to cook them on the wood stove.

Our family was part of the foundation of the Bethel Baptist Church in Unionville, where we grew up. As adults, all of the church family members would return to Virginia annually for the church's anniversary and revival on the second Sunday in August. The dinner was served on homemade wooden four-foot-high tables draped with crisp white linen tablecloths. The meal was served between the morning and afternoon services. Edna traditionally prepared fried chicken, potato salad, corn pudding, baked ham, sliced tomatoes and onions, and freshly squeezed lemonade. People scurried to the end of the table looking for her delicious peach cobbler, blackberry cobbler, and homemade vanilla ice cream. Wherever she was in the country, coming home for Second Sunday was always on her calendar.

Edna was quiet, warm, and sincere, and was especially loving and kind to her family and to others. She was very respectful and looked for the best in people. She didn't have her own children but dearly loved her three nieces—Mattie, Nina, and Amelia—and her nephew, Douglass. She would buy special toys for them even on her meager salary. As they grew older, she shared with much pride in their accomplishments.

Edna never forgot her family and her roots in Freetown.

Two of my moments of greatest pride in my sister were when she received an honorary doctorate from Johnson and Wales University, and when the U.S. Postal Service unveiled her Celebrity Chef stamp; she was one of only five celebrity chefs on the first stamps honoring those in the culinary world. As Edna's only living sibling, I was asked to speak on behalf of my family about Edna Lewis, who many have only come to know since she was honored by the Postal Service stamp.

My sister Edna and I were very close, and I am honored to continue to cook her recipes, to wear the lapel pin I've had made with a rendering of her stamp, and to be able to speak on behalf of her and our family.

Nina Williams-Mbengue, niece of Edna Lewis

My memories of Aunt Edna—my mother's older sister—revolve around food, family, and Virginia. I remember hot summers picking wild blackberries and her laughter as she shared memories with her sisters, Jennie-Mae and Ruth, or laughed with my mother, Naomi, over something that happened at her work that day.

When I was about ten years old, Aunt Edna and her husband, Steve, moved in with my mother and me in the South Bronx. My mother had become very ill with pneumonia and had to be hospitalized for a time. Aunt Edna and Uncle Steve remained with us after my mother returned home. Edna had already written *The Edna Lewis Cookbook*, and soon she began working on *The Taste of Country Cooking*. I had just learned how to type and was given a new typewriter. Aunt Edna asked me to type up the manuscript for the book because her "chicken scratch" would be difficult

Ruth Lewis Smith and Nina Williams-Mbengue

for her editor, Judith Jones, to read. Aunt Edna would give me her recipes on long yellow legal pads that I would then do my best to type. I asked her lots of questions if there was something I didn't understand or tried to get her to go into more detail or explain a recipe more clearly as I typed and retyped each page.

I will never forget her descriptions of springtime "sweet-faced baby calves" and the long lists of food from the fields, woods, and streams that her mother and the other women of Freetown joyously prepared for various events such as Emancipation Day, Christmas, and Revival Dinner. I could just close my eyes and smell and taste the food as I typed.

The best part was testing all the recipes in our tiny apartment. Aunt Edna would painstakingly cook each dish and revise recipes if something didn't taste just right. If she was unsure about how to prepare a dish, or the best ingredient to use, she called her older sister, Jennie-Mae (whom we called "Aunt Jen"), who still lived in Virginia on the family farm near Freetown, to go over the recipe.

I spent my summers in Virginia, just up the road from Freetown, attending the same Revival dinners at Bethel Baptist Church that Edna wrote about in the book. During those summers, Aunt Edna would visit Aunt Jen, and the sisters would spend hours walking through the fields discussing how the "old folks" lived, raised crops, cattle, and chickens, and prepared ham, jellies, and jam. I often walked behind them as they picked fresh blackberries to make into cobbler or jelly and relished the sound of their sparkling laughter.

Edna's descriptions of Freetown — how the farm families prepared for planting in the spring, wheat threshing, hog killing, summer harvesting and canning, the putting up of fruits and vegetables, and fall and Christmas activities — introduced millions of people to a vibrant, creative and hard-working community of families who, while newly freed from slavery, dreamed of a bright future for their children and grandchildren. While Edna described how to make pear and damson plum preserves and the importance of always having biscuits on hand for unexpected guests, she talked about how her grandfather, a former slave, set up the first school in the area for African American children. He hired a teacher from Ohio and held classes in his living room. Families sent their children from miles away to attend the school. The families worked together to build a church and an entertainment hall and to hold great events such as Revival Week at the church and Emancipation Day, a holiday that honored their freedom from chattel slavery and was more important to them than celebrating Thanksgiving.

As Aunt Edna's reputation grew, she was featured in magazines all over the country and accepted offers to head up the kitchens of several great restaurants up and down the East Coast. Her love of freshly prepared, local food grown in good, rich organic soil grabbed the attention of people all over the nation. Edna helped southern food's reputation change; it was no longer just fried chicken and greens but came to include sage-flavored pork tenderloin, stewed tomatoes, hot buttered beets, scallion and lentil salad, quail in casserole, homemade peach ice cream, and wild strawberry preserves. I can still hear Aunt Edna's voice describing the Freetown of her childhood as I typed up those recipes.

It was not until I became an adult that I understood the impact of what Aunt Edna passed on to us. I have only recently come to grasp that my life has been profoundly affected by a woman who sat at the feet of former slaves, listening intently to their experiences, learning their foodways, and absorbing their wisdom. I don't think Edna thought that she would launch a movement advocating freshly prepared, seasonal, and locally available foods; she just wanted to share what she knew to be so good and so true.

As I am writing this essay on what would have been Aunt Edna's 101st birthday, I dearly miss her wonderful food, sparkling laughter, and stories about the people of Freetown. Aunt Edna was so proud of them and always felt as though their spirits walked alongside her. Freetown is where she learned to cook biscuits, apple brown betty, blackberry cobbler, cymling squash, and pan-fried chicken.

I continue to be amazed to meet young chefs and scholars who talk about how Edna influenced their way of thinking about food. I can only think that she would giggle in her quiet, unassuming way and shake her head in amazement.

I know that the people of Freetown would be proud and astonished to learn that Edna took their stories and dreams with her when she journeyed north with her brothers and sisters. I hope that people who discover Aunt Edna's cooking and are inspired to become chefs, be part of the farm-to-table movement, or just cook some incredible food will remember them, too.

One of the last times I was with her before she died was the summer of

Ruth Lewis Smith and Nina Williams-Mbengue

2005, after my mother passed. I brought my very young daughters to meet her and spend several hours with her in her apartment in Atlanta. Aunt Edna watched them in amazement, laughing and shaking her head as they played "restaurant" and pretended to cook Play-Doh pizza and pie. I pray that one day they will realize that they, in their turn, were blessed to sit at the feet of one of the "old saints" from Freetown and that they will carry on Freetown's hopes and dreams.

Acknowledgments

To Judith Jones, for telling me about Edna Lewis with such candor and admiration. Thank you for recognizing the value in Lewis's stories and recipes, and for guiding her work into print. I owe so much of what I know and think about to you. Thank you for inviting me into your home that freezing January day, for tea and conversation, for laughter and toughness, for Vermont and New York, and for all the fine work you've given to all of us. My admiration knows no bounds.

This book owes its existence to Marcie Cohen Ferris. Marcie, for facilitating a conversation between Nathalie Dupree and me in Charleston—the spark for this project—for reading my "just a thought" email where I soft-pitched the idea for this volume, and for introducing me to your own wonderful editor, I will be forever grateful. Your generosity and brilliance never cease to amaze me.

My sincere thanks to my editor, Elaine Maisner, for jumping on board with such immediacy and enthusiasm. Your ability to calmly manage the logistics of a project with such sprawl was awe-inspiring. Thank you for your patience, your skill, and, mostly, your faith. To the entire team at UNC Press, thank you for your excitement about this project, for your careful editorial eyes, for putting up with my technological ineptitude, and for shepherding this project into existence.

To all my contributors, thank you for picking up your phones and answering when I called to ask you to lend your voices to this work. I've met many of you through talking about Edna Lewis and working on this book; my life, and understanding of Miss Lewis, is all the richer for all of you.

To my North Carolina–born husband, chef Chris Bradley, thank you for baking me biscuits way back when—what (still meager) understanding I have of the nuances and complexities of southern food and culture really began there. Thank you, too, for keeping a straight face and offering your support while I pitched this project during a moment of great tumult and uncertainty in our lives. You have always put up with my many (perhaps *too* many) irons in the fire with such grace and, since day one, have made our home — and especially our kitchen — a true haven.

To our children, Calvin and Eliza, thank you for putting up with my time away from you in your earliest months of life while I tended to this book's final touches. You two have brought immeasurable meaning and joy to all areas of my life, but feeding and beginning to cook for you two has been a particular pleasure.

And, most important, to Miss Edna Lewis: I ache at having missed the opportunity to meet you in the flesh. Your recipes and prose, while no substitute for your physical splendor, are beloved proxies. Through sharing of yourself, you revealed a world to so many. We are all deeply grateful. I hope this book begins to do justice to your wisdom, grace, fortitude, deftness, knowledge, and fineness.

Contributors

＊

ANNEMARIE AHEARN is the founder of Salt Water Farm Cooking School, a farm and cooking school for home cooks, located on the coast of Maine. She attended the Institute of Culinary Education and cooking schools in Europe. After nearly a decade in New York City, Ahearn moved to Maine to build a life and career focusing on food education and farming. Salt Water Farm celebrates a deep appreciation for traditional methods of cooking locally sourced ingredients. Her seaside café and market in Rockport has earned praise in *Bon Appetit*, the *New York Times*, and the *Wall Street Journal*. *Food and Wine* named Ahearn as one of the "Top 40 under 40: Changing the Way America Eats and Drinks." She is a regular contributor to *DownEast Magazine* and the author of *Full Moon Suppers at Salt Water Farm: Recipes from Land and Sea*.

MASHAMA BAILEY is the chef and partner of The Grey, an award-winning restaurant she opened in late 2014 in a former Greyhound bus station in Savannah. The Grey is the first solo effort by Bailey, who trained under Gabrielle Hamilton at New York's Prune. The gig represents a homecoming of sorts for the Bronx-born chef, who spent nine years of her childhood in Georgia. Here, she's doing southern food, her way—with an emphasis on seasonal, local produce.

SCOTT ALVES BARTON holds a Ph.D. in food studies and teaches food studies and anthropology. Formerly an executive chef, Barton was named one of the top twenty-five African American chefs by *Ebony* magazine. Barton serves on the James Beard Foundation's Cookbook Awards committee and is a former board member of the Southern Foodways Alliance. His research on northeastern Brazil interrogates the intersection of secular and sacred foodways as a marker of cultural and ethnic identity. Recent publications include "Now You Are Eating Slave Food," in *The Making of Brazil's Black Mecca: Bahia Reconsidered*, edited by Scott Ickes and Bernd Reiter (forthcoming), and "Race, Faith, and Cake," in the journal *Culture and Religion*.

PATRICIA E. CLARK is associate professor and chair of the Department of English and Creative Writing at SUNY Oswego. She teaches courses on African American, twentieth-century, and contemporary American literature and culture and on black women writers. Her recent work examines how popular notions and stereotypes of race and gender play within classic literary motifs, narrative structures, and genres in contemporary black American literature. Clark's published work focusing on gender, cookbooks, comparative foodways in western Africa and the United States appears in the journal *Callaloo* and in the collection *Gendering Global Transformations: Gender, Culture, Race, and Identity.*

NATHALIE DUPREE is the author of fourteen cookbooks and the winner of four James Beard Awards. She has hosted PBS and Food Network cooking shows and has written for many national publications. Founding chairman of the Charleston Wine and Food Festival, she was also a founding member of the Southern Foodways Alliance and the International Association of Culinary Professionals (where she was two-time president and served on the board many years). She has worked as a chef in several restaurants and for ten years directed Rich's Cooking School in Atlanta. She was named "Grande Dame" by Les Dames d'Escoffier, which she considers her highest honor. In 2013 the French Master Chefs of America named her Woman of the Year, and in 2015 she was named to the James Beard Foundation Who's Who in Food and Beverage in America. She regularly writes for the *Charleston Post and Courier* and lives in Charleston.

JOHN T. EDGE has directed the Southern Foodways Alliance since its founding in 1999. Around that same time, he began writing for the *Oxford American*, where an earlier version of the essay in this book first appeared. He is the author, most recently, of *The Potlikker Papers: A Food History of the Modern South.*

MEGAN ELIAS teaches in the gastronomy program at Boston University. She is the author of *Stir It Up: Home Economics in American Culture* (2008), *Food in the United States, 1890–1945* (2009), and *Lunch: A History* (2014), as well as her recently published book *Food on the Page*, a comprehensive history of cookbooks in America.

SARA B. FRANKLIN is a writer and oral historian whose work focuses on culinary history, food writing, and agriculture. Her oral history of legendary Knopf editor Judith Jones is archived at the Schlesinger Library at the Radcliffe Institute for Advanced Study. She holds a Ph.D. in food studies from New York University and studied documentary radio and nonfiction at both the Salt Institute for Documentary Studies and the Center for Documentary Studies at Duke University. She teaches courses on food and writing at NYU Gallatin and via the NYU Prison Education Program at Wallkill Correctional Facility. She lives, cooks, and gardens with her husband, chef Chris Bradley, and their children, Calvin and Eliza, in New York's Hudson Valley.

JOHN T. HILL was the cofounder and first director of Yale University's Department of Photography, where he taught photography and design for nearly two decades. He was the executor of the Walker Evans Estate and has written, edited, and designed many prize-winning books on Evans and other artists, including *Walker Evans at Work, Walker Evans: Lyric Documentary*, and *Walker Evans: Depth of Field*. His books have accompanied comprehensive national and international exhibitions, which he also designed. As a working photographer, throughout his career he has made pictures for books, magazines, and other publications. He was a longtime friend of Edna Lewis and photographed her in multiple settings, including the image used for the United States Postal Service stamp honoring her as one of America's great chefs. Hill grew up in Georgia and shared many of the delights of southern cooking with Edna Lewis.

VIVIAN HOWARD is a chef and storyteller from eastern North Carolina. She is the host of the PBS series *A Chef's Life* and the author of *Deep Run Roots: Stories and Recipes from My Corner of the South*. On television, on the page, and in the kitchen at her flagship restaurant, Chef and the Farmer, Howard works to exalt the food traditions of the frugal farmer, to connect people to their food source, and to reveal common ground between rural and urban palates.

LILY KELTING is a postdoctoral fellow associated with InterArt, a research center at the Freie Universität, Berlin. Her two academic research projects focus on new food movements around the world and the relation between food and the concepts of theatricality and performativity. As a journalist, she reports on arts and culture for NPR Berlin and is an editor at the English-language magazine *Exberliner*. Kelting is originally from New York City and has a Ph.D. in theater from the University of California, San Diego.

FRANCIS LAM is the host of the public radio show *The Splendid Table* and is editor-at-large at Clarkson Potter. Previously, he was a columnist at the *New York Times Magazine*. His writing has earned multiple James Beard and International Association of Culinary Professionals awards, and he has appeared in all but one of the editions of *Best Food Writing* from 2006 to 2016 (his parents are very disappointed about that one year). He is a graduate of the University of Michigan and the Culinary Institute of America and serves on the board of the Southern Foodways Alliance.

JANE LEAR is a food and travel writer based in New York City. She writes a food advice column for TakePart.com, the digital arm of the media company that produced the film *Food, Inc.*, and about what makes her hungry at janelear.com. The former senior articles editor at *Gourmet* and former features director at *Martha Stewart Living*, she has written for the *New York Times*, the *Wall Street Journal*, *The Magazine Antiques*, *Martha Stewart Living*, *Rachael Ray Every Day*, *Garden Design*, and other publications. A contributor to *The Oxford Companion to Sugar and Sweets*, Martha Stewart's *Martha's American Food*, *The Gourmet Cookbook: More than 1,000 Recipes*, and *Gourmet Today: More than 1,000 All New Recipes for the Contemporary Kitchen*, she is also the coauthor, with New York City chef Floyd Cardoz, of *One Spice, Two Spice: American Food, Indian Flavors*.

DEBORAH MADISON is the author of fourteen books, including *The Greens Cookbook*, *Local Flavors*, *The New Vegetarian Cooking for Everyone*, and *Vegetable Literacy*. Her most recent book is *In My Kitchen: A Collection of New and Favorite Vegetarian Recipes* (2017). She is also the author of *What We Eat when We Eat Alone* and has just completed a memoir. Known as a chef as well as a writer, her specialties are seasonal vegetable recipes with an emphasis on farmers' markets produce, heritage varieties, and food from the garden. She has managed her farmers' market and served on many boards and at present is involved with the Southwest Grassfed Livestock Alliance. Deborah gardens and writes in Galisteo, New Mexico, where she lives with her husband, painter Patrick McFarlin.

KIM SEVERSON is a *New York Times* domestic correspondent covering food trends and news across the United States. She was previously the New York Times Southern bureau chief and, before that, a staff writer for the *New York Times* dining section. Since her arrival at the *Times* in 2004, she has pushed the food beat in interesting directions and onto page 1. She previously wrote about cooking and the culture of food for the *San Francisco Chronicle*, following a seven-year stint as an editor and reporter at the *Anchorage Daily News*.

RUTH LEWIS SMITH, Edna Lewis's sister, was born on leap day, February 29, 1924. She currently lives with her daughter and son-in-law in Galesburg, Illinois, where she drives, cooks, irons, is active in church, and enjoys raising chickens, guinea, and quail and gathering eggs from a dozen laying hens. She attends any events she can that are related to her sister

Edna. She spoke at the unveiling of the United States Postal Service Celebrity Chef stamp in honor of her sister.

TONI TIPTON-MARTIN is a culinary journalist, author, and community activist. She is the author of the *The Jemima Code: Two Centuries of African American Cookbooks*, the winner of a 2016 James Beard Book Award and a 2016 Art of Eating Prize and the recipient of a 2015 Certificate of Outstanding Contribution to Publishing from the Black Caucus of the Library Association. She founded SANDE, a nonprofit organization that promotes the connection between cultural heritage, food, and health. She is a member of the James Beard Awards committee and a cofounder of Southern Foodways Alliance and Foodways Texas. Toni was invited twice by First Lady Michelle Obama to the White House; was the first African American food editor of a major daily newspaper, the *Cleveland Plain Dealer*; the nutrition writer for the *Los Angeles Times*; and a contributing editor at *Heart and Soul Magazine*. She is a member of the advisory board for Oldways' African Heritage Diet Pyramid.

MICHAEL W. TWITTY is a culinary and cultural historian and the creator of Afroculinaria, the first blog devoted to African American historic foodways and their legacy. Twitty has appeared on NPR's *The Splendid Table* and *Morning Edition* and has written for the *Guardian*, *Ebony*, *Local Palate*, and the *Washington Post*. He is a Smith Fellow with the Southern Foodways Alliance and a TED fellow and speaker, was the recipient of the Taste Talks's first Culinary Pioneer Award, and received a readers' choice and editors' choice award from *Saveur* for best food and culture blog. Twitty's book *The Cooking Gene* is published by HarperCollins.

ALICE WATERS is a chef, author, food activist, and founder and owner of Chez Panisse Restaurant in Berkeley, California. She has been a champion of local, sustainable agriculture for more than four decades. In 1995, she founded the Edible Schoolyard Project. She has been a vice president of Slow Food International since 2002. She conceived and helped create the Yale Sustainable Food Project in 2003 and the Rome Sustainable Food Project at the American Academy in Rome in 2007. She was elected Fellow of the American Academy of Arts and Sciences in 2007; given the Harvard Medical School's Global Environmental Citizen Award in 2008; and introduced into the French Legion of Honor in 2010. Most recently, she was awarded a National Humanities Medal by President Barack Obama. Waters is the author of fourteen books, including *New York Times* best-sellers *The Art of Simple Food I & II* and *The Edible Schoolyard: A Universal Idea*.

KEVIN WEST is author of *Saving the Season: A Cook's Guide to Home Canning, Pickling, and Preserving,* coauthor of *Truffle Boy* and *The Grand Central Market Cookbook,* and a contributor to *America: The Cookbook.* He is from Blount County, Tennessee, and splits his time between western Massachusetts and Los Angeles.

SUSAN REBECCA WHITE was born and raised in Atlanta, earned a B.A. in English from Brown University, and then lived in San Francisco for several years before moving to Virginia to earn her MFA in creative writing from Hollins University. White has published three critically acclaimed novels: *Bound South, A Soft Place to Land,* and *A Place at the Table.* She has also published narrative nonfiction in *Tin House, Salon, The Bitter Southerner,* and *Atlanta* magazine. White has taught creative writing at Hollins, Emory, and the Atlanta branch of SCAD (Savannah School of Art and Design.) During the spring of 2017 she was the Ferrol A. Sams Jr. Distinguished Writer-in-Residence at Mercer University in Macon, Georgia. She lives in Atlanta with her husband, Sam, and son, Gus.

CAROLINE RANDALL WILLIAMS is a cookbook author, young adult novelist, and poet. She received her MFA from the University of Mississippi, where she cowrote the Phillis Wheatley Award–winning *Diary of B. B. Bright, Possible Princess* and the NAACP Image Award–winning *Soul Food Love.* A Cave Canem fellow, she has published poems in several journals, including the *Iowa Review, Massachusetts Review,* and *Palimpsest.* Her debut collection, *Lucy Negro Redux,* came out with Ampersand Books in 2015. She is currently writer-in-residence at Fisk University.

NINA WILLIAMS-MBENGUE, Edna Lewis's niece, works on child welfare policy for the National Conference of State Legislatures (NCSL) in Denver, Colorado. Before joining NCSL, she worked in the Children's Division of the American Humane Association, where she provided research assistance on child maltreatment issues to child welfare professionals, researchers, and the general public. She has a B.A. in Latin American studies from the University of Virginia. She lives outside Denver with her husband, Mustafa, and two daughters, Salymata and Amina.

JOE YONAN is the two-time James Beard Award–winning Food and Dining editor of the *Washington Post.* He has written two cookbooks, *Eat Your Vegetables: Bold Recipes for the Single Cook* (Ten Speed Press, 2013), and *Serve Yourself: Nightly Adventures in Cooking for One* (Ten Speed Press, 2011), and is consulting editor of *The Great American Cookbook,* a project to benefit No Kid Hungry. He writes the *Post's* Weeknight Vegetarian column, for five years wrote the Cooking for One column, and has written frequently about his efforts to grow food on his 150-square-foot urban front yard. His work for the *Post* and the *Boston Globe,* where he was a food writer and Travel editor, has won multiple awards from the Association of Food Journalists, and his stories have appeared in multiple editions of the *Best Food Writing* anthology. He grew up in West Texas.

Index

⟶⦅⟵